Teaching, Tenure, and Collegiality

SUNY series in Asian Studies Development

Roger T. Ames and Peter D. Hershock, editors

Teaching, Tenure, and Collegiality

Confucian Relationality in an Age of Measurable Outcomes

MARY K. CHANG

Cover: Fiber art titled "The Moving World—Winter" (2012). Original design by Lin Hsin-Chen. Reprinted with permission of the artist. This is a collective production by 孔詩尹 (Kong Shi-Yin), 王淑惠 (Wang Shu-Hui), 王麗君 (Wang Li-Chun), 王郦君 (Wang Li-Chun), 吳美珠 (Wu Mei-Jhu), 吳翠秀 (Wu Tsui-xiu), 杜淑瀛 (Du Shu-Ying), 林幸珍 (Lin Hsin-Chen), 林美惠 (Lin Mei-Hui), 林瑞雪 (Lin Rei-Xue), 洪瑛鍈 (Hong Ying-Ying), 徐珮盈 (Xu Pei-Ying), 張月媛 (Chang Yue-Yuan), 張秀幸 (Chang Hsu-Hsing), 張素屏 (Chang Su-Ping), 梁英雅 (Liang Ying-Ya), 莊惠蘭 (Chuang Huei-Lan), 陳怡汝 (Chen Yi-Ru), 陳春香 (Chen Chun-Hsiang), 陳麗鳳 (Chen Li-Fong), 陳鶯 (Chen Ying), 陳艷秋 (Chen Yen-Chiu), 曾蓮招 (Tseng Lien-Chao), 曾譯瑤 (Tseng Yi-Yao), 黃明美 (Huang Ming-Mei), 黃欣雯 (Huang Hsin-Wen), 黃美玉 (Huang Mei-Yu), 黃鈺芸 (Huang Yu-Yun), 黃慧純 (Huang Hui-Chun), 葉蕙珍 (Yeh Hui-Chen), 蔡沛縈 (Tsai Pei-Ying), 顏惠芳 (Yan Hui-Fang).

Published by State University of New York Press, Albany

Printed in the United States of America

For information, contact State University of New York Press, Albany, NY
www.sunypress.edu

Library of Congress Cataloging-in-Publication Data

Name: Chang Mary K., author.
Title: Teaching, tenure, and collegiality : Confucian relationality in an age of measurable outcomes / Mary K. Chang.
Description: Albany : State University of New York Press, [2022] | Series: SUNY series in Asian Studies Development | Includes bibliographical references and index.
Identifiers: ISBN 9781438487458 (hardcover : alk. paper) | ISBN 9781438487472 (ebook)
Further information is available at the Library of Congress.

10 9 8 7 6 5 4 3 2 1

Contents

Acknowledgments vii

Foreword xi

Introduction 1
Value of Cohering Faculty Roles 4
Marketizing Higher Education 8
Normalization of Individualization Separates 13
Distinguishing Confucian Relationality 16
Attending to Processes 20
Linking Time and Space 26
Juxtaposition as a Way to Enrich Relation 30

PART 1
A DYNAMIC CONFUCIAN TRADITION

CHAPTER 1
The Exam Is Not the Text 37
Emphasizing a Commentarial Tradition 39
Taking an Interpretive Approach 41
A Complicated Conflation 44
Toward Agential Reading 59

CHAPTER 2
A Familial Way Forward 65
Parents and Children 67
A Process Orientation Harmonizes 73
Framing People as Events 80
Personal Cultivation Emerges Through Relationship 83

PART 2
UNIVERSITIES: TOWARD SHARING RESPONSIBILITY

CHAPTER 3
The Tenure Expectations Paradox 93
Product Paradigm Stresses Efficiency 99
Abstraction Decontextualizes 104
What About Teaching? 107
Addressing the Paradox 112
Engage the Core Values 116

CHAPTER 4
Foregrounding Collegiality 121
More Than a Method 125
Generating Collaborative Space 130
Taking Experiences Seriously 133
Beyond Measurable Outcomes 139
Developing Inner Circles 141

CHAPTER 5
Responsive Pedagogy 143
Unlearning Positions of Privilege 146
From Personal Cultivation to Critique 156
All About Relation: Juxtaposition With Feminist Perspectives 161

CONCLUSION 173
Embracing the Complexity of Learning: Some Implications 181
How Will You Respond? 188

APPENDIX A
University of Hawai'i Strategic Directions, 2015–2021 191

APPENDIX B
Criteria and Guidelines for Faculty Tenure/Promotion 201

BIBLIOGRAPHY 223

INDEX 229

Acknowledgments

Engaging a concept of Confucian relationality suggests that people's activities necessarily emerge through engagement with others. This is certainly the case with the writing of this book. I am grateful to Roger Ames and Peter Hershock, editors of the Asian Studies Development book series, for seeing the potential in this book. Roger's inspiriting seminars and our far-ranging conversations encouraged me to explore an interpretive approach to reading classical Chinese texts, and they shaped the concept of Confucian relationality that emerged. An exemplary scholar-teacher, his encouragement and discerning feedback have been sustaining. I thank him for writing a foreword for this book.

Hannah Tavares astutely pointed out ideas that needed unpacking in the earliest drafts of the manuscript. She encouraged me to explore how power manifests in institutions, which led to my explorations with juxtaposition of various epistemologies. Hannah invited me to present in the Spaces of Pedagogy symposium at the American Educational Research Association Conference in Washington, DC, an experience that spurred my growth as a scholar and helped me refine my ideas about faculty learning communities.

Eileen Tamura closely read the manuscript with her incisive historian's eye. Eileen's questions about the role of Chinese classical texts as part of the civil service examination process led to my exploration of how the process shaped normative meanings of the texts. Her thoughtful comments also inspired the emergence of framing themes during the revision process. I appreciate her mentorship and feel fortunate to be able to consider her an exceptional friend.

Numerous scholars and friends have offered advice and encouragement along the way. I consider among these Baoyan Cheng, Sarah Twomey, Xu Di, Chisato Nonaka, Jacquelyn Chappel, Shannon Brown, Kevin Lima,

Kavita Rao, Marsha Ninomiya, Amy Sojot, David Kupferman, Youxin Zhang, and members of the College of Education Doctoral Students Association. I am grateful to the faculty whom I took classes with and to those who have been my informal teachers. They have helped expand my thinking in immeasurable ways. The University of Hawai'i at Mānoa and East West Center Hale Kuahine communities provided an engaging context to undertake research and writing. I express my appreciation to Carol Bradof, who gave generously of her time to read portions of the manuscript and whose asides helped me appreciate more deeply the resonances among formidable traditions. Ned and Janet Trombly have rooted for me throughout the writing process. The sustaining friendship of Asha John, Jennifer Phillips, and Katherine Gould-Martin, strong and incisive women, have helped me grow as a person and scholar; they, along with friends I met at the University of Michigan, continually show me that friendship is indeed an important "way forward."

I thank James Peltz, SUNY Press editor-in-chief, whose professional aplomb, expertise, and warmth helped facilitate the production of the book. My thanks go to the SUNY Press team, including Diane Ganeles, Laura Tendler, Alicia Brady, Michael Campochiaro, and Sue Morreale, for their thoughtful attention.

I thank the following publications for permission to use earlier versions of the works noted. The introduction and chapter 4 are derived in part from an article published in the journal *Policy Futures in Education* on August 4, 2017, volume 16, issue 7, 2018, copyright Sage Publishing. The original publication is available online at https://journals.sagepub.com/doi/full/10.1177/1478210317722285

Chapter 1 is derived in part from an article published in *Educational Studies* on August 19, 2020, copyright American Educational Studies Association, available online at https://www.tandfonline.com/doi/full/10.1080/00131946.2020.1799217

Chapter 1 is derived also in part from an article published in *The Encyclopedia of Teacher Education* on November 8, 2019, copyright Springer Link. The original publication is available online at https://link.springer.com/referenceworkentry/10.1007%2F978-981-13-1179-6_291-1

A Confucian relationality suggests that people live in mutuality, and family is a primary relation. I am grateful to my parents, who, as immigrants to the United States from Taiwan, devoted their adult lives to their children, providing me with strong models of commitment. I owe my love of reading in part to Johanna Chang, who took her children on regular trips to the library. She was a model of resourcefulness, for instance relying on books to teach her children to swim and on herself to undertake home repairs. Peter Chang's work ethic knew no bounds. He spent evenings washing dishes at restaurants to supplement his graduate teaching stipend to support his then-young family and later creating design patents after work. Johanna and Peter's family commitment reflected that of their own parents, whose lives were upended by war. My grandparents' dedication to their families was shaped by their ancestors' devotion to theirs—the mothers, fathers, farmers, and scholars whose contributions I cannot trace but nonetheless matter because they shape the person whom I continue to become. I am grateful to my extended family near and far and to my siblings, Margaret Chen, Lawrence Chang, and Stephen Chang, who are attentively encouraging of my work and of me as a person.

I am deeply appreciative to Jonathan Trombly, who offered me a chance to think aloud about the writing and research process. His inquisitive feedback and clear-eyed observations enriched my thoughts about the implications of engaging a Confucian relationality and extends to all that we share. He has been with me through the whole process, resolutely and intrepidly. Ness and Nas, you forge my way forward. I love you beyond words. You inspire me continually to put a conception of relational personal cultivation into daily practice, and for that, and so much more, I am grateful.

Foreword

It is with great pleasure and very fond memories that I sit down to write this foreword for Mary Chang's monograph, *Teaching, Tenure, and Collegiality: Confucian Relationality in an Age of Measurable Outcomes*. Over the several years Mary spent as a graduate student in educational foundations at the University of Hawai'i, she took and excelled in several of my seminars in Confucian and comparative philosophy. In addition to the formidable task she faced in making the Confucian philosophical classics her own, I suspect that at least in some degree she found a vocabulary that enabled her to confirm and give expression to her own cultural intuitions as a Chinese American. As a member of her PhD dissertation committee, I had the occasion to watch as she embraced the project of challenging what have been increasingly dominant if not sometimes oppressive ways of thinking about educational metrics within the Western academy. Mary turned to Confucian ideas drawn from the canonical texts that, although ubiquitous in the ancient cultures of East Asia, are in many ways unfamiliar to a Western audience as a resource for critiquing recent market-oriented, quantitative trends in American education. While it has been an all-too-common phenomenon in the contemporary academy for scholars, both Chinese and Western alike, to theorize and to discipline Chinese culture through a Western conceptual structure, a unique feature of Mary's approach has been to turn this asymmetry on its head by reading contemporary American education through a Confucian lens. In the process of reading, discussing, and responding to her work, I watched as she invested her best efforts in trying to reconceive the institutions and culture of tertiary education in a way that is more capacious and inclusive.

Like many colleagues particularly but certainly not exclusively in the humanities, I have personally both looked askance at and long resisted the trends in contemporary education toward market-based quantification that Mary has so thoroughly appraised and critiqued in this work. Certainly the ways in which the product of faculty members is commodified and packaged in the tenure review process sets real limits and can have a deleterious effect on how we understand our work and interact with our colleagues. But for me, it is what such quantification does to the classroom experience for the students that I have found most frustrating. The word "curriculum" L. *currere*, meaning "to run the course," has its root in the Latin word for "track" or "racecourse," and from there it came to mean a course of study or syllabus. To the extent that we live by our metaphors, I could never be interested in professing an education that can be conceived of as students running in repetitive circles around a racetrack vying to win.

Perhaps for an introductory course in philosophy, an argument can be made for the value of a comprehensive course syllabus with a list of all the assigned readings, the responsibilities of the students in mastering the subject matter, and the instructor's basis for evaluation, and then made complete with the obligatory cautions about the consequences of plagiarism. Even at this introductory level, however, I have struggled with the constant administrative demand for a list of student-learning outcomes to be an exercise that seems to me to be so general as to be trivial, or to be a contrived misrepresentation of the meaning of education itself.

There is for me a profoundly important distinction that is sometime elided in service to such educational metrics between "education" and "training." Often these terms are taken as near synonyms with the difference being construed as more theoretical learning versus practical application. But I never thought of my own education as training for a job, and I have never regarded my students as my apprentices. For me, real education is transformative of one's person and has to do with how we live our lives, where the theoretical emerges out of practice to make it more intelligent and productive. Real education has perhaps more to do with what we do in our free time as a way of life than with the business of making a living.

When we move from an introductory course to the level of a graduate seminar, I have always thought that we need a good question to pursue in our course and a direction set for the first three or four weeks of classes. While we need a clear and focused beginning, it is important that, rather than setting constraints on where our question is going to take us by fixing the readings and defining the content of our sessions in advance, we have the intellectual freedom and honesty to follow an open-ended path forward. A graduate seminar that begins from a predetermined answer is for me a disingenuous pretense in what should properly be the shared teacher and student project of producing new knowledge.

The etymology of the English word "education" is helpful in expressing this concern. The word "education" has two principal roots—L. *educare* and *educere*. The first root means "cultivating, rearing, bringing up," while the second means "educing, evoking, leading forth, drawing out." *Educare* resonates with the sense of education as rationally ordered, generic guidance; it is the logical and more systematic mode of education that we associate with transmission of cognitive understanding. Education in a "discipline" certainly requires discipline (L. *disciplina* meaning "instruction and training" from the root *discere* "to learn"): a knowledge of its history, its key figures and their stories, its theories and terminologies. Even though there is much that is common and rote in laying a solid foundation, this formative aspect of education is essential. On the other hand, this customary, habitual, and ritualistic phase of education as *educare* needs to be properly managed because it does lean in the direction of programming and indoctrination.

Educere as a second root of education suggests a more creative, personal, and expansive understanding of its goals and outcomes. Education so construed is a transactional, collaborative process including teaching and learning that entail both continuity and creativity in the growth of both *this* able teacher and *that* able student. The evocative sense of *educere* as "educing" resonates with the engagement of one's inner genius and feelings through novel and imaginative elaborations of one's own mode of personal cultivation in the student-teacher relation. It is decidedly prospective in the sense that it reaches for, shapes, and addresses issues that have heretofore been in important degree unknown by both parties to the project. Indeed, in this phase of education, the distinction between student and teacher is often blurred and sometimes reversed as both participants in the process exercise their insight and imagination to press against and break through the boundaries of existing knowledge. This teacher-student reversal has certainly been the case for me in my role of helping to supervise Mary's dissertation, where I have been brought into a relationship with and learned much from some of today's most formidable voices in pedagogy and philosophy of education.

In the first part of this monograph, where Mary is constructing her conception of Confucian relationality, she underscores the persistent centrality of family as a model for personal, social, political, and indeed cosmic order in this worldview. Indeed, the distinguished late-Qing scholar Yan Fu 严复 (1854–1921), who translated and introduced the works of Adam Smith, T. H. Huxley, John Stuart Mill, Herbert Spencer, and others into the Chinese academy, once remarked that if we ask after the source of social and political order in imperial China over the past two millennia, 30% can be attributed to emperor, and 70% to family lineage.

The traditional Confucian way of life does not embrace the Aristotelian asymmetrical distinction between *oikos* and *polis*, between family/household and the realm of politics, with his *Politics* (*ta politika*) being understood as "the affairs of state." Instead, witnessing a persistent isomorphism between family and state (*jiaguo tonggou* 家國同構) throughout the early Confucian canons, we come to understand that the perceived primary source of both social and political order in this tradition is the institution of family as it is grounded in the prime moral imperatives of "family reverence" (*xiao* 孝) and its complement, "an achieved propriety in one's roles and relations" (*li* 禮). While Confucian texts certainly regard the abstract rule of law and the application of punishments as necessary institutions, at the same time they construe appeal to law as a clear admission of communal failure. At its most fundamental level, it is the proper functioning of roles in family and community and the commensurate sense of shame such roles produce within ritually choreographed relations that serve as the primary source of social and political order. A dynamic *li*-structured family and community is a concrete and powerful guarantee of social solidarity, while the application of abstract laws and policies can at best serve as only secondary injunctions.

We would be hard-pressed to find any family-centered philosophical notion that is any way comparable to or has had the vital importance that "familial reverence" (*xiao* 孝) serves in its role as its prime moral imperative for Confucian philosophy. If we rehearse the contributions of our principal philosophers in the Western narrative, few indeed have invoked family as a productive model for organizing the human experience. This disinterest in the always partial relations that emerge from family feeling is perhaps due to the perceived centrality of impartiality as a necessary condition for ethical conduct among those philosophers who would look to moral reasoning as the ultimate source of adjudication.

Such a lack of appeal to the institution of family as a model of order in our philosophical narrative contrasts starkly with the Confucian worldview in which family is *the* governing metaphor, and in which in fact *all* relationships are ultimately perceived as familial. The signature of Confucianism is that morality as it is cultivated through a commitment to the achievement of "consummate conduct in one's roles and relations" (*ren* 仁) is an extension and expression of immediate family feeling. The underlying judgment in this Confucian tradition is that, if a superlative harmony achieved through relational equity and an achieved diversity is the desired goal, it is the family that is the single human institution to which persons are most inclined to give themselves utterly and without remainder: time, money, a body part, their very lives. A positive sense of shame expressed as identification with the family and community values guarantees that relations are prosocial and thus preemptive in minimizing antisocial behaviors. Family is the entry point for the growth in relations that is the substance of Confucian morality, and as these vital relations expand outward radially into the community, they have the primary role not only of transforming mere association into the Great Community, but the Great Community itself into the Great Family.

The concept of family lineage that was such a powerful source of social and political order in traditional China has largely been replaced by the nuclear family structure, but the force of family feeling still permeates the society and is especially relevant to the institutions that govern education. Teachers in the classroom are either "teacher-father" (*shifu* 師父) or "teacher-mother" (*shimu* 師母), and students are "older-sister student" (*xuejie* 學姐) and "younger brother student" (*xuedi* 學弟). There is a popular expression: "a teacher for one day is a father for a lifetime" (*yiriweishi, shenzhongweifu*一日為師身終為父).

Having taught at several Chinese universities for extended periods over my career, I would contend that this continuing commitment to family is not just a matter of language. The classroom culture is one of family. And again, family feeling is also very much a part of departmental culture, where older faculty who have made their careers in an institution are still included in the life of the department. Just as family feeling is integral to what Mary calls "relation-ing" in the various kinds of mentoring processes and faculty activities that go on among colleagues in their roles in the faculty, her emphasis is properly on family as a long-term process: the "family-ing" of a department. Again, it is the department as family that is the locus of one's own regimen of personal cultivation across one's career in education. When I thus look back on my own career, I see in Mary's appeal to the promotion of family values within the institution to be a productive complement to our more familiar ways of providing our students the best education that we can.

Roger T. Ames
Peking University

Introduction

In an age when market values shape political, cultural, and institutional practices in countries like the United States, metrics emerge to determine normative merit. For universities, this means they face product-oriented pressures to quantify the value of academic endeavors. Instructional faculty members, as a result, face the difficult task of navigating mixed expectations from universities. Mission statements, on the one hand, discuss the importance of cultivating wise global citizens and academic excellence. Hired in part to realize these goals, faculty members are tasked to cultivate the craft of teaching to encourage students to undertake processes of learning that can vary for persons and whose outcomes are uncertain. At the same time, university strategic directions documents express a business ethos when they articulate institutional aims using a product-oriented parlance that prioritizes returns on investments. From this perspective, faculty prestige is largely determined by research contributions.

Problematically, the use of metrics as a way to determine the value of the breadth of faculty contributions heightens the delineation of faculty roles, and it sets the roles up in competing ways. The emerging complication is that those aspects of faculty endeavors that can be more easily measured, then, risk becoming normatively viewed as more institutionally valuable. For instance, when teaching and research are viewed in product-oriented terms as separate, even competing, endeavors, faculty members must make deliberate choices about how to expend limited energy and time. These choices have extensive implications for their academic communities.

For instructional faculty members, the product-oriented phrase "publish or perish" may seem like an open secret. A normative market-oriented focus on outcomes suggests that publishing research contributes the most to institutional prestige, implying that those who choose to emphasize teaching may jeopardize the success of their tenure and promotion applications. As higher educational institutions face increasing scrutiny by lawmakers and the public to justify their expenditures, tenure guidelines for instance reflect a reliance on the production of measurable evidence to assess the "big three" of faculty activities—research, teaching, and community and institutional service. How faculty members make sense of their academic roles amid tension between normative market pressures to publish and relative institutional quiet on the relation among their activities has a profound impact on their and other's experiences of academia.

A product orientation functions in part by fragmenting faculty activities and framing them as separate and competitive endeavors. While evidence of research expertise in the form of peer-reviewed publications is normatively regarded as sufficient for review committees to determine research contributions, providing evidence of expert teaching or quality of engagement in service may be more difficult to describe in standardized, quantifiable terms. Situating these activities through the lens of measurement implies that the big three of faculty endeavors are separate because they require different ways to compare their outcomes among different faculty. Given that tenure guidelines often refrain from explicitly weighting their activities, faculty and tenure review committees are left to infer institutional priorities and make decisions about the value of particular faculty activities.

A product orientation institutionally frames faculty foremost as producers. A focus on outcomes simplifies faculty activities because it narrows a notion of value, especially given that some faculty activities are not easily measurable. Situating faculty members as expert producers of research, teaching, and service overlooks the complexity and value of what they do as colleagues, mentors, and people who are part of extensive academic communities. A market orientation that implies that faculty endeavors can be characterized in a quantifiable way relies on a major assumption—that for tenure and promotion purposes, faculty members can delineate their achievements in clear, evidence-based ways. It assumes that people's activities can be abstractly extricated from their engagement with others with a rational, orderly method. It situates faculty members as independent of the colleagues in their departments and broader institutional community rather than as inextricably connected. It overlooks the complexity of the processes involved in their activities and the learning that they involve.

More broadly, engaging a market orientation to shape higher educational practices including faculty activities masks the limits of such an approach through deflection and redirection. It deflects by deemphasizing the influence of those relational aspects of faculty activities that refuse measurement. Consider the myriad conversations that take place among people on any given day at a university: the classrooms, labs, departments, administration offices, hallways, and parking lots, among others. Higher educational institutions are massively complex organizations often involving tens of thousands of people. How is it possible to comprehend the varied activities and their affective nuances in measurable ways and how they influence teaching, learning, and research? It may be quite difficult, if not impossible.

Rather than acknowledge this, a product orientation instead redirects by driving attention to those aspects of university function that are more easily measurable, overlooking the complexity of many academic endeavors. For instance, while a university mission statement may affirm a stated core value of "academic rigor"—a value that may be difficult to quantify—its strategic directions may be preoccupied with achieving specific retention rates and the preparation of workers for the state where a university is located. While engaging a product orientation can contribute productively to discussions about an educational institution's directions, an overreliance on evidence-based determinations of value without acknowledgement of its limits narrows envisioning the potential breadth of educational institutional endeavors.

Political scientist Wendy Brown (2012) suggests it is the drive to economize human endeavors that means success needs to be measured. Scholars, for instance, need to provide evidence of their contributions to show their value to institutions. They must prepare to "go on the job market" by distinguishing themselves with niche research areas, build CVs featuring prizes and publications, and provide evidence of the ability to acquire grants to ensure an institution is making a good investment through a hiring. Even after achieving a faculty position, tenure and promotion rely on showing metrics of contributions mainly via publications, in which teaching, ironically, gets devalued: "Tenure and promotion, let alone targeted recruitments and lucrative counteroffers, are never based on teaching excellence in research universities" (Brown, p. 197). The professionalization of scholars, Brown warns, positions them as "human capital" rather than teachers and thinkers. For those who have risen through the ranks in this system, there is little alternative view, and many are left feeling resigned to and pressured to perpetuate current norms.

In a time of globally scaled challenges, such as issues related to climate and health, people are increasingly turning toward collective integrative problem solving to seek to address them. Higher education institutions and faculty members in particular are poised to participate. However, interdisciplinary approaches, which necessitate attention toward the cultivation of inclusive and diverse processes, imply the importance of relational activities, for instance, cross-disciplinary learning among participants of multidisciplinary collaborations and academic programs. Because global challenges resist any particular disciplinary approach to address them, universities need to acknowledge and even embrace complexity, not seek to reduce it. The broad challenges require that faculty members not only be situated in market-oriented ways as expert producers of research, teaching, and service, but also as connected, adaptive learners open to change. For faculty members and universities, this means they are compelled to look beyond product-oriented ways of understanding their activities to attend to the processes and contexts of generating possibility, which may be risky because the outcomes may be uncertain and hard to measure.

Value of Cohering Faculty Roles

This book explores the use of a concept of Confucian relationality as a way to assist universities to make good on their commitment to cultivating wise global citizens. It does this by putting forward the value of developing the craft of teaching. But it does this not in the sense that it suggests teaching is a unidirectional activity that simply involves faculty members communicating with students to produce wise citizens, but rather suggests a more complex process that implicates and influences all involved. The distinction between a reductive and a more complex view of the value of teaching hinges on one critical aspect—how people are situated. While a product orientation reflects a broader normative and culturally dominant assumption that people are "individuals" in order to be able to quantify their perceived attributes and achievements, a Confucian relationality assumes just the opposite—that people are necessarily relationally constituted.

What engaging a Confucian relationality does more broadly is to show the limits of a product orientation that situates people as separate from each other. Instead, the process-oriented concept of a Confucian relationality offers the notion that people are relationally constituted as an alternative and valuable framework to engage contemporary phenomena that privilege the notion that people continually construct the contexts they engage through their activities. To view people as necessarily constituted by others suggests that while attempts may be made to normatively fix identities and quantify achievements, these are ultimately acts of decontextualization that may be somewhat arbitrary in their determinations.

What a Confucian relational view means for teaching is that it necessarily involves a process of learning. The two are aspectual in part because they are activities that necessarily emerge through engaging others. When people are seen as relationally constituted, it is through engaging others that personal distinctiveness emerges and enriches the contexts people generate through their activities. To undertake a process of personal cultivation that involves reflection on how a person engages others does not simply influence those undertaking the process themselves but also impacts how they relate with others. To try to achieve the broader goal of cultivating wise citizens means recognizing in part the shared responsibility for complex and unpredictable processes that occur not only within classrooms but beyond them too. Such processes defy complete description in quantifiable terms because they necessarily take into account particular relational contextual considerations.

More specifically, this book engages Confucian relationality as an interdisciplinary process-oriented framework to inquire about some higher education institutional product-oriented priorities and practices and considers their implications for faculty activities. While tenure guidelines and norms may prioritize publications over teaching and service, Confucian relationality compels a more comprehensively integrated view of faculty member endeavors as part of relational networks that may not be easy to quantitatively pin down. In brief, the concept situates people as necessarily constituted by others, foregrounds a process orientation that engages a view of time and space as related, and frames personal cultivation as relationally resonant. Engaging Confucian relationality calls attention to the value of complex educational processes deemphasized by a product orientation like support for the craft of teaching, reflective pedagogical research, and the value of faculty collegiality. It is a valuable approach because it situates the world as changing, foregrounds experiences, and fosters inquiry about the contextual field of higher education.

A concept of Confucian relationality is constructed from reading a translation of the *Zhongyong*, a classical Chinese philosophical text. Rather than an occasion to mainly focus on the analysis of Confucian texts and tradition, this work constructs a concept of relationality to use as an inquiring lens to encourage reconsideration of some normative priorities in a case study institution. The Confucian relational concept emerges informed by the work of comparative philosophers such as Roger Ames, David Hall, Li-Hsiang Lisa Rosenlee, Sor-hoon Tan, Henry Rosemount Jr., Peter Hershock, and Thomas Kasulis, among others. These scholars suggest that the classical Chinese tradition is relevant to contemporary philosophical discussions when situated as flexible and dynamic. In other words, it continues to change when people read classical Chinese philosophical texts from their own particular spatial and temporal locations. They have written extensively about the differences between substance-oriented and process-oriented worldviews and the impact they have on the construction of people's identities. Whereas a substance-oriented perspective emphasizes defining "what things are," a process-oriented worldview focuses on situating life as happenings, events. This shift from "being" or "thing" to "happening" has profound implications regarding how to situate people. Engaging a broader worldview of processual change envisions people as contingently relation-ing rather than as individuals. As a result, a process-oriented concept of Confucian relationality foregrounds the importance of complex relationships without a need to quantify them because it assumes their value.

Engaging a concept of Confucian relationality suggests a more comprehensive view of faculty roles because it foregrounds a process-oriented view, which complicates a notion of faculty as producers. A process orientation situates faculty as learners, a move that calls attention to the effort, time, and risks involved in engaging the processes of conducting research and developing the craft of teaching, among others. I mention risks because emphasizing processes also reminds that outcomes may not always emerge as predetermined; the processes can be intricately nuanced and outcomes uncertain. At the same time, this unpredictability also calls attention to the emergence of valuable possibilities. In other words, a focus on processes may return more unexpected and complex outcomes than a product-oriented focus might. The value of these may be missed if there is tunnel vision on some expected outcomes. To broaden a notion of faculty from producers to learners frames the nature of faculty work as ongoing, of faculty in the midst of their activities—not simply as researchers but as researching, not simply as teachers but as teaching and continually developing the craft of teaching.

Confucian relationality integrates faculty activities by reframing them not simply from the perspective of outcomes but primarily as changing experiences. It situates universities as constituted by people foremost who are relating, performing various roles, and continually vitalizing institutional structures through their activities. Instead of human "beings," as mentioned earlier, a notion that assumes an independent state, people are envisioned as necessarily constituted by others. By situating people in this way, Confucian relationality insinuates that people emerge through experiences, which necessarily emerge in relation with others. Our relation-ing continually shapes us. This perspective engages a process-oriented worldview that considers life as ongoing. When faculty activities are seen as ongoing processes, then this shifts attention from a focus on measurable outcomes to the importance of attending to people's experiences. When experiences of people are foregrounded, then faculty activities emerge as integrated aspects of each other because this focus calls attention to the people themselves who generate the activities. Faculty activities, then, cannot wholly be considered separate from each other because they cannot be separated from the people and contexts from which they emerge. Learning from the context of featuring experiences emerges from relation and influences relation.

A concept of Confucian relationality informs a notion of faculty activities by highlighting the relational implications of personal cultivation. When considered relationally, learning has extensive implications because it impacts people and how they relate with others in unpredictable ways. Because people are envisioned as intricately enmeshed with others in changing ways, learning emerges from and assumes the primary importance of relationships. This means envisioning universities foremost as constituted by people's activities. In other words, people construct the university. For faculty, this means that what they do matters. How they learn matters. From a process perspective of the world where people are deeply connected, faculty who undertake the activity of learning influence not only themselves but also their "relation-ing" with others in unpredictable ways. This enriches normative notions of value.

While a market orientation focuses on outcomes, Confucian relationality legitimizes multiple notions of value with its focus on process, people's connectedness, and subjective experiences. By foregrounding experience, what is considered valuable may differ for different people in different contexts. Engaging Confucian relationality inspires questions related to whom, how, and why? For faculty members, engaging Confucian relationality suggests that while they may feel the need to respond to institutional normative focuses on outcomes, at the same time, they can see the limits of this focus and seek to develop their own notions of value to guide their activities. In fact, Confucian relationality urges taking a longer-term view. The faculty who at one point must undergo tenure review will later constitute tenure committees and take on positions to review tenure guidelines and institutional strategic directions. Having reflected on their own notions of value throughout their institutional employment, they will be poised to thoughtfully shape the guidelines for others.

Engaging a Confucian relationality is a valuable approach to considering universities because it calls attention to the relational aspects of the complex contextual field of higher education. Engaging Confucian relationality as an adaptive, process-oriented resource and a methodological approach suggests the frame itself, rather than seeking to compete with other orientations, becomes enriched when engaging others. For instance, while it recognizes the usefulness of situating the university from a normative, product-oriented perspective of higher educational institutions as producers for the state, of jobs, employees, and research, at the same time, it encourages a stance of modesty about its capabilities and complicates notions that outcomes can be wholly attributable and fixed in a measurable way. It serves to remind administrators and faculty to continually ask what institutional directions leave out, to consider what might be unknown along with the perceived known. A process-oriented Confucian relational framework challenges normative notions of faculty identity from one of a producer of knowledge to one that emphasizes that even the experts are always learning—through relation and informing relation. Rather than separate activities, it suggests that teaching, research, and learning, for instance, are aspectual and contingent. More broadly, it situates the university as a learning community.

Marketizing Higher Education

What I have been referring to as a market or product and outcomes orientation has a more formal moniker: neoliberalism. The rationality of neoliberalism, expressed as a relationship between a country and its citizens that is primarily economic, dominates current social, political, and educational constructs (Biesta, 2010; Brown, 2015). In other words, this framework strongly emphasizes a free-market and deregulation orientation with regard to government policies, situating people and institutions in a producer-consumer oriented relationship. From this perspective, managerial accountability through the provision of evidence is necessary to provide, as Gert Biesta calls it, "quality assurance" of institutional activity to ensure that the perceived needs of its stakeholders are met. Such a market orientation influences contemporary university structures, directions, and values, positioning people as independent and in generally competitive ways.

How does neoliberalism influence higher educational institutions? Patrick Fitzsimons (2002) suggests that a neoliberal culture has two major tasks. The first is that all institutions need to be reshaped in the form of commercial enterprises that are consumer oriented. For universities, this means they should be organizationally structured like corporations and operate using business practices. Higher educational institutions already employ a heightened level of bureaucracy with regard to their organizational structures in that they share so-called production systems of "mediums of exchange" such as diplomas, transcripts, and certificates that allow people to move among institutions and institutions to control participant entry (Green, Ericson, & Seidman, 1997). Building on these structures, institutional mission statements and strategic plans, which publicly articulate a university's values and goals, openly express their interest in becoming more business oriented. For example, the University of Hawai'i's Strategic Directions for 2015–2021 (2015) cites as one of its four goals the development of a "high performance mission-driven system," committed to "accountability, transparency and managing costs by leveraging our unique status as a unified statewide system of public higher education." Furthermore, for each of the four goals, the document identifies specific "productivity and efficiency measures associated with these outcomes [to] provide clear, measurable goals and the ability to effectively monitor progress over time." The institution's strategic directions showcase a market orientation not only through its articulation of institutional goals but also in the structures and how it evaluates outcomes.

The use of business language to describe institutional purposes and goals is not only evident at the University of Hawai'i—the institution I refer to as a case example throughout this book—it is common in many universities and colleges, public and private, across the United States. For example, at the University of California, Berkeley (2002), a strategic academic plan refers to the university as an "academic enterprise" tasked with "maximizing the potential for interdisciplinary synergy . . . to ensure our investments in both academic programs and physical improvements . . ." At the University of Michigan (2016), the president's office lists six areas of interest on its webpage, each with a link to its own strategic directions that describe strategies for "recruitment, supporting innovation, and creating equity." The area of "Academic Innovation" works closely with the "Academic Innovation Initiative Steering Committee" during the 2016–17 academic year to "assess the constraints that inhibit academic innovation and explore ways to overcome them" and "propose a transformational approach for leveraging academic innovation to shape the future of education and further realize our mission," among others. At Harvard University (2017), the president and fellows of Harvard, known as the corporation, is an entity that "engages with both questions of long-range strategy, policy, and planning as well as transactional matters of unusual consequence. It serves as a confidential sounding board for the President on matters of importance . . . and is responsible for approving the University's budgets, major capital projects, endowment spending, tuition charges, and other matters."

Such consumer-oriented language suggests the importance of economic considerations in numerous higher educational institutions and reflects market-oriented perspectives with regard to institutional directions.

Engaging a predominant product-orientated view compels administrators and policy makers to value perceived measurable outcomes and deemphasize those deemed not relevant to achieving specific goals. For instance, in the University of Hawai'i's strategic directions document, one "tactic" noted for the goal of a "high performance mission-driven system" is to "implement world-class business practices to advance efficiency, transparency and accountability with sound risk management." Biesta (2010) points out that discussions and research about educational function, which impact institutional directions, necessitate judgments about desirable expectations. If administrators emphasize the construction of efficient institutional standards to evaluate institutional developments, then they may overlook those aspects of educational endeavors whose outcomes are difficult to quantify in economic terms.

As a matter of fact, Fitzsimons (2002) suggests that the second task of a neoliberal culture is to background or even reverse any initiatives that do not contribute to the development of "enterprise." This suggests administrators tend to value the activities that fit more cleanly into an economic-driven frame, while undervaluing those aspects thought to complicate specified goals. Furthermore, Fitzsimons suggests that neoliberalism is also an ethic that implies market operations are values in and of themselves and need not be connected to the actual production of goods and services. To engage a market orientation, then, is to strive to determine value according to its principles even when such categorizations may seem incompatible, for instance, with regard to complex processes or relational phenomena of educational institutions.

A neoliberal orientation has a more inadvertent, even unassumingly extensive, implication for faculty members. In higher education institutions, faculty members may feel pressure to perceive their roles in simplified ways. Brown (2015) warns that the reach of neoliberalism, as a rationality and language, extends toward marketizing areas of life that have been traditionally noneconomic. In other words, it frames all aspects of life from a market-related perspective in a narrow way that suggests that people should be situated as entrepreneurs (Fitzsimons, 2002). Fitzsimons describes neoliberal or "enterprise" culture as one where a market orientation is reflected in people's beliefs, notions of self, which influence professional and personal activities. It reflects a status-oriented attitude that infuses all aspects of life such as choice of partners, friends, and hobbies, among others. While these choices may not necessarily be assigned a dollar value per se, they can be seen as a way to raise a person's status in the perceived eyes of future employers or for particular employment-related purposes. Biesta (2010) argues that to situate the state as a provider of public services and citizens as consumers depoliticizes and formalizes their identities, limiting their relationships with each other. For instance, product-oriented institutional expectations pressure faculty members to prioritize publishing of research over their teaching endeavors to achieve tenure and promotion. This situates faculty as producers of research and teaching, a view and expectation that can influence how faculty members construct their own roles as part of higher educational institutions. For institutions to situate faculty mainly as producers reflects a construct that narrows relationships, suggesting they can be understood in financial terms, and implying that the value of particular activities, like research, teaching, and service, can be measured as isolated endeavors.

The dominating influence of a culture of measurement on educational institutions informs not only how institutions situate people but also how people, through the use of an evidence-based lens, view each other's roles. A formal economically framed relationship between state and citizen resonates in the relations between state officials and educational administrators, departments and faculty members, and faculty members and students. For instance, faculty members and administrators may determine the breadth of student learning based mainly on test scores, a focus that may overlook and even devalue the learning that may have occurred outside an evaluatory scope. Administrators and colleagues may determine faculty members' instructional success largely based on end-of-semester teaching evaluations from students, a limited measure of the complexity and impact of teaching. They are limited especially given that they reflect students' own performance in classes and biases rather than serve as a standardized evaluation of teaching quality. For instance, students' gender bias emerges when female junior faculty are systematically given lower evaluation ratings than their male colleagues (Mengel, Sauermann, & Zölitz, 2019). Also, racial biases influence teaching evaluations—the race and language of instructors influence how students rate their instructors in evaluations (Subtirelu, 2015). Not only do the terms of a culture of measurement shape people's views of each other in a product-oriented way, but they also influence our expectations of and behavior toward each other.

Although the frame of a culture of measurement can be useful—it provides data on educational phenomena for faculty, administrators, and policy makers—it has limitations as a dominant paradigm for educational considerations because it can obscure the vast complexity involved in educational initiatives. For instance, how does one quantify or describe "quality" or "expert" teaching? Or calculate the value of a colleague's input on reading a draft of a syllabus or of gaining a deeper understanding of a concept that one learned in a class decades ago? How can one really measure learning about teaching—an ongoing process that one may not be completely aware of oneself—when there may be multiple desired outcomes? The complexity of educational endeavors may be impossible to usefully characterize in terms of measurement. Elizabeth Ellsworth (1997) goes so far as to argue that if teaching is envisioned as the transfer of information from one person to others, then it is "impossible" because teachers cannot control what students will hear and think, and should not assume that they can. Ellsworth suggests that an acknowledgment that teaching is impossible opens up new possibilities. It does not mean one does not try to teach, but, rather, teaching with awareness that one cannot expect to have complete control over what others hear and how they will react influences how one approaches and what one expects from the activity of teaching. This is an example of how it may be impossible to wholly comprehend the complexity of educational endeavors.

A product orientation limits consideration of complex phenomena such as relationships and experiences. As a result, institutions can overlook important aspects of educational function such as support for the development of faculty members' collegial relationships and attention to the broad value of reflective pedagogical research. To participate unquestioningly in a normative culture of measurement can be problematic because such an orientation conveys a sense of false confidence that one can understand or describe educational endeavors and their value completely with such a framework. It also influences how people understand their roles as part of an institution and are situated in relation to one another. In particular, a neoliberal orientation relies on a critical assumption: it situates people as necessarily autonomous and is reflected by an interest to foster competition between so-called "individuals."

Normalization of Individualization Separates

A neoliberal orientation functions largely by deliberately individualizing people. For instance, formalized educational systems function to organize relations among people for the purposes of individualization (Foucault, 1995). Often from the ages of four and five, if not younger, people are expected to attend school through to the age of 18, and often beyond to college and graduate school, if they want access to certain jobs and perceived social status. A person must move through each level of the system to move onto the next. Institutional structures are in place to evaluate people at each stage to determine when a person can move on. These structures are used largely for organizational purposes and only work if a person's perceived characteristics or performance can be captured somehow in order to compare with others. This has a normalizing impact on situating people as separate from each other. In institutional contexts, it situates learning largely as an "individual's" responsibility too.

To draw on the writing of Michel Foucault (1995), educational institutions are formations that make use of disciplinary methods such as time tables in the form of schedules, evaluation through examinations, and enclosures in the forms of classrooms and office spaces that are designated for specific functions. The purpose of these methods, in neoliberal terms, is to distinguish people from each other in hierarchical and competitive ways to make it more efficient for interested parties, such as employers, to identify people as qualified for particular positions. Individualization has a productive purpose, which can also have a normalizing effect. Educational institutions influence societal notions of what it means to learn, to teach, and to be "schooled"—even "educated" implying that these activities happen for people as individuals. Disciplinary methods introduce a scale around norms that influences people's relations in part because they seek to organize relations and to situate a person as separate from another.

Engagement of a neoliberal orientation by higher educational institutions situates people in economic terms. The framework does this to distinguish people from each other, further reinforcing the importance of documentation and evaluation of people for the purposes of realizing institutional goals. A neoliberal rationality provides a power/knowledge construct that situates people as objects and subjects of power. From a neoliberal perspective, people are objects because reliance on the use of disciplinary methods to organize relations through a process of individualization insinuates that people can at some level be understood or described through those methods. In other words, a transcript or CV, among other documents, reflects a simplified rendering of a person. People become subjects to such disciplinary methods because the methods influence how people feel about themselves, whether one is good at school or a subject, and the extent to which one feels educated. Norms influence how we behave, relate, think, and judge others and ourselves. Participation in an institution oriented by economic terms and business practices, to some extent, encourages internalization of those terms—and their rationality. The emergent norms not only suggest that quality research and teaching can be adequately quantified, that grades do reflect what students learn, that retention rates indicate institutional success, among others, but also imply that people are necessarily separate from others and situated in a competitive way.

While a neoliberal orientation reflects a power/knowledge regime that seeks to situate people as objects and subjects and emphasizes the differences between people to distinguish them from each other, Foucault suggests that people cannot be autonomous because we are necessarily socially constructed (Bevir, 1999). A notion of autonomy would suggest that a person could exist outside society. Foucault implies this is not possible because one cannot escape the influence of some kind of societal normalization because people are born into and live in relation. This is not to say that people cannot become aware of normalizing influences and seek to act in ways that counter them. Mark Bevir (1999) suggests one can engage reason, senses, the development of perspective, reflection, among others, to consider how to act within institutions and society. While one's responses and actions may influence how one experiences social constructs to an extent, one cannot be separate or autonomous from these constructs.

A Confucian relationality shares the same assumption—that people are not autonomous—but takes it in a different direction than Foucault does. A framework of relationality drawn from classical Chinese philosophical texts envisions life as processual and, because people are situated necessarily in relation, it suggests that relationships are of utmost importance. One has some choice about how one engages with others in ways that can influence the robustness of a relationship. For instance, people who act toward one another with a sense of reciprocity, respect, and care may have stronger, more enriched relationships. People grow through their relationships. To be clear, a notion of relation does not mean that people cannot have their own personalities and differences, but, rather, Confucian relationality suggests that our individualities emerge through our engagement with others. While Foucault suggests that power/knowledge regimes can situate people as objects and subjects generating societal norms that mask the complexity of people causing oppression and suffering, a concept of relationality emphasizes that people can influence norms because they generate and perpetuate them continually through their activities.

A Confucian relational perspective offers a profoundly distinct view of institutions as formations that seek to organize relations, which can generate norms and knowledges, impacting how people act and what they believe without a need to situate people as individuals. This is not to shy away from the fact that institutions can function in oppressive ways to keep certain groups of people out of them. Rather, this orientation suggests that because relation is primary, it reminds that institutions exist because people construct them continually. Because institutions exist only because people in relation constitute them, how people relate influences them. In fact, educational institutions could be situated not only as organizing relations between people, but also as generating roles and chances for relating. While the roles reflect varied levels of institutional power, from a relational perspective they could also be perceived as creating opportunities for unintended activities that have the potential to unsettle the product-oriented aims of the institution including the construct of people as autonomous individuals.

Distinguishing Confucian Relationality

A neoliberal framework, which situates people as autonomous for competitive purposes to distinguish them from each other, is largely a product-oriented perspective that tends to be reductive in nature because it backgrounds complexity to make it easier to compare people. In other words, it is an approach that tends to exclude those aspects that may serve to complicate comparative identifiers. But a Confucian relationality, on the other hand, situates people as necessarily constituted by others and in doing so assumes and foregrounds complexity. Because it is process oriented, it is more inclusive in nature because perceived differences do not have a pressure to be framed as having competitive implications. Rather, considering activities as emergent welcomes diversity because differences may enrich the activities themselves in part by initiating inquiry. Because outcomes are not the sole valued focus, the experience of the ongoing activity itself matters. This direction of thinking when extended to considering broader notions of relationality implies that varied frameworks of relationality need not be viewed as competitive but rather as complementary. Different characterizations of relationality emerge as a matter of inclusive emphasis rather than exclusive. While this book engages a concept of Confucian relationality, I want to point out that there are other related notions, which differ with regard to their focus and purpose.

Eurocentric perspectives, for instance, generally employ the term "relationality" as a useful metaphysical concept, often framed as a reverse discourse deployed to challenge epistemological, ontological, or methodological norms. For instance, it can be a way to resist notions of dualistic beliefs and ways of knowing reflected by Platonic and Rousseauian educational theories (Stone, 1988/2013). Lynda Stone suggests that a relational epistemology is largely feminist and potentially transformative because relation is basic; emphasizing relation challenges the notion of transcendental truths. This construct echoes poststructuralist interests in considering how power relations shape notions of truth and knowledge, destabilizing assumptions that there exists some kind of direct link between them (St. Pierre, 2000). For instance, engaging relationality loosens notions of positionality from being essentialist and fixed.

In addition to providing epistemological challenges to binary thinking about mind/body, subject/object, and sciences/humanities, among others, Barbara Thayer-Bacon (2010) makes a more specific case for a relational epistemological perspective when framing knowing as transactional. This pragmatist social feminist view, as Thayer-Bacon calls it, situates beliefs, expectations, and standards as socially constructed, requiring continual critique and adjustment; people construct what we know through our relationships with others. An idea, for example, cannot be isolated but exists in a web of knowing that emerges through people's embodied social environments. The characterization of a relational epistemology can be useful for "active engagement" and "democratic inclusion" as a way to connect educational theory and practice (Thayer-Bacon, 2010, p. 3). For educators, this means not prioritizing ideas (or abstractions or objectivity) over experiences (often seen as subjective, concrete, temporal) or vice versa, but rather to envision their connectedness. This move emphasizes the importance of developing awareness of the role of contexts and beliefs in the construction of knowing while also accommodating ambiguity. When people are situated as active participants in a natural world that is contingent, this focus considers a view of what phenomena are possible rather than what may be perceived as actual.

While Thayer-Bacon uses a concept of relationality as a way to reframe philosophical notions of epistemology, Karen Barad (2007), drawing on quantum physics, suggests that relationality can be used to consider how notions of epistemology, ontology, and ethics are mutually implicative and inseparable. Barad offers a concept of "agential realism" to destabilize scholars' perceptions of the normative boundaries among humanities, social sciences, and traditional sciences to provoke more far-reaching conversations. In particular, Barad suggests that a relational ontology provides the basis for a "posthumanist performative account of material bodies," which indicates that agencies form through relation. A key part of the conception of agential realism is the notion of intra-action, which is described as different from interaction because it implies that identifiable agencies do not precede relation but emerge from it. Agencies are enmeshed and only become distinctive through relation.

Barad further invokes relation between humans and nonhumans through the suggestion that there is reciprocity between "thinking about something and knowing your intentions (concerning the matter)" (Barad, 2007, p. 21). The nature of intentionality needs to be rethought because circumstances inform thinking. As a result, intentions cannot preexist relation. In fact, Barad (2007) states—provocatively—that

> Perhaps intentionality might better be understood as attributable to a complex network of human and nonhuman agents, including historically specific sets of material conditions that exceed the traditional notion of the individual. Or perhaps it is less that there is an assemblage of agents than there is an entangled state of agencies. (p. 23)

Humans and nonhumans, then, cannot ever be considered as existing separately from others but, rather, as necessarily actively embedded in particular changing contexts. While one may seek to describe a person or "thing" in particular ways, the act of description itself is always partial because it entails the act of selection, which smacks of artifice because to select is to distinguish and background relation. For Barad, relationality can be a useful theoretical tool to reconfigure notions of meaning and boundaries that envision the world, human and nonhuman, as deeply connected.

While Barad discusses relationality with regard to the inextricability of agencies and its implications for the entangled relations between humans and nonhumans, Bruno Latour (2004) invokes it epistemologically with a cultural context in mind. Latour argues for a repositioning of the critic not simply as one who participates in a process of critique and deconstruction of objects for the sake of it, or for possible misuse, but one, who through thoughtful, even ethical analysis, can contribute to the generation of meaning. In particular, Latour argues that epistemological matters of fact are situated as emergent and relational to matters of concerns, implying a reality that is not bound by matters of fact. They are limited representations of experience: "Matters of fact are only very partial and, I would argue, very polemical, very political renderings of matters of concerns . . ." (Latour, 2004, p. 232). For example, the intention of identifying something as an object or fact implicates it in a web of matters of concern. Latour uses relationality to consider how matters of fact are always embedded in matters of concerns rather than existing in isolated or transcendent ways devoid of contexts.

While the renderings of Eurocentric notions of relationality that I have described so far emphasize a largely epistemological perspective, a concept of relationality drawn from reading classical Chinese texts, instead, has a different focus. Rather than an emphasis on perceptions of knowing, Confucian relationality largely engages a notion of the world as specific and embodied, taking as its focus the human realm of conduct. This compels a view of people as constituted by others in particular ways. I discuss this in more detail in chapter 3. In brief, however, people are not seen as abstractions but emerge in specific relation. Because people are particular and emergent, this implicates a process-oriented view of life as changing. When we accept there is no individual, no essence of a person, then it suggests that people are contingent and foregrounds the importance of experiences.

I want to point out that engaging a specific notion of relationality does not reductively devalue others. Choosing to use a Confucian relationality to read higher educational institutions does not presume that, for example, Barad's considerations of the connections between humans and nonhumans or relational epistemologies are moot. Rather, I see them together as generating a broader field of relationality; rather than antithetical, the frameworks have different emphases that can coexist and complement each other. While it may be difficult to characterize "relationality" beyond a general notion of connection without delving into intentions and specific contexts, I suggest the term's flexibility reminds educators that our endeavors are particular—necessarily spatially, sensorially, and temporally experienced. In fact, the more ways that relationality as a conception is theorized in specific contexts, the more complex the field of relationality that develops. The multiplicity of purposes for its use presents an opportunity to consider how the term's meanings take specific shape from engagement. The frameworks develop meaning when they are engaged contextually, and I situate myself as one of many exploring the implications of these constructions. In the case of this research involving educational institutions, I use a Confucian relationality to consider the primary contextual value of enriching human relationships and communities through dynamic intra-actions. More broadly, this view of a notion of relationality as continually emergent and accommodating of differing notions and informed by them suggests that rather than a product-oriented, dualistic notion of winners or losers, better or worse, a Confucian relationality features creative and generous conjunctive notions—"and," "if"—encouraging focus without losing complexity.

Attending to Processes

The purpose of the book is twofold. First, it seeks to construct a concept of Confucian relationality through the reading of a classical Chinese text. To do this, I situate the Confucian tradition as a relationally dynamic one in part because its commentarial practices suggest that textual meaning is continually constructed through readers' engagement. I explore this perspective in more detail in chapter 1. If the activity of reading is considered a way to construct meaning about the classical texts, then this suggests that the particular temporal and spatial locations of readers influences the meaning of the texts too. In other words, textual meaning emerges through the activity of reading. In chapter 2, I share my reading of a translation of the classical text *Zhongyong* and use it to construct a concept of Confucian relationality, a process-oriented concept that situates people as necessarily constituted by others. This suggests that classical Confucian texts have relevance as interdisciplinary resources for contemporary contexts.

Second, the book explores how the concept can be used to foster inquiry about contemporary higher educational contexts by drawing attention to the product-oriented nature of some practices and values. In particular, engaging the concept of Confucian relationality suggests the value of attending to process-oriented aspects like developing the craft of teaching and the faculty collegiality that emerges through participation in learning communities that foster imaginative collaborative learning, which enrich academic communities in unexpected ways. In fact, what emerges from this exploration is the surprising resonant value of teaching, which rather than a normatively considered unidirectional activity becomes an important context for faculty learning too. The engagement of the concept with specific contexts at the same time also elaborates various aspects of a Confucian relationality, which contributes to ongoing contextualizing of a notion of Confucian relationality. The inquiry challenges educators to envision faculty roles beyond product-oriented notions of separation and competition to situate them as relational and changing.

More specifically, I use the concept to examine three specific examples of higher educational phenomena. In chapter 3, I use the concept of a Confucian relationality to consider orienting documents (strategic directions and tenure requirements) of the case study institution to show, in part, the tensions between product-oriented outcomes like research and situating the value of process-oriented ones such as teaching. Engaging a Confucian relationality as an analytical framework emphasizes a process-oriented perspective of faculty endeavors, one that complicates normative notions of teaching and learning. A concept of Confucian relationality, rather than situating people as separate beings who enter into relation and leaving them in the same way, frames relating as occurring among people who are part of the same expansive networked field. To see people not as separate from others but in synergistic relation influences the implications of what it means to engage, relate, and learn. Rather than "interact," people from a relational perspective "intra-act." As mentioned earlier, Barad (2007) distinguishes between interaction and intra-action from the perspective of a notion of agency. Interaction assumes that agency precedes relation, while intra-action implies that agencies emerge through relation. To extend this view of intra-action to learning then is to situate it as an activity that emerges through relation, and because relation is ongoing, so is learning. That people are inextricably enmeshed has profound implications for teaching in higher educational institutions in part because a Confucian relationality views teaching and learning as dimensions and features of people's activities rather than as clearly delineable.

To engage a Confucian relationality draws attention to the value of existing writing of scholars from various disciplines that complicate normative notions of teaching and learning by situating them as intra-active processes. Educator Ernest Boyer (1990), for instance, suggests that teaching is "a dynamic endeavor" that involves thinking and learning; in fact, Boyer argues that while a critical part of a conception of scholarship involves conducting research, so should reflection on the connections between theoretical constructs and teaching practice. For instructional faculty members, a notion of scholarship should envision the endeavors of research, teaching, and service as related. Along the same lines, John Dewey (1916) makes the point that in educational contexts, subject matter cannot be separated from method: "The method of teaching is the method of an art, of action intelligently directed by ends" (p. 170). With an expert understanding of materials and tools, painters, for instance, must learn how to use them. "Attainment of this knowledge requires persistent and concentrated attention to objective materials. The artist studies the progress of his own attempts to see what succeeds and what fails" (p. 170). Teachers, like artists, Dewey argues, embrace the challenge of shifting contexts and conditions by continually learning through experimentation in ways that can be transformative. Urban planner Donald Schön (1983), similarly, views those who teach as professionals and experts who give artistic performances in their practice of teaching: "his artistry is evident in his selective management of large amounts of information, his ability to spin out long lines of invention and inference, and his capacity to hold several ways of looking at things at once without interrupting the flow of inquiry" (p. 130). Philosopher Roger Ames (2016) suggests that teaching and learning are abstractions of educational endeavors, which could be envisioned as an enmeshed activity of what he calls "holistic" learning. Anthropologist Tim Ingold (2018) suggests that education is not about transmission of information at all but about living and "leading life" rather than teaching and learning, and, in particular, cultivating attention regarding the sharing of experience; education emerges through participation in people's lives.

Engaging a concept of Confucian relationality draws attention to scholars' writings that already complicate normative notions of teaching and learning. It highlights their resonances and inquires about their implications. In particular, if envisioned as intra-active processes that emerge through experience and taking this further by adding a Confucian relational notion that situates communities not as collections of autonomous persons but considers people as necessarily associative, then the activities of teaching and learning take on a synergistic, mutually implicative quality necessarily involving others. More broadly, for higher educational institutions, engaging the expansive notion that people intra-act suggests that those aspects that generate contexts to cultivate relationships, such as teaching and support for teaching, become eminently valuable because to enrich relations is to enrich communities. While a neoliberal perspective emphasizes those aspects of institutions that are measurable, a Confucian relational orientation foregrounds educational endeavors that cultivate relation. Engaging a Confucian relationality, in particular, draws attention to collegial faculty groups such as learning communities that gather to support the activity of teaching-learning through discussion and reflection about classroom experiences, which emerge in university contexts as forums for fostering dynamic collegial relationships.

In chapter 4, the concept of Confucian relationality is engaged to examine how research about faculty learning communities situates collegiality in the context of encouraging faculty to develop the craft of teaching. Used as an analytical framework, Confucian relationality emphasizes the importance of collegiality to support learning about teaching as part of a community, showing the value of attending to the development of the quality of relationships. Faculty learning communities, for instance, have developed in part because of faculty interest in finding ways to support teaching in an academic culture where the practice of teaching is often perceived as a so-called "private enterprise" that is not often subject to open discussion, peer review, or constructive criticism (Glowacki-Dudka & Brown, 2008). Jason Ritter (2011) points out that because higher educational institutions assume that institutional support for teaching is largely unnecessary, new instructional faculty may feel reluctant to ask for assistance because it might be perceived as a move that positions experts in particular areas of study as learners about teaching. This can evoke emotions of vulnerability and uncertainty about how to respond to events in classrooms (Pinnegar, 1995). Michelle Glowacki-Dudka and Michael Brown (2008) posit that when faculty do seek to improve their teaching craft, they often turn to campus centers for teaching that offer short workshops on developing specific teaching techniques. While these workshops may be useful to address some aspects of teaching, the experiences may not encourage the development of a thoughtful teaching philosophy and a comprehensive teaching methodology that might emerge as part of a more collaborative setting. Faculty learning communities that encourage the development of philosophies of teaching and learning through the cultivation of collegial relationships, on the other hand, provide a space for the exchange of ideas between colleagues that fosters collaborative imaginative learning, which in turn also contributes to strengthening collegial networks.

The concept of the faculty learning community emerged from descriptions of student learning communities by Alexander Meiklejohn (1932) and John Dewey (1933) that suggested that shared study and collaborative inquiry were keys to active learning (Cox, 2004). In particular, the notion of cohorted study included the practice of having groups of students take courses together throughout a program. Some higher educational institutions found that participation in learning communities increased student retention because it helped students adjust socially and personally to university cultures and deepened their intellectual engagement. Interdisciplinary faculty members voluntarily participate in faculty learning communities (generally between six and 12 or so in each group)

(Furco & Moely, 2012). The generally cohort- or topic-based gatherings tend to be goal oriented and create a collegial environment where faculty members feel comfortable to discuss their classroom experiences. Groups meet regularly for a designated period of time and may discuss shared readings that foster reflection about teaching experiences or learn about new teaching approaches, among other activities.

While research about faculty learning communities describes the effectiveness of group activities to support the learning of teaching innovations, it often misses the broader value of the development of collegiality that emerges. If we consider a relational perspective of the development of collegiality, in which relationships are prioritized, it has an extensive impact on a university community by reconceptualizing the whole notion of community that situates people as necessarily associative and the world as processual. Efforts to develop collegiality through participation in faculty learning communities can enrich relationships beyond the scope of the learning community by fostering the potential for future intra-actions. Rather than a need to fix outcomes, a relational perspective values the cultivation of relationships to consider what is possible. It also situates personal cultivation as having expansive implications.

In chapter 5, the concept of Confucian relationality is engaged to explore how the reflective pedagogical research of Elizabeth Ellsworth situates faculty members as learners; the classroom may be viewed as a context for learning not only for students but for faculty too. Engaging a Confucian relational concept emphasizes the extensive impact of personal cultivation in the context of classrooms and beyond. Engagement with reflective pedagogical research supports envisioning teaching as an ongoing practice and as a process of personal cultivation. When institutions see the value of reflective pedagogical research as broadly relevant to various disciplines in a university, they insinuate the notion that teachers are learners. For instance, educator Elizabeth Ellsworth has published reflective theorizations about pedagogy that emerged from her experiences in the classroom, where Ellsworth examines the complexity of the classroom space and the relationships between participants through situating herself as continually learning. In particular, Ellsworth offers a critique of critical pedagogical approaches, examines the importance of destabilizing notions of student and teacher, and suggests that communication in the classroom should not be viewed as a matter of direct transfer of information but rather as a conversation that might return the unexpected. Ellsworth's research reflects, in my view, an undertaking of a process of relational personal cultivation in a classroom context, which could be seen as relevant to instructional faculty in various academic disciplines. From a Confucian relational perspective, because people are enmeshed, personal cultivation involves a process of learning through relation that can have extensive implications.

The three examples show how the concept of Confucian relationality may be used to inquire what might be missed by a product-oriented view of higher education. A neoliberal framework situates teaching and learning in a reductive, separate manner. While a culture of measurement seeks to describe quality teaching in quantifiable terms such as "products" and "outcomes," teaching is too complex a process to adequately and comprehensively describe in quantifiable ways. Fitzsimons (2002), crediting Jean-François Lyotard, suggests that a neoliberal framework situates the function of a teacher as a consumer of cultural products in order to reproduce them via teaching for consumption by students in classrooms with the goal of producing a labor force. The function of students from a product orientation is to consume (learn) content that teachers provide along with the various social hierarchies embedded as part of the schooling process. This suggests that faculty members are in the business of teaching, and students in the business of learning. In other words, teaching involves the production and conveyance of content for students. As a result, it may be difficult to prioritize support for teaching from a neoliberal perspective because the practice of teaching is so contextual. Because the purpose of this research is to foster inquiry, the examples I examine are specific because I interpret Confucian relationality as an approach more interested in particular contexts rather than making generalizations about them; the book does not intend to provide comprehensive examinations of those examples mentioned.

What a neoliberal perspective leaves unexamined is how learning about teaching can enrich a university more broadly in part by situating faculty as learners and a university as a learning community itself. In the concluding chapter, I consider how a Confucian relational concept frames the university as a learning community that is continually constructed. Engaging a notion that people are continually in relation suggests that perceived lines between teaching and learning are not so clear, challenging normative notions of teaching to some extent that include the direct transfer of information from teacher to student. More broadly, what engaging a Confucian relationality does in part is to call attention to existing conceptions of teaching and learning as intra-acting processes and frames them as a family of related endeavors. In doing so, a Confucian relational framework further encourages exploration of the implications for educational institutions' priorities and inquiry about normative notions of faculty member's activities.

Linking Time and Space

My interest in exploring a process-oriented view of higher education emerged in part from a prior experience of teaching in a three-week intensive writing program for incoming first-year students at a liberal arts college. The program embraced its faculty as learners by creating a supportive context for faculty to learn about writing-to-learn practices with a weeklong training for new faculty and two faculty-led weekend workshops for all faculty before teaching in the program prior to the fall semester. What made the approach distinct was that the faculty learned the practices as their students might by engaging writing as a way to construct ideas and gain innovative access to reading theoretical and creative texts rather than viewing writing simply as a product to be evaluated. Instead of conveying the practices in a didactic way, the program encouraged faculty members, drawn from institutions nationally, to experience various approaches and then develop their own ways to engage an anthology of multidisciplinary readings with their students. Rather than solely focus on discussing the desired outcomes for students, the program trusted that attending to developing an enriching learning process for faculty would shape how they worked with their students.

By taking the time and effort to create a faculty learning community, the program cultivated a context for faculty in which the sought-after outcomes emerged naturally and in more ways than administrators could have hoped because faculty were motivated to take risks as part of a supportive collegial peer community. What the program did was focus on cultivating the process of learning for faculty in a way that attended to developing collegiality among faculty, which included engaging the practices together, undertaking assignments as their students might, and sharing writing with faculty peers. As a result, team-teaching collaborations emerged naturally, for instance, through the open sharing of lesson plans and informal conversations about teaching. Attention to faculty as learners encouraged faculty members to explore new teaching approaches in part through engaging their experience of feeling vulnerable and challenged as learners as part of a community. The program emphasized collegiality and in doing so broadened normative notions of learning about teaching.

However, what surprised me was that the writing practices, which helped faculty and students to connect with texts across disciplines, were not used more widely, even on a limited basis, in the regular semester courses offered at the college. A question that emerged from this teaching experience was why it was so difficult for the college to share among all its faculty members a pedagogical approach used in a program required for all their students. Students spent the equivalent amount of time and energy as required of a semester-long course to learn a process approach to writing (and along with it accompanying terminology) that could be useful in fostering active discussions and generating ideas for academic papers in many traditional disciplinary classes. Instead, it was often the first and last directed experience students had with this type of process-oriented writing.

My provisional thinking led me to consider how faculty of many disciplines of higher educational institutions tend to be "university trained," and as a result, our views of teaching are shaped by our often disciplinary experiences of teaching and learning at universities. Although liberal arts colleges often normatively tout the importance of teaching, their administrative structures such as faculty tenure requirements often reflect those of universities to some extent. In short, scholarly value emerges from research productivity rather than teaching excellence. This led me to consider, more broadly, why it is difficult for universities to actualize the importance and value of some of their relational aspects, like teaching, beyond market-oriented perspectives, calling into inquiry their priorities.

I came to appreciate a process perspective without quite knowing it. As a child who was born and raised in the United States and brought up Chinese American, this largely meant having different cultural practices from my Midwestern school friends—my family left our shoes at the door upon entering our home; ate "fusion" food, for instance, like rice with stir-fried vegetables along with breaded fish sticks and mayonnaise on the side; and spoke Mandarin at home and English everywhere else. My early direct notion of classical Chinese texts came shaped in part by my mother's memories of memorizing texts like the Confucian *Analects* in grammar school in Taiwan. Her frustration at not knowing what the texts meant as a child yet having to spend quite a bit of time studying them likely contributed to her gravitating toward an interest in math—

the clarity of geometric proofs!—to majoring in math in college and to choosing accounting as a profession. But she tells me her feelings of the texts have changed through time. While she did not like the pressure of reciting the texts in front of her classmates, she has come to appreciate how the texts contributed to how she makes sense of life in profound ways. She noticed the meanings of the texts emerged and changed as she changed, rather than having fixed meanings.

The lessons about how learning can emerge through time came in other ways for me. Once when my grandfather came from Taiwan to visit my family, we took a trip to the Rocky Mountains. Grandfather had limited education because of political upheaval in his childhood, lost his father at a young age, and ended up pressed to serve in the military, as did many young men of his era. Along the way, we took a rest stop alongside a gusty mountain river. My siblings and my nine-year-old self rock-hopped along the bank. Without thinking, I picked up a small smooth stone and tossed it into the river, enjoying the plunking sound it made. My grandfather sat down on a rock near me and asked, "What if everyone who stopped by tossed a stone in the river?" In the moment, I wondered what I had done wrong. How could tossing a stone in the river matter? He did not tell me not to throw a stone in the water in an authoritarian way. Instead, he left me with a question that stayed with me, although I did not come up with more varied responses until later in my life, years after he had passed. The river would fill with stones; people could change the flow of a river and a landscape without knowing how. What people do matters; even the action of a child, who tossed a stone in the water to hear the plunking sound, has a consequence. It mattered to some extent because one is necessarily part of a broader world—physical, material, human. It is important to view people's actions relationally in context, as a part of time and space.

Linda Tuhiwai-Smith (2012) writes that Eurocentric philosophies and languages tend to regard notions of time and space as separate: "This view generates ways of making sense of the world as a 'realm of stasis,' well-defined, fixed and without politics" (p. 55). This notion that they can be considered separately insinuates the idea that space can somehow be measured, reflecting an ideological position encoded in language preoccupied with what Smith calls "exactness" and "parameters." In fact, this notion of space as fixed undergirds normative notions of science in that it foregrounds an idea that knowledge can be attained through the ability to reason in part by giving space dimensions. The notion that knowledge, expressed through language and the ability to reason, can be gathered and accumulated gives humans a hubristic sense of superiority over nature. It's a limited concept, Smith suggests, because it removes context. It makes it easy to think we understand more than we do, even to magnify what we think we know. Smith discusses how a notion that space can be somehow measured also foregrounds the view that people are individuals, a perspective that gets expressed in how people are viewed in communities—as a basic social unit and building block of society from which a capitalist mode of production develops.

The importance of the notion of viewing time in relation to space leads me back to reflecting on my teaching experience. Perhaps I cannot wholly fault the college at not building more broadly upon the innovative program that they supported given the inertial heft of disciplinary traditions and structures that treat teaching and learning as separate. The implications of Smith's ideas about a deep fissure of conceptions of time and space suggest it resonates broadly, encoded not only in language but also in institutional practices and priorities in ways that are difficult to perceive when one is an active part of it by contributing to it through one's actions. Experiences, while viewed as personally valuable, simply do not have the same value in a language that merits outcomes and evidence. Even in academic research, consider how normatively science and its production of quantitative data carries more political and social value with its promise of "generalizability" and "replicability" even as it may to some extent omit or background contextual aspects in its study designs—how it somehow normatively seems more "true" than qualitative and humanities-oriented research, which involves engaging interpretive approaches and seeking to inquire about contexts.

A developing appreciation for a process-oriented perspective, one that embraces a relation between concepts of time and space, leads me to inquire about the value of attending to experiences and relation, to collegiality, to reflective engagement in the context of faculty activities in higher educational institutions, even if their value may be difficult to measure in outcomes-focused ways. Trying to explore a relational view when a predominant product-oriented one is already entrenched is a tall order. But I am reminded that part of the project here is to make more visible the value of what already exists as part of higher educational phenomena, to inquire about the implications of considering the value of relational experiences. My grandfather, with his question about the consequence of tossing a stone in a river, insinuated considerations of anthropocentric as well as geologic time. To consider a relation between time and space beyond one is to consider that there are resonances to one's actions impossible to know. Engaging a Confucian relationality requires a certain amount of trust that when attention is given to enriching people's experiences, it opens up unpredictable possibilities, suggesting that even those aspects that defy measurement may be profoundly meaningful.

Juxtaposition as Way to Enrich Relation

So far I have been mostly referring to Confucian relationality as a useful theoretical framework to read higher educational contexts to emphasize the value of those aspects of educational institutions that prioritize relation, but I want to point out that I do not engage the framework in a fixed or static way. In fact, I use the concept as an approach to frame this research more broadly when I envision it as an inquiry that is not meant to be definitive or conclusive. A process orientation insinuates that change is continual, implying that no perspective can be totalizing, suggesting that research endeavors are necessarily partial to some extent. To acknowledge the partialness of research approaches at the outset positions researchers as always engaging some doubt, with certainty always out of reach. Juxtaposition, for instance, is intentionally a partial method that does not seek to provide comprehensive analysis or understanding of a text or concept. Rather, it inquires rather than essentializes. To juxtapose is to intentionally choose to set side by side, but the choice also leads to a question about what to leave out. The awareness of leaving some aspects out contributes to the acknowledgement of the partiality of one's research approach. When change and process are emphasized, to juxtapose theoretical frameworks, for instance, implies that the activity of inquiry enriches their existing relation.

Throughout the book, I build on Elizabeth Ellsworth's (1997) conception of juxtaposition as a way to invite questions about the texts and concepts that I examine. Ellsworth writes, "Reading two texts side by side can destabilize the sense I have made of each text separately" (p. 14). It is a practice that makes visible assumptions by attending to the resonances and differences that emerge from the experience of reading. The point is not to make differences match up but to ask what they mean. To undertake a process of juxtaposition highlights the process of reading as a decidedly subjective, ongoing, and generative activity, rather than one that assumes objectivity or considers an act of reading as the uncovering of essential meanings. While a process of comparison and contrast largely seeks to see differences between two texts in order to view them more clearly as separate objects, a process of juxtaposition, on the other hand, emphasizes the construction of meaning. The use of juxtaposition as an approach to inquiry is inspired by a notion of "concept as method" put forth by post-qualitative scholars who express concern that qualitative research approaches have fallen into increasingly narrow patterns of knowledge production (Lather & St. Pierre, 2013; St. Pierre, 2014). To use a concept like juxtaposition is an attempt to engage in exploratory inquiry as part of particular contexts and at the same acknowledge the partialness of such an approach.

While Ellsworth may not view her work within the context of a Confucian relationality, I suggest that her articulation of how reading is a way to construct meaning resonates with a Confucian relational notion that juxtaposed phenomena are part of the same connected field. From a Confucian relational perspective, juxtaposition does not create relation, which would insinuate that there was no relation prior to juxtaposition, but enriches ones that already exist. To ask about resonances and disjunctures between, for instance, concepts, then, is to engage the potential to transform them through enriching relation. Not only does this approach acknowledge partiality, it suggests that through engagement, frameworks change. Because anything can be juxtaposed with anything else, the act of juxtaposition reminds that texts and concepts are always part of a contextual field that is specific and emerging. The texts and concepts do not and cannot exist in isolation. To juxtapose then is to deliberately enrich interpretations of the selected texts or concepts through influencing their relation. This positive or productive activity of contextualization creates resonance and disjuncture and at the same time insinuates what is left out. Why juxtapose this and not that? It is the deliberateness of juxtaposition and also the element of randomness that acknowledges that the question of choice is always there. To read two texts or concepts in juxtaposition compels me to see them differently even if I return to consider them separately. My notion of them changes from considering their relation.

Throughout the book, I use juxtaposition in varied contexts—documents with other documents, concepts with other concepts, concepts with educational phenomena, research with other research, among others. The intention is in part to try to make visible the assumptions I have about reading them, to notice resonances and disjunctures that emerge from their juxtaposition and to ask about what they mean, and to insinuate the breadth and complexity of the field of educational institutional endeavors. I take this approach to inquire about the possibilities that engagement with a relational concept can return in the specific contexts of universities. Juxtaposition is a relational method because it inquires. It also takes on an ethical dimension from this perspective because when phenomena are seen as related, then activities such as questioning norms, personal cultivation, and institutional reflection, among others, necessarily have extensive impacts on others.

I want to point out that engaging a Confucian relational framework does not mean that one dismisses a neoliberal one in toto. I am not suggesting that there is no room in a product-oriented perspective to accommodate people in relation or that a Confucian relationality as an orientation completely negates the value of measurement in some capacity in educational contexts for particular purposes. Engaging a Confucian relationality, rather than having an exclusionary intention, implies that the two theoretical frameworks have different emphases to some extent. To engage them in juxtaposition can enrich them and the contextual field of which they are a part.

Universities would benefit from reflecting on the priorities that emerge from their practices because valuing what can be measured simply does not capture the complex relational richness of educational endeavors. To engage a concept of Confucian relationality is one generative way to actively inquire about how a neoliberal framework influences the constructs of higher educational institutions by making visible the assumptions this approach has on institutional expectations of faculty activities. It suggests that while institutions may continue to engage a neoliberal approach because it reflects broader political-cultural-economic global trends, participants can at the same time strive to be critical of it, and to take care to reconsider notions of what institutions normatively value. It offers institutions a chance to resist neoliberal pressure by situating the orientation not as an essential framework but as a constructed one.

Engaging a Confucian relational framework implies that participants in an educational institution do not exist as independent from others but as necessarily already in relation. Because it situates people as intraconnected and invokes a worldview of change, it suggests that relation is not a thing, it is a doing and happening. In other words, what is important from a Confucian relational perspective is *how* people relate. Such a perspective implies the value of attending to relational aspects of educational institutional phenomena, for instance, those that prioritize the development of collegiality and support the development of teaching. It challenges participants to look beyond a predilection to use metrics to measure the quality of a university community and instead to see its activities as constructed continually by people's actions in ways that cannot be fixed or wholly described or quantified—and do not need to be.

While instructional faculty may continue to feel neoliberal pressure to emphasize publishing over teaching to achieve tenure and promotion, engaging a Confucian relational perspective suggests faculty might want to continually inquire about institutional expectations that influence their professional experiences in part by asking questions not only about what institutions value, but also about what they do not. Adopting a position of inquiry about university norms is important because it impacts faculty activities in ongoing ways, can lead to changing institutional practices, and can even contribute to the revision of various guidelines themselves. A Confucian relationality is a radical framework for reading universities, especially in an age of neoliberalism because it, through envisioning time and space as contingent, reminds that institutions exist only because people in relation perform them. People, in other words, constitute institutions, and their activities construct institutional communities continually. From this perspective, learning is a process of personal cultivation that influences others in ways we may not know, shaping the contexts of each other's lives.

PART 1

A DYNAMIC CONFUCIAN TRADITION

Chapter 1

The Exam Is Not the Text

To construct a notion of a Confucian relationality using a translation of the classical Confucian text *Zhongyong*, which I do in the next chapter, it is helpful first to situate the Confucian tradition as a dynamic one. Historically contextualizing the tradition brings to the foreground the role of commentators, translators, and readers in shaping the normative meanings of the classical texts and the Confucian tradition. It also shows how particular contexts in which the texts were engaged influenced normative meanings of the texts as in the case of the use of the texts as content for the imperial civil service examination process. More broadly, a focus on the tradition's commentarial aspects from an interpretive perspective suggests that agential readings of the texts from people's particular contexts encourages the use of the texts as contemporary resources. From this perspective, engaging the texts contributes to a changing Confucian tradition.

Confucianism, often viewed as a major component of traditional Chinese culture from sociocultural, political, and historical perspectives, emphasizes the importance of improving relationships to foster ethical living. It addresses a broad range of values and governance-related questions, including how to cultivate learning and leadership abilities. The term Confucianism often insinuates for English speakers a monolithic tradition drawn from a group of classical texts that reference a particular figure, Confucius (551–479 BCE). Confucius lived in Shandong province in the state of Lu, raised by his mother and her family after his father, an oft-called low aristocrat, passed away when Confucius was 3 years old. Scholars credit the invention of the term "Confucianism" to John

Francis Davis, second governor of Hong Kong, who used it in his 1836 publication *The Chinese*. They also point out that Jesuit missionaries to China in the seventeenth century employed the term because they felt compelled to find a perceived counterpart to Christianity.

English-language translators have shaped normative Eurocentric notions of the Confucian tradition in part by encoding their worldviews into translations of classical Confucian texts. Roger Ames and David Hall (2001) note that some English-speaking translators of Confucian texts impose post-Enlightenment ideals, Christian beliefs, and substance-oriented worldviews onto the Chinese language. For instance, when the Chinese character *tian* is translated as "Heaven" with a capital "H," it takes on a Christian gloss that indicates a place where "God" resides, assuming a separation between a powerful divine being and people. This becomes mistakenly read as part of classical Chinese culture, which did not have such conceptions.

The Eurocentric views that inform translations of the classical Chinese texts are ontological in nature. For instance, some translate the texts by assuming there is some sort of definitive understanding and take on a role of interpreter in an attempt to provide a universal translation. Ames and Hall (2001) discuss how Eurocentric normative worldviews, reflected as part of English language and philosophy, engage an Aristotelian substance ontology, which has emerged from the classical Greek tradition that foregrounds a notion of "things" over "happenings." Substance ontology privileges objects over processes, descriptions over functions, and permanence over change. Within this essentialist cultural framework, a view of objectivity as truth and people as autonomous informs the construction of institutions, law, government, and people's relationships. Engaging a substance-oriented view that privileges permanence over change promotes the problematic notion that the classical texts that form the basis of the Confucian tradition and the tradition itself are unchanging.

While the terms "Confucianism" and "Confucian tradition" give an impression of a cohesive and largely unchanging tradition, scholars point out, however, these are relatively recent Eurocentric constructions that actually reference the discussions of literati/scholars throughout the last two millennia. In Chinese, the term "Confucianism" is a translation of the term "*ruxue*," which references a social class that predates Confucius. Michael Nylan (2001) calls the term "Confucianism" a useful abstraction, which masks the tradition's practice of active intellectual engagement.

Nylan points out that the classic philosophical texts could be considered related to Confucius the person in two aspects. First, Confucius and his followers may have used some of the texts for the purpose of drawing inspiration for moral guidance. Second, some traditions claim that Confucius compiled some classical texts. Prior to 136 BCE, the followers of *ruxue* dressed in particular ways and performed rituals that may have contributed to their identification as a group; the scholars supported a number of concepts including cultivating empathy to improve relations with others. They also contributed to the transmission of the concepts orally and through commentary.

Taking a closer look at the historical context of the Confucian tradition supports the view that the texts are part of a tradition that continually changes. By focusing on the commentarial aspect as a way to situate the classical texts, I suggest that it is valuable to see the texts and their meanings as necessarily changing through how people engage them rather than view them as unchanging objects with fixed and definitive meanings. Taking an interpretive view of the Confucian tradition creates a context for engaging the texts that encourages contemporary readers to focus on how the texts have been engaged through time and varied contexts. This approach also suggests that, rather than assume one has to be an expert to engage the texts, nonspecialists can do so from their own perspectives with the understanding that their readings (and all readers' readings) will not, and could not possibly, be definitive. Situating the Confucian tradition from the perspective of its commentarial tradition implies the value of situating it as multivocal and changing. This chapter lays the groundwork for understanding how and why I take an interpretive approach in engaging a translation of the *Zhongyong* in the next chapter, where I construct a conception of Confucian relationality.

Emphasizing a Commentarial Tradition

What contextualizing the Confucian tradition historically makes evident is that the tradition and the constitution of the texts themselves have emerged as part of a relatively fragmented and multivocal process. Throughout the last two millennia, the Confucian tradition materializes in part from a commentarial tradition constituted by ongoing interpretations of a family of so-called Confucian texts. In addition to the *Zhongyong* text (sometimes translated as *Doctrine of the Mean*), these include the

Analects (*Lun Yu*), *Mencius* (*Mengzi*), and *Great Learning* (*Daxue*), among others, which are normatively viewed as constituting the basis of a Confucian tradition. The commentarial tradition, which involves scholars writing interlinear textual commentary, situates Confucianism as vitally changing because it suggests the value of continually engaging the texts from readers' particular historical contexts and positioning the texts as valuable resources to contemporary contexts.

One reason the tradition is multivocal and fragmented is that the texts have changed form through time. They have changed to an extent that scholars would find it difficult to identify "original" texts. What a focus on the commentarial tradition does in fact is to challenge the normative notion that there exist fixed "originals" of the classics. Given that many people participated in the authoring of the texts, some commentary likely became part of what might be considered today a classic "text." There may be no identifiable definitive "pre-commentarial texts" available to contemporary readers. It is likely that some texts in their current form include more recent commentary that even suppressed older commentary (as was likely the case with Song period scholar Zhu Xi, who "edited" and commented on a set of classical texts, and through his selection of texts emphasized some texts and perspectives more than others). This also may not have happened intentionally but may have occurred through time when some textual versions and commentary were read more than others.

Written running commentary of classical texts, which became a major mode of scholarly discourse, appeared during the Han period (206 BCE–220 CE) (Gardner, 1998). Scholars would insert their reflections about parts of the texts into the narratives themselves, generating a form of interlinear conversation. Scholars, through their commentary, would attempt to bring coherence to the fragmented texts and persuade others of the relevance of particular texts to the Confucian canon. Attempts at commentarial persuasion include bringing together the views of other scholars' textual interpretations or at times refuting them, underscoring the notion that classical textual meaning is constructed by the activities of a community of readers. (For an example of how vastly commentaries can differ, see Daniel Gardner's 2003 book *Zhu Xi's Reading of the Analects: Canon, Commentary, and the Classical Tradition*, in which he compares Song period scholar Zhu Xi's written commentary with that of Han period scholar He Yan's.) Scholars traditionally read commentaries along with various texts because the commentaries "mediate" the texts through time. Put another way, in response to particular historical contexts, commentaries give the texts new meanings and even create new textual artifacts, which continually reshape the Confucian tradition.

To focus on the commentarial aspect of the tradition is to situate the Confucian tradition as changing in part because it elucidates several inconsistencies in its transmission including the disrupted nature of the construction of the texts themselves. In fact, commentary is embodied in the forms of the Confucian texts often read today. Many unknown scholars contributed to the actual construction of the texts, suggesting that commentary itself constitutes the bodies of the texts. For instance, contemporary scholars attribute the writing of the *Analects*, a collection of 500 passages and 20 books between 475 BCE and 220 CE, to Confucius's students after his passing. The text, a central one to the tradition, narrates purported events of Confucius's life, describes him as a person, and includes anecdotes about Confucius and his students. However, actual authorship of the text, which was written with brush and ink on bamboo strips bundled together by string, is a mystery. Robert Eno (2015) points out that while some passages seem to have dominant themes, the disjointedness of the passages suggests that multiple commentators sought to deliberately disrupt the text to influence readers' interpretations. That said, scholars also point out that the string that held the bundles of text together sometimes broke, contributing to a possible rearrangement of the passages. Even the bodies of the classical texts in forms engaged today have changed through time, reinforcing a view of *ruxue* that is continually constructed rather than one that is essentialist.

Taking an Interpretive Approach

Along the same lines of historically situating the Confucian tradition as changing by emphasizing its commentarial aspect is for readers themselves to take the role of engaging the texts actively, including their translations and commentaries. One way to be an active reader is to take an interpretive approach to situating the texts and the tradition. This means adopting a process-oriented view of reading the classical texts that suggests that there can be no fixed or essentialist reading because the texts have different meanings for different people through time. A Confucian commentarial tradition, from an interpretive perspective, situates Confucianism as a dynamic philosophical tradition constituted by readings of texts that necessarily reference readers' specific locational and ontological orientations. Situating Confucianism as multivocal, then, accommodates the fragmented nature of a complex tradition, which is continually constructed by those who read and write about the texts rather than constituted by purported universal truths about the texts. Written commentary, from an interpretive perspective, generates new texts with new meanings.

Taking an active role in reading includes positioning the translations of the classical texts one engages as a form of commentary about the texts. While scholarship about the commentarial tradition often focuses on Chinese literati contributions, engaging a notion of "commentary" as textual construction also encompasses translators' interpretations of Confucian texts. Translators contribute to the commentarial tradition too because the act of translation involves textual interpretation. Rather than interlinear in form, they embed their interpretations in the body of the translated texts, which necessarily reflect their worldviews. To consider translations as part of commentarial tradition, then, insists that they must also be read as part of a changing Confucian tradition. While translations may impose translator views on the texts albeit at times inadvertently, the onus is on readers, in part, to acknowledge there is no definitive meaning of the classical Confucian texts. Rather, meaning is constructed by people's interpretations of the texts. This view places an inquiring emphasis on how readers read and translators translate within their particular contexts, leading to questions about how their aims, assumptions, and worldviews influence the readings of the texts.

Not all translators seek to provide definitive translations of the classical texts, making the framing work of readers easier. For instance, some scholars engage an interpretive approach to translation. Rather than seeking to translate words directly from one language into another, they approach translation reflectively through more elaborate descriptions, taking into account how differing worldviews and assumptions influence their perspectives. Some comparative scholars engage an interpretive approach to draw attention to seemingly incommensurable cultural notions. Ames and Hall (2001), for example, undertake a translation of *Zhongyong* informed by a relational gestalt, which reflects a process-oriented worldview resonant with the language of the classical texts. For instance, instead of translating *tian* as "Heaven," they acknowledge the complexity of translation when, for example, they choose to leave *tian* untranslated within the text or refer to it instead as "propensities of things," among other descriptive phrases. An interpretive relational worldview considers form and function always in mutual relationship. It insists on considering a view of life as processually affective, suggesting relation is necessarily intrinsic and ongoing. Meaning, then, emerges from specific contextual experiences.

For readers who take an active and interpretive approach to engaging the texts, what emerges is the changing nature of a multivocal commentarial tradition that accommodates even Eurocentric takes on the Confucian tradition by positioning English-language translations of the classical texts not as universal readings but as part of a field of multiple interpretations. Engaging an interpretive approach to translation puts the onus on readers to acknowledge translators' assumptions and consider how they may influence the bodies of translations. While some translators may strive to interpret the classical texts in a universal way, readers can read the translations with the understanding that they cannot be definitive. Readers who actively engage the texts and their translations through an interpretive lens assist with situating the Confucian tradition as dynamic because they need not wholly accept commentaries and translations from an essentialist orientation.

More broadly, to situate the Confucian tradition as dynamic draws attention to the point that literati established the *ruxue* tradition through commentaries written from particular contexts and for their own purposes, including attempts to cohere the tradition in order to address the issues of their particular time periods. Literati maintained the tradition through continual elaboration and engagement with it, suggesting its changing nature. Taking an interpretive approach suggests the inordinate importance of readers to engage the texts critically and to consider the interpretations and translations we encounter as reflective of multiple voices with multiple intentions. It also suggests the value of reading the classical texts from our own perspectives and contexts.

That said, while commentators have sustained the texts through centuries, this engagement has also generated powerful normative notions about the texts, which have emerged as culturally laden (for instance that they promote authoritarian views) so much so that they become viewed as inertial rather than continually emerging. Some historical contextualization about how the classical texts and their commentaries have been used, for instance, for imperial political purposes as part of the civil service examination process, expresses the sociocultural-political implications of the commentarial tradition as well as encourages continued engagement with the texts.

The civil service examinations provided an extreme context that influenced the way the texts were read and shape normative interpretations about them even in the present day. The reason for the weight of that particular context is valuable to explore because the norms about the texts that emerged from the use of the texts in the examination process (that they are inflexible and narrow in scope) may deter people from reading them. To explore the exam context in detail is to suggest that it is one context of many, and it need not be a dominant one from the perspective of contemporary readers who seek to engage the texts as contemporary resources.

A Complicated Conflation

A potential hindrance to seeing the Confucian tradition as dynamic is the cultural norms that have emerged about the tradition and the classical texts in relation to their role in the imperial civil service examination process. A powerful feature of the commentarial tradition is the ability of commentators to make the texts and tradition historically relevant through their interpretations. The success of commentators has meant the survival of the classical texts over two millennia. Because commentators made these texts relevant to their particular historical contexts, this meant that people read them and encouraged others to read them. They created new texts, new meanings, making the texts historically pertinent. Their success has also resulted in perhaps the inevitable development of normative simplified notions about the classical texts, influencing impressions and beliefs about their content.

An emergent concern is that norms from particular contexts may deter those with limited familiarity with the texts from directly engaging the texts, or they may inadvertently shape the experience of those who do engage them. Nowhere is this more evident than in the case of the imperial service exams, which used the classical texts as their basis. Norms about the texts, for instance, that suggest they promote authoritarianism and rigid pedagogical approaches to engaging the texts among others, emerged in part because of conflation of the texts with exam contexts. Historically contextualizing the civil service examination phenomena and considering the role classical texts played can provide examples of how normative notions about the texts have been shaped by their contexts.

In particular, historical contextualization encourages exploration of how the use of the texts as part of the civil service examination process served to publicize and magnify some commentators' interpretations about the texts. Discussing how the exams were used for imperial political purposes, how exam processes became public spectacles, how participating in the exam processes became related to a desire for success, and how the exam process abstracted textual meanings shows how the exams and the texts became conflated and intimates some of the implications. Historical contextualization suggests that while the texts were used as the content for the exams, it is important to question the assumption of the view of the texts as essential extensions of the extreme exam contexts that emerged from deployment by imperial powers. More broadly, it suggests the importance of engaging an interpretive approach to view the civil service exam context as one of many past contexts (and potential future ones), from which various textual meanings emerge.

Serving Imperial Purposes

Civil service examinations were used for specific imperial purposes, and classical texts served as their basis. On and off during the Han period (206 BCE–220 CE) through the Qing period (1644–1912), imperial governments used classical texts as the content for civil service examinations to select civil service personnel. The use of an examination process for civil service purposes first appeared during the Han period to select imperial librarians who had an understanding of classical texts. Benjamin Elman (2000) points out that records show that around 134 BCE, those who completed study in an imperial academy underwent oral examinations about their knowledge of classical texts before being granted government positions. The exam process to select librarians became a forerunner to the imperial examinations that emerged during the Tang (618–907) and Song (960–1279) periods and throughout much of the next millennium to select civil service personnel. Despite the differing periods of imperial powers, many of the rulers found that maintaining the exam process, while it could not necessarily stave off war from invading groups, could be used to some extent for practical, political, and social purposes to support their rule. The examinations provided a pathway for elites to access government positions, generating social stability by reinforcing class divides while at the same time legitimizing imperial power (Elman, 2000).

While the examination process served a practical purpose to identify qualified people for office, imperial powers used it at the same time for political purposes. It increasingly became a convenient way for imperial powers to destabilize the authority of local elites who often relied on family connections to gain government positions. Empress Wu in the Tang period (618–907), Elman (2000) notes, found that officials chosen via examination "served as a countervailing force to entrenched aristocrats in capital politics" (p. 7). The exam process gave the Empress a way to interrupt the authority of families who had continually maintained footholds on the staffing of some official positions. While imperial powers sought to limit the elites' power, the examination process also gave the elites just enough access to official positions to curb their collective interests to revolt. Elman suggests that the examination process served a largely political function because rulers used it to gain the support of gentry elite to legitimize their power. Northern Song rulers (960–1126), for instance, used the promise of access to government positions through the examination process to draw in the sons of elites from newer territories in Southern China to serve in official capacities.

Imperial powers also used the examination process to promote social stability. The exam process served to encourage people, especially those of low income, to believe they had access to official positions when it actually contributed to societal stability through reinforcing class divides. For instance, Elman points out that the examinations in late imperial China from 1400 to 1900 were not designed to increase social mobility but rather institutionalized a system of inclusion and exclusion, which became manifest in the selection of officials in a public and legitimizing way by reproducing the "status quo" (Elman, 2000, p. xxix). In other words, the examination process favored the sons of literati and merchant elites to obtain official appointments because the educational curriculum required scholars to undertake years of resource-heavy preparation, which often necessitated extra expense. The expectation of linguistic mastery of nonvernacular classical texts proved to be a barrier for many of those from lower classes.

From the rulers' perspective, the examination process also served another valuable function—to restrict military power within their governments. Ichisada Miyazaki (1981) argues that the content of the examination system, with its focus on literary studies, which promoted the notion of intellectuals as leaders and officials, served to limit military power. This framework allowed the ruling group to reserve the most important official positions for civilians. For instance, in the Qing period (1644–1911), officers in the military could rise no higher than the rank of unit commander because the posts of minister of war and chief of staff could only be filled by civilians; civilians also served as front-line generals. A government culture developed in which military personnel were not expected to distinguish themselves in politics, which restrained military power.

Imperial powers used the exam process for almost two millennia because it helped them find people to serve in their governments in a controlled way that promoted social stability and reinforced their legitimacy. The examination served their purposes because it proved to be a particularly effective method of disciplinary control. According to Foucault (1995), this approach makes people visible to one another for the purposes of differentiation, classification, ranking, and judgment. In other words, exams identify and create differences among people for competitive and hierarchical purposes. Imperial powers used examinations to generate a system to provide a pathway for elites to participate in governance while also deterring those of low income from achieving power because of the amount of preparation required to perform well on the exam. The sleight of hand the examination achieved was the promise of equality and access to all, when actually it reinforced class divides, keeping imperial powers in charge.

Which texts were used as content for the exams? Because the examinations served as gatekeepers to powerful positions, various groups contested the examination questions, resulting in exam changes, which meant, as a consequence, some classical texts were privileged, depending on which exam designers and leaders considered most relevant at a particular moment. While the classical texts became normatively viewed as an integral part of the exam process because of their use as exam content, it is important to note that the exam content changed through time. For instance, Song period scholar Zhu Xi's (1130–1200) commentaries about some classical texts became part of the basis for the civil service examination process after 1313. Zhu Xi privileged particular texts by writing extensive interlinear commentary about *Analects*, *Mencius*, *Great Learning*, and *Zhongyong*, volumes that became known as the *Four Books*, which became a focal point for the civil service exams, a move that had reverberating sociocultural influences.

Zhu Xi selected the *Four Books* from the earlier canonical texts: The *Analects* and the *Mencius* were included as part of the thirteen classics; *Great Learning* and the *Zhongyong* were two chapters from the *Book of Rites*. Prior to 1313, the texts that formed the basis for the early civil service exams included the *Five Classics* of the "Confucian" canon: the

Odes, the *Documents*, the *Rites*, the *Changes*, and the *Spring and Autumn Annals*. By the Tang period (618–906), there were nine classics used in the exams and 13 by the Song period (960–1279). While the texts used for the exams previously discussed a broad range of topics from varied perspectives, Gardner (2007) points out that the *Four Books* were considered more philosophical and preoccupied with exploring the nature of people and morality and how people are situated within the cosmos, which contributed to the development of what is today considered Neo-Confucian thought. After 1313, exam takers were expected to have mastered the *Four Books* along with Zhu Xi's interlinear commentary and, to a lesser extent, the *Five Classics*.

Why did Zhu Xi choose particular texts to write about? Scholars suggest that Zhu Xi's work on the *Four Books* was a concerted response by literati to historical pressures of the time. Some literati felt that political and social reforms of the time were failing and perceived cultural and physical threats from non-Han groups (Gardner, 2007, p. xxii). The threats of attack by tribes to the north and northwest were not unfounded—after the fall of the Tang, the Song rulers were forced to give land to the Liao. Another pressure that spurred literati to reinforce classical studies, or as Gardner refers to it, the "native tradition," was the increasing popularity of Buddhism. Buddhism, considered a foreign influence given what Gardner describes as its "metaphysical interest in human nature," intrigued those at all levels of society. Gardner credits the "inward shift" toward an interest in human morality on the part of Song-period literati, to some extent, to a growing awareness of Buddhism. The *Four Books* became emphasized by scholars during the Song period because of a confluence of events including a weak economy, dissatisfaction with government to deal with political and social problems, and society's developing interest in ideas about human nature due to the influence of Buddhism. The emergence of the *Four Books*, whose circulation increased because of its emphasis in the civil service examination process, contributed to further identification of the classical Confucian texts as embodiments of traditional Chinese culture.

In summary, because the exam process served imperial purposes, its deployment was political and often contested. The classical texts became viewed as part of this particular context as evidenced by the changing nature of the exams and the texts used. For instance, when Zhu Xi generated the framing of the *Four Books*, some texts that may have been less studied in the past became prominent and vice versa.

While the examination process made some classical texts public in the sense that it necessitated those seeking civil service positions to read them to prepare for the exams, it also deemphasized their connections with the contexts from which they emerged by conflating them with the examination process. The conflation of the texts with the exam process began with the start of the exam process. However, it is important to note that the classical texts predated the exams. The texts became convenient exam material. The exam process was extremely politically charged, and this generated a similarly heightened political and increasingly public context for engaging the texts.

Spectacle Reinforcements

The examinations made the classical texts increasingly public as part of the context of imperial power displays, thereby shaping engagement with the texts. As the examination system became increasingly institutionalized, the civil service examination rituals of the late imperial age became manifest in society as public spectacles that fostered a "festive marketplace atmosphere" (Elman, 2000). The visibility of these public displays notably emerged while imperial rulers increasingly became hidden. As content for the examinations, the classical texts became subject to and objects of power along with the scholars who studied them. As the civil service examination process increasingly became a spectacle, it implicated the texts as part of the extreme circumstances.

The public displays of the classical period served political purposes (Nylan, 2005). For instance, Nylan describes how the Qin emperor hosted events for thousands of guests from newly conquered territories, which involved the provision of sumptuous meals and often gifts of the lacquer serving dishes, to show his generosity:

> By the prevailing rationale, the gracious condescension of a superior sharing objects and experiences through public spectacles revealed that laudable self-abnegation, freedom from selfishness, and political transparence that alone could sustain, to the mutual benefit of all, an equitable, stable sociopolitical order. (p. 24)

Display culture conveyed the message that harmonious social behavior benefited all in a community, reinforcing hierarchical constructs.

Ceremonial displays were meant to build lasting relationships based on reciprocity through a process of tribute. In this way, leaders sought to solidify their positions especially during the Warring States period to appease new populations with which they did not have hereditary ties. Leaders needed to gain support especially from the elites in the areas they conquered, and they used the displays to send a message that while they would collect taxes, they would also be giving something back.

Rather than being perceived as a method to mark the differences between classes, participation in or witness of a spectacle encouraged people to feel they were part of, as Nylan describes it, a "unified" whole. This spectacle culture had a ripple effect in the sense that local elites would also assert their authority in a similar way. These formalized exchanges through public acts of giving and receiving created mutual obligations that assisted in the provision of security for varied social groups and became a force for social stability.

Whereas the spectacle of the pre- and early first millennium visibly connected the emperor as a powerful benefactor of the people, the spectacle of the civil service examination displays of the late imperial age intriguingly shielded the emperor from public view yet maintained, even magnified, the emperor's power. The "festive marketplace" of the examinations garnered much public attention in part because it required great government expense, especially with regard to the provision of personnel—police, clerks, readers, copyists, and examiners—to maintain the examination (Elman, 2000). During a late Ming period (1368–1644) prefectural examination that took place every 3 years, 4,000 to 5,000 candidates would enter the examination compounds. Elman (2000) describes how outside the compounds' shops sold examination-taking supplies, friends and relatives of the candidates crowded about, and clerks sounded gongs and horns to mark the beginning and end of the examination periods. While the most prestigious ceremonies took place at the imperial capital examination hall, there was "pomp and ceremony" (p. 177) at many examination compounds: "the provincial compounds became venues simultaneously for cultural rituals, the deployment of police, and the testing of Ch'eng-Chu learning" (p. 178). "Ch'eng-Chu" learning refers to a Neo-Confucian interpretation of the texts featuring commentary by Song period scholars Zhu Xi, Cheng Yi, and Cheng Hao. Nylan (2005) writes, "The great social theorists of Warring States and Western Han times, after all, had sold public display as a way to balance hierarchy with reciprocity" (p. 33). The civil service examination process itself became an expression and embodiment of the practice of spectacle.

The spectacle of the examinations shifted public focus from the emperor to the exams, the texts, and the scholars who vied for limited civil service positions. This shift magnified imperial power by making it less visible yet omnipresent as the overseer of the examination process, thereby leaving its power unquestioned. While the early spectacles featured the emperor giving gifts of food and dishware to people, the civil service examination process gave to those who were successful (and to their families) the gift of lifelong status. For those who were not, the exam process gave the gift of the hope of the possibility of achieving status. The public displays implied the magnanimity of the imperial powers while at the same time keeping the imperial powers, which included those who sought to influence the content and structures of the exams, away from public view and from too much scrutiny. Emperors did, however, often preside over the final level of examinations held at the imperial palace, making their power quite visible to those fortunate few to make it to the last stage, emphasizing the preeminent place of the emperor as head of the examination process.

Besides shifting public emphasis from the emperor to the examination process and the classical texts through the use of spectacle, power is exercised through the disciplinary mechanism of the examination by influencing what is normatively considered knowledge and how it is manifested (Foucault, 1995). For instance, those who decide test content can to some extent frame for others a notion of what is normatively valuable simply because test takers must attend to mastering the designated test content. Attention to test content became what scholars valued—what they spent their energy and time studying—for the specific purpose of preparation for the examinations. The context in which the texts were read became quite focused. In brief, the scholars, in Foucauldian terms, became objects of power when they chose to study for the exams because they had to focus on the texts that the exams emphasized and try to perceive examiners' perspectives about them. Their lives and beliefs, to some extent, became influenced by power. They became subject to power when their performance on the tests influenced how successful they might have felt as scholars. The examinations normalized notions of how "educated" or "learned" scholars might be perceived as by the public as well.

In short, civil service examination spectacles contributed to the conflation of the texts with the examinations in that, similar to that of the scholars, they reinforced the texts also as objects and subjects of power by publicly intensifying the acts of exam taking by visually and experientially involving the community. The texts became objects of power when contestation of the examination format led to emphasis on some texts rather than others, shifting the contexts in which scholars might have engaged them or not. Because the classical texts constituted the material for the exams, more people engaged the classical texts because "mastering" them became linked to the possibility of obtaining civil service positions. Because the examination publicized and circulated some classical texts, it also impacted which texts were widely read. Classical texts became subject to power through their use in the civil service examination process because mastery of the texts became connected to performance on the examinations. The exams provided a specific context in which the texts were read and shaped the experience of engagement. The spectacles of the examination-taking process manifested in elaborate displays magnified this especially by involving even those who may not have been taking the exams. For the test takers, imagine the feeling of walking into an examination hall surrounded by all the pomp and hubbub, the swell of emotion tempered by an attempt to ease tension, and the fervent hope of doing well on the test not only for one's own sake but also for one's family and even one's village.

ELEVATING STATUS

As the civil service examination exams became increasingly perceived as a vehicle for success, the connection between studying the texts for the purposes of taking the exam and social status grew. For the scholars preparing for the exams and the public they sought to serve in government positions, the texts, and mastery of them, represented a pathway to realize a desire for perceived economic benefit and social status.

Historically, the ability to read in China contributed to a person's social status. For instance, before and during the Warring States period (479–221 BCE), texts had an important, although limited, place in rituals connecting power with past and memory (Nylan, 2005). Tomb excavations have uncovered writing on bone, wooden strips, bamboo, and silk, among other materials, usually given special placement in lacquer boxes with other ritual objects such as flutes, oyster shells, and plant branches, which helped establish the status of the deceased. Written and oral texts, critical to ceremonies as much as gesture and dress at the time, were thought to reflect what Nylan calls "patterned workings" and information about the cosmos: "text and ritual served as 'framing devices' within which to interpret the inexplicable changes occurring outside the confines of text and ritual, converting the incoherence and unintelligibility of the mundane and the merely personal into 'usable' insights of broader relevance" (p. 10). Those considered masters of text and ritual gained social status because they were perceived to bring a meaningful coherence to aspects of living.

However, when the civil service examination emerged during the later part of the first millennium, the ability to read and interpret the texts tremendously upped the potential to increase and maintain social status. For instance, mastery of the texts for the purpose of exam taking became an avenue toward achieving power, especially for elites. The elites enabled the exam process through their participation, and while their efforts to game the system could be seen as a way to undermine the process, it also encouraged imperial powers to adapt it by generating more bureaucracy, thereby institutionalizing it. For instance, during the Tang period, elites sought to identify and then bribe civil examiners (Elman, 2000). When the government learned about the pressure they put on their examiners, they created a new department in response—the Ministry of Rites—to ensure those who proctored the exams were not the same as those in the Ministry of Personnel who made the civil service appointments.

For those with less power and money, communities would support the education of some local children with the hope that their success would benefit their communities. If they did well in the exam process and were awarded official positions, they might contribute to their hometowns' economic development and pride. For instance, these benefits might include a stable salary and perceived access to political power and the influence that comes with a civil service position and knowing other civil servants. Mastery of the texts became viewed as a way to realize a desire for officialdom and power, although those who succeeded were few. Some local elites of small townships and counties figured out that, even without real hope of obtaining official positions, they could improve their own and their families' statuses somewhat through capitalizing on the fact that they or their sons had participated in the lowest-level examinations. But the harsh reality was that the majority of test takers, especially those with less wealth, were not likely to pass the examinations to obtain the official positions they wished for because it would be difficult for their families to marshal the resources necessary to support their exam preparations.

As the exam became institutionalized, the number of applicants who sought positions through participation in the exam process increased. During the Qing (Manchu) period (1644–1911), the number of civil service positions available was about 120 each year, but the population had grown steadily throughout the centuries to about 300 million in the 18th century, and, as a result, competition increased for a limited number of spots (Rosenlee, 2006). The exam offered a pathway to officialdom and wealth. While most people did not obtain a government position, they did all study the classical texts.

The possibility of achieving officialdom proved to be quite a powerful motivator to study classical texts and also influenced pedagogical approaches to engage the texts, a legacy manifest in contemporary *guoxue* or cultural Chinese schools' practices, which, for instance, emphasize memorization of classical texts even before children can read (see Teo, 2015). While memorization was often used as a method of oral transmission of the *ruxue* tradition prior to the examinations, as the number of applicants increased, study strategies became rigid and formalized because of the pressure to succeed. During the Qing dynasty (1644–1911), the civil service examination apparatus had become extensive (Miyazaki, 1981). Preparation for the examinations began with teaching boys to read and write even from the age of 3. By 7 years of age, formal education began when boys were sent to village or communal schools staffed by scholars who had failed the examinations or were former officials. At these schools, students would be expected to begin to master the classical texts through memorization. Schools prepared students to take a series of examinations, which began with the district and prefectural exams. If they passed, they would take a qualifying examination, then the provincial examination, and, finally, the palace examination.

My point here is that the exam process could be rightly viewed as an extreme context. It was highly contested. Some exam answers were judged as better than others. Success was linked to increased status. The exam context influenced how the texts were read, shaping the experiences of those studying the texts. However, while the demands of the exams may have required extreme methods to "master" the content of the texts, the texts themselves did not necessarily support them. In fact, texts like *Zhongyong* and others, for instance, situate learning through personal cultivation as having an extensive impact on people's roles and engagement with others where the purpose of education is to help people live with integrity and care for their communities (see Ames, 2016; Chang, 2017). Engaging a relational worldview where people are considered constituted by others rather than perceived as "individuals," the texts suggest that teaching and learning are aspectual (teachers are always learners too) and that academic education includes character development. While the pedagogical approaches used in civil service examination preparations to "master" the texts may have emerged inadvertently because of the increasing demands of the examinations, they became normatively viewed as connected to and supported by the texts. The institutionalization of the examinations increased the status of the texts, deeply linking them to the pedagogical processes used to prepare for the exams too. Together, the texts and the exams and the methods that emerged to prepare for them became conflated with notions of economic and social success. This had sociocultural reverberations in the form of the generation of normative ideas about the meaning of the texts.

Norms Emerge From Textual Abstraction

One way the normative meanings were shaped by the examination process was that some commentarial scholarship about the texts became part of the examinations, especially after the Song period, shaping not only what texts were read but also their meaning. As the philosophical texts became more widely engaged through their connection with the exams, the exams (including methods used to prepare for them) and the texts became increasingly synonymous, contributing to the abstraction of the texts from the contexts from which they were produced and influencing engagement of the texts by those preparing for the examinations. Because of the increasing social significance of the exams and by implication the texts, the conflation of the two had broader sociocultural implications by influencing normative textual meanings that became used to control people's behaviors.

The metaphysical turn of classical scholars in the Song period (960–1279), as mentioned earlier, resulted in moralizing interpretations of the classical texts that formed what is now called Neo-Confucian thought. Hongyu Wang (2001) suggests Neo-Confucian scholars' interpretations of the texts foreground a metaphysical view of moral principles as an ethic by privileging principles. These views were reflected in the civil service examinations after the Song period. Exam designers requested that exam preparers master Zhu Xi's interlinear commentary and adopted his emphasis of the *Four Books*. Zhu Xi argued that the *Four Books* and the *Analects* in particular should have canonical status over other texts and wrote extensive interlinear commentary integrating and justifying the Neo-Confucian metaphysical perspectives that have reoriented normative philosophical Confucian tradition since that time (Gardner, 2003). The content of later civil service examinations reflected his views—scholars after the Song period were expected to master the texts Zhu Xi foregrounded and also his interlinear commentaries to prepare for the civil service examinations.

As moralizing Neo-Confucian views became institutionalized via the exam process, the exam process itself also became more restrictive. For instance, during the Qing (Manchu) period (1644–1911), the scope of the examination questions had become quite narrow (Rosenlee, 2006). Philosopher Li-Hsiang Lisa Rosenlee writes that scholars complained that the standardized essay format, the "8 legged essay," which had been instituted in the late 15th century, limited the scope of creativity of candidates, and the examination questions themselves had shifted from an emphasis on ability to write social policy to a focus on primarily providing explication of the meaning of the *Four Books* and their commentaries. Recitation of the classics became the focus, rather than detailed responses to questions related to state affairs. Rosenlee notes, "The kind of *Ru* that the Qing court produced through the standardized examination format and the narrow scope of the orthodox *Ru* learning was more of a specialized vessel or bureaucratic clerk than a high level advisor fully participating in governance" (p. 32). The examinations became less to do with discussions of governance and more oriented toward candidates' mastery of classical knowledge, their ability to write in the style of official documents, and consideration of candidates' ethnicities.

At the same time, whereas Confucian texts might have been interpreted initially more commonly as ideals and advice about approaches to governance and fostering harmonious living through personal growth, later normative interpretations, especially after the Song period, were at times expressed as rigid rules meant to control people's actions. According to Sor-hoon Tan (2003), Confucian ritual practices over the centuries lost their flexibility, and guidelines became perceived as rules that "sometimes ended up as social shackles that oppressed the heart and paralyzed the mind" (p. 88). For instance, pat normative dictates about submitting to authority overlook textual content that suggests the importance of reciprocity in relationships. To provide an example, Tan juxtaposes a passage from *Mencius* that suggests that genders should refrain from touching each other as a matter of courtesy (except within relationships between parents and children, between spouses, or in situations of danger) with a "severe admonition" from Neo-Confucian Cheng Yi (1033–1107). Cheng interprets the passage to mean that widows, even out of economic necessity, should not accept a new spouse because starvation would be preferred "to a loss of chastity" (p. 88). Zhu Xi echoes these extreme sentiments when he hierarchizes relations between genders as a principle that he draws from reading the classical texts: "According to Zhu Xi, such a differentiation is the basis for proper relationships with children, practicing filial piety, pursuing righteousness, and performing rites" (Wang, 2001, p. 164).

The broader point here is that some appropriated the classical and increasingly canonical texts for particular purposes when they interpreted them as providing narrow dictates intended to control and judge the conduct of others. And such views had an impact on normative meanings of the texts because the texts continued to develop cultural significance as part of the civil service examination process. The inclusion of the texts in the examination process meant that perceived mastery of the texts came to represent a desire and pathway toward a societally recognized success, as discussed earlier. As a result, a normative notion of success became connected with mastery of the texts for the purposes of participation in the civil service examination process, and this also contributed to the growing cultural significance of the texts, which influenced normative textual interpretations.

While genuine engagement, including inquiry, with textual content might have been the purpose of the earliest civil service examinations for test takers and test designers, as the examination system changed, mastery of the texts for many became perceived as a conduit toward achieving officialdom. This development likely narrowed the scope of textual interpretations in part because for those who studied to take the civil service examinations, engagement with the texts had less to do with rigorous or imaginative interpretations of textual content and more to do with attempts to figure out what one needed to know to pass the test. Because classical Chinese philosophical texts provided the content of the exams, making mastery of the texts part of the civil service exam system, engagement by test takers shifted from a personal one to one that became politically charged because it had material outcomes determined by others (most simply: pass the test—earn position/fail the test—no position). How one read a text for the purpose of test taking may look quite different from the engagement with a text for one's personal interest or other purpose. The examination process is an extreme context to situate the texts that necessarily influences why and how one might read the texts, contributing to reductive normative interpretations of the texts.

The examinations at the same time ensured that the sheer numbers of people who encountered the texts increased. Because employment, wealth, and social status were at stake, preparation for the exams required that serious test takers spend inordinate amounts of time to study the texts. As a result, mastery of the texts came to signify notions of achievement—it came to represent the desire for success through test taking. While those who prepared for the exams engaged with the texts directly, the family members and neighbors of the scholars, while they may not have read the texts themselves, would have known something about them, perhaps enough to develop normative notions about the texts and their content.

While the context of the exam process influenced interpretations of the texts more broadly, I want to point out that I do not propose that examinations do not have their productive uses. In the case of the civil service examination, scholars have pointed out that it was an effective way to stabilize a society by providing pathways for elites to participate in governing. It also served as a useful check on ruling and military powers by offering civilians a pathway to leadership positions, suggesting that institutional and centralized processes with hierarchies can function to generate social stability. Power differentials among institutional roles could be envisioned as necessary toward a broader goal of establishing efficient societal function. Foucault (1995) writes,

> We must cease once and for all to describe the effects of power in negative terms: it "excludes," it "represses," it "censors," it "abstracts." it "masks," it "conceals." In fact power produces; it produces reality; it produces domains of objects and rituals of truth. The individual and the knowledge that may be gained of him belong to this production. (p. 194)

For Foucault, power emerges from formations that seek to organize relations and conduct. It creates. That said, when there are complex systems at work in organizing a society, the manifestations of such systems can directly impact the lives of the specific people of a particular society. They influence relations, behavior, and shape normative beliefs and practices.

While people were situated as subjects and objects of power through the examination process, the process also influenced normative notions about the philosophical texts themselves, which returned to shape the process too. The texts gained a strong social presence as cultural phenomena but at the same time also became subjects and objects of power, interpreted and evaluated for particular purposes. While manifestations of power with regard to the design and use of the civil service examination may necessarily emerge from the activity of trying to organize society and government, consideration of the function and effects of power contribute to theorizations about how the texts that were used as part of the exam influenced how people perceived them more broadly. However, people of a contemporary time do not have to feel relegated to simply accepting the norms that emerged about the texts from their involvement in the context of the exam process. The norms about the examinations that emerged from the extreme context of test taking—that the exams were inflexible and narrow in scope, for instance, need not be imposed on the bodies of the classical texts that were used as the basis of the exams. The onus again is on contemporary readers to consider the exam process as a particular context that shaped the meanings of the texts and to consider how different meanings will emerge from readings from different historical contexts.

Toward Agential Reading

Just as the worldviews of translators and commentators influence their interpretations of the classical texts, generating specific textual meanings, so do particular contexts similarly shape normative textual meanings. The examinations were by scholarly accounts an extreme context. The exams were political in nature and often contested by various parties; they became perceived by many as a pathway to fulfill a desire for status and success. While the exam process itself may rightly deserve normative notions that they were rigid in nature, the troubling issue is that the classical texts themselves, which constituted the basis of the exams, are sometimes viewed as an essential extension of the exams. As a result, they may bear the normative qualities of the exam, implying that the content of the texts support authoritarianism and rigid pedagogical practices, among others. Historically contextualizing the exam process and the role of the texts to show their conflation is to trouble this normative assumption. The point is not to attempt to decontextualize the texts to infer some sort of essential version of the texts, but rather to encourage readers to extend an interpretive approach to situating contexts when reading the texts. While the civil service exam process was an extreme context that shaped people's experiences of reading the texts that generated textual meanings, it could be situated as one context of many in which the texts were read and could be read, contexts that influence the meanings of the texts in different ways. This suggests the importance for contemporary readers to engage the various texts themselves directly, thereby lessening the reductive impact of normative notions about the texts.

Imperial powers found that the use of the classical texts as part of the civil service examination process served their particular purposes, inadvertently shaping temporally resonant cultural notions of success and the texts' normative meanings. Moreover, political powers continue to use the texts in contemporary contexts. For instance, the texts are implicated in controversial politically driven initiatives such as the establishment of Confucius Institutes globally, including a hundred or so located on U.S. higher educational campuses, that seek to promote a narrow notion of "Chinese culture" for propaganda purposes (Epstein, 2018). However, contextualization of the relation between the classical texts and the civil service examination process reminds contemporary readers that the texts do not need to be solely read for the purposes dictated by political powers. It reminds readers that engaging the texts also need not condone a nation's contemporary politics and policies. Despite the use of the texts for political purposes, it is valuable to remember that people reading the texts within particular contexts, including varied purposes, also generate meaning.

That the activity of reading continually generates meaning assumes a relational perspective that reading itself is an agential activity of construction. Notably distinct from a substance-oriented view that would situate textual meanings more as essences fixed to the body of the texts, a shift to undertaking a processual relational orientation suggests that interpretations of texts can change when texts are read for varied purposes and from specific spatial, personal, and temporal perspectives. To clarify, I do not suggest that one attempt to read the texts in a historically decontextualized way; rather, I emphasize the value of recontexutalization toward recognizing the constructive act of reading in order to inquire, in part, about the complexity of the emergence of normative interpretations and how they influence how and what we read. Contextualization insinuates that all interpretations of the classical texts, then, will always be partial because they emerge from particular contexts that influence their meanings. But rather than see this perspective as a limitation, to directly engage these texts could be framed more broadly as part of an ongoing conversation about the texts, contributing to their use as innovative resources to address contemporary issues. In short, engaging the texts would be participating in a complex and dynamic commentarial tradition.

In fact, a focus on the commentarial tradition also has pedagogical implications. For instance, the act of writing commentary itself, Gardner (1998) suggests, is an activity that can contribute to personal cultivation. To dialogue with the classical Confucian texts through writing commentary requires active engagement with a deep focus that involves a "savoring process," which familiarizes people with the words of the texts through internalization. Writing commentary offers an experience of the texts that generates meaning about the texts through a process of deep reflection that involves engaging people's contexts that may influence how they choose to live.

Engaging an interpretive approach encourages reading the classical texts in their contemporary forms from a relational perspective rather than a substance-oriented one, which has affective implications for the subjects under discussion. For instance, this has particular ramifications for those parts of the texts that discuss learning because they situate learning as a process of personal cultivation that emerges from relation with others rather than one undertaken by oneself for the benefit of oneself. This view suggests people's roles cannot be separate or fixed. The roles of teacher and student, for instance, are considered aspectual, implying that teachers who teach must also be continually learning from their students and relationships with others. Engaging a relational perspective when reading the texts may offer a way to reflect on normative notions about teaching and learning.

A historically contextualizing approach to learning about Confucianism fosters comparative inquiry. For instance, juxtaposing different commentaries and translations raises questions about the contextual nature of reading. The dissonance and gaps that emerge from comparing interpretations generates space for new interpretations. Inquiries that ask what is left out and why may lead to examination of the sociocultural influences and politics about specific contexts of when particular readings occurred, disrupting notions that there can be any kind of definitive or universal reading of the texts. These pedagogical implications suggest readers participate in the dynamic tradition of Confucianism through engaging classical Confucian texts.

People interpret the texts through their specific contexts, implying that the meaning of the texts will continue to change. Because the tradition is multivocal, readers need not feel pressure to be experts about the Confucian tradition to engage the texts. Instead, it may be more relevant to see engagement as part of a broader ongoing conversation. In fact, it is this ongoing conversation that situates the Confucian tradition as a resource for addressing contemporary issues. For instance, recently scholars have used their interpretations of Confucian texts to generate innovative perspectives on democracy, feminism, and environmental ethics. While Confucianism could be perceived as an immense fragmented tradition, engaging its commentarial aspect features its changing nature and how educators who interpret the classical texts influence it.

Philosophers Hourdequin and Wong (2005), for instance, draw in part on classical Confucian texts for inspiration to situate environmental ethics. Relational identities that encompass human and nonhuman worlds provide an alternative approach to instrumentalist (the belief that the environment is provided for human use) or intrinsic (the environment as having value in and of itself) views with regard to situating the environment. They, referencing Ames and Hall (1998) and Rosemont (1991), situate people as constituted necessarily by others to describe a humanity that can be broadly interpreted. For instance, they extend a notion of appropriate conduct from the human realm to the physical environment by discussing how propriety must be couched in particular circumstantial terms in order to have meaning. A relational identity brings social and ecological connections to the forefront. It draws support for bioregionalism movements, ecological restoration, and a view of humanity that includes "experiencing oneself as accountable to others and as an agent with an active role in the world. In relationships, one learns that one's actions *matter*" (p. 29).

While the classical texts have been and continue to be used for political purposes, historical contextualization of the texts contributes to a notion that the texts can be read as valuable resources toward addressing contemporary issues. It also encourages inquiry about how continuing influences perpetuate narrow textual normative interpretations. For instance, this type of inquiry might include how the pedagogies employed by contemporary *guoxue* schools that take as their focus the study of traditional Chinese culture were influenced by the extreme civil service examination demands that test takers "master" the content of the texts. Inquiry about these practices leads to questions about why schools continue to perpetuate the civil service exam preparation legacy when the purposes of reading the texts have changed. Also, historical contextualization of the texts encompasses consideration of those translating the texts. How do translators' cultural and personal contexts, including beliefs, influence how they read the texts?

More broadly, historical contextualization of the texts' relation with the civil service examination process reminds us that reading is an agential activity that can have contemporary implications. While today's local and global issues often require interdisciplinary approaches to address them, engaging the classical texts directly may spur resonant thinking that enriches new contexts, meanings, and cultures. While Confucianism may rightly be viewed as a vast complex tradition, drawing attention to its commentarial aspect brings into focus its changing nature. This also encourages inquiry about how readers of the classical texts can contribute to a dynamic tradition, shaping the new normative textual meanings that emerge like a concept of Confucian relationality.

Chapter 2

A Familial Way Forward

People "are" what they do, according to the *Zhongyong*. For when the world is viewed as changing, then how people relate matters foremost. This notion is a central aspect of Confucian relationality, which engages a view of the world as process oriented, situating all life's aspects as events because it frames them as in-motion. From a process-oriented perspective, events emerge in relation to specific contexts located in space and time. They express energy occurring from actions and responses that are necessarily intra-related. Second, another related aspect of Confucian relationality, then, suggests that when people are situated as continually emergent from specific contexts, people can be viewed foremost as living in mutuality implying that how people relate matters. Third, a Confucian relationality positions personal cultivation as extensive because it is through people's committed relation-ing that radially shapes the growth of others and generates the contexts of their lives. From this aspect of a Confucian relationality, a process of personal cultivation, which seeks to harmonize relationships, involves developing an emotional maturity that includes the capacity to imagine a person in the place of others. This process requires people to do the potentially difficult reflective work of genuinely cohering their feelings with their thinking to try to understand their own and others' experiences in order to act in thoughtful ways every day.

A concept of Confucian relationality is drawn from reading a philosophical and interpretive translation of the *Zhongyong* by Roger Ames and David Hall (2001) called *Focusing the Familiar*. The *Zhongyong* is credited to Confucius's grandson Kong Ji (c. 483–402 BCE). However,

Kong Ji did not likely write the text. As part of the commentarial tradition, the *Zhongyong* was probably the work of many people through generations that would later be attributed to Kong Ji who was considered a notable person. The text was initially considered part of the *Liji* (*Record of Rites*), a collection of ritual documents, which emerged first in the Han dynasty (202 BCE–220 CE). It later gained status from its inclusion in the *Four Books* when compiled and commentated upon by Song period scholar *Zhu Xi*, who organized it into the form of 33 parts/chapters of varying lengths (one as short as 8 characters, one over 800) in which it is most often read today.

To draw a concept of Confucian relationality from Ames and Hall's (2001) philosophical interpretation of *Zhongyong* is a matter of emphasis. To clarify, the concept emerges from the work of Ames and Hall and other comparative philosophers whose theorizing builds to some degree on others as part of an ongoing commentarial tradition. As a result, the three aspects that I emphasize as part of a concept of Confucian relationality—a process-oriented view of the world; the notion that people live in mutuality; and the extensivity of personal cultivation—will be familiar themes. However, the framing is what I offer as an emerging development—the way I interpret the aspects and relate them, and how I use the concept in later chapters as a lens to read aspects of higher education. I want to point out that I envision my discussion of a concept of Confucian relationality as one of many possible perspectives and consider how even my view of it will continue to change through time.

In my reading of the *Zhongyong* in order to construct a concept of Confucian relationality, I emphasize the development of emotional maturity in the context of relationships in order to consider how personal cultivation emerges through relation-ing. I explore this because the process has potential to incur a broad impact—how people choose to live as expressed by what they do can have an influence on those they engage and shape the contexts in which they live. In particular, examining how the *Zhongyong* situates familial relationship as a context for personal cultivation provides a way to explore the three intra-related aspects of a Confucian relationality that I emphasize. Engaging a process-oriented long-term perspective shows the complexity of responsibility for the development of emotional maturity and the importance of genuine regard for others. To view people living in mutuality is to consider how people are necessarily constituted by others and how experiences shape them at a neurological level. The extensivity of personal cultivation becomes even more evident considering how personal cultivation emerges through relation. Personal cultivation requires people to reflect on their own experiences to understand others in order to conduct themselves in thoughtful ways.

Parents and Children

The notion of what it means to live ethically is a broad preoccupation in the Confucian tradition that influences a conception of Confucian relationality. The discussion in a nutshell follows: If people's activities matter foremost, then those who seek to become exemplary do so through attending to their relationships, especially familial ones. The *Zhongyong* suggests that a refined emotional maturity achieved through a process of personal cultivation conveys itself to others effortlessly and clearly through a person's actions. In chapter 33, in the last chapter and part of the *Zhongyong*, the *Book of Songs* is quoted describing the seemingly effortless way the natural world moves and implies this reflects how exemplary people relate with others, "Harboring the highest excellence in your breast, you have no need of loud words or intimidating looks" (p. 115). It continues, "The natural world around us goes about its work without using sound or scent." In other words, the natural world goes about its work of providing an abundant context for so many events spontaneously. It simply happens without hesitation continually. Regarding these lines in the *Zhongyong*, Ames and Hall suggest, "It is in this sense that the model of the *junzi*, the middle ground between the ordinary and the extraordinary, anticipates and is entailed in the emergence of the most exalted category of personal cultivation, the sage" (p. 69). An exemplary person need not communicate through loud or forceful speech or bearing. Yes, this would describe a sage, and I would add, a wise parent.

The *Zhongyong* presents kin relationships and political roles as contexts that rely on the same methods for personal cultivation. Chapter 20 states, "Ruler and minister, father and son, husband and wife, older and younger brother, friend and mentor—these are the five ways forward in the world. Wisdom, authoritative conduct, and courage—these are the three methods of excelling in character. How one advances along the way is one and the same" (p. 102). While the text is focused on exemplariness in public life in regard to people's relations—"ruler and minister"—at the same time, it makes a deliberate connection to what may be conceived of as private family life, for instance, "father and son," when it situates these relationships as "ways forward in the world" that require the same methods "of excelling in character." While the words designate the relations between father and son, I extend this, inspired by the commentarial tradition of reading the texts from one's own time and spatial context, to include father and daughter, mother and son, mother and daughter, and perhaps most broadly, parent or primary caretaker and children. To focus on this relation between a parent and child as a way forward in the world offers a through line to interpret some aspects of the *Zhongyong*. In particular, it provides a fruitful context to explore how a process of personal cultivation emerges through relation. The parent and child relationship is a valuable context to explore in part because of the important role parents play in the personal cultivation of young children and how it challenges parents to personally cultivate themselves.

While people may not be rulers or government officials or married or have younger siblings or mentors, they certainly have been children to parents/caretakers and may be parents to children. Of the five relationships mentioned in the *Zhongyong* that serve as contexts for personal cultivation, the one between parent and child emerges as primary in part due to its implicit ubiquity. The *Zhongyong* suggests that "ordinary people" have the capacity to become as exemplary as sages even though the text often focuses on discussions of personal cultivation in political contexts. For instance, the *Zhongyong* makes clear its interest in political leadership in part by identifying those who might serve as examples of exemplary conduct: from chapter 17, "The Master said, 'Now Shun—there was a person of great filiality (*xiao*)! His excellence (*de*) was that of a sage (*shengren*), he was venerated as the Son of *tian* (*tianzi*), and his wealth encompassed everything in the world . . .'" (p. 96); and from Chapter 18: "The Master said, 'It was only King Wen who suffered no grief. He had King Ji for a father and King Wu for a son. His father forged the path, and his son continued along the proper way'" (p. 97). However, the text also suggests that the way to become exemplary is accessible to all people: from chapter 12: "The proper way (*dao*) of exemplary persons (*junzi*) is both broad and hidden. The dullest of ordinary men and women can know something of it, and yet even the sages (*shengren*) in trying to penetrate to its furthest limits do not know it all" (p. 93); also from *Zhongyong* chapter 12: "The proper way of exemplary persons has at its start the simple lives of ordinary men and women, and at its furthest limits sheds light upon the entire world" (Ames & Hall, 2001,

p. 93). Family is a specific type of relational context kings share with those referred to as "ordinary" people.

The *Zhongyong* identifies the importance of kin relationships and their critical role in personal cultivation for those seeking to become exemplary—from chapter 20: "Thus, exemplary persons (*junzi*) cannot but cultivate their persons. In cultivating their persons, they cannot but serve their kin. In serving their kin, they cannot but realize human conduct. And in realizing human conduct they cannot but realize *tian*" (p. 101). It is through trying to harmonize relationships with family members that people can cultivate themselves to the extent they can wisely lead others. Family, Ames and Hall (2001) point out, is a governing metaphor in the text and of the tradition (p. 38). Family is a critical and model institution that can allow one to develop as an ethical person. It is what Ames and Hall call a "radial locus" for human growth that suggests that one becomes a person through cultivating relations with family members foremost.

> The underlying assumption is that persons are more likely to give themselves utterly and unconditionally to their families than to any other human institution. Thus, the family as an institution provides the model for the process of making one's way by allowing the persons who constitute it both to invest in and to get the most out of the human experience. Promoting the centrality of family relations is an attempt to assure that entire persons, without remainder, are invested in each of their actions. (p. 39)

A person becomes exemplary through developing ethical relationships with family members in part because it is through those close relationships that one becomes a person, literally and metaphorically. Because we are all born from relational contexts and into relational contexts, the family institution is a familiar and natural context that is shared by all.

To consider a notion of personal cultivation from the perspective of a familial context raises the implication that it is at times a process out of a person's own conscious control. For instance, parents are to some extent responsible for the emotional personal cultivation of their young children. The first line of chapter 1 states, "What *tian* commands (*ming*) is called natural tendencies (*xing*); drawing out these natural tendencies is called the proper way (*dao*); improving upon this way is called education (*jiao*)" (Ames & Hall, 2001, p. 89). "*Tian*," Ames and Hall (2001) write, "is the environing social, cultural, and natural context that is brought into focus and articulated by sagacious human beings" (p. 27). To dwell for a moment on the "natural context" of *tian* leads me to focus on a part of chapter 26, which offers an illustrative description of this context: "The way of heaven and earth can be captured in one phrase: Since events are never duplicated, their production is unfathomable. The way of heaven and earth is broad, is thick, is high, is brilliant, is far-reaching, is enduring" (p. 107). A natural context within a conception of *tian* is process-oriented—changing, robust, and productive. The productive natural activity of *tian* is evident in general in children from 0 to 5 years of age. Young children seem to grow effortlessly and robustly in a way that reflects a natural changing context of *tian*, which reflects their *ming*, "what *tian* commands," and their *xing* ("natural tendencies"). They do not have to consciously try to learn to speak, walk, and act because the natural tendency is for them to do so in a flourishing way. They learn at a pace their physical and brain development allow. However, to develop in a natural way, children rely on their parents to pursue *dao*, the "proper way," in order to help them learn to harmonize relationships and improve on this way through education (*jiao*) by caring for them physically and psychologically.

Parents must provide a nourishing context for children to develop naturally. More specifically, the proper way (*dao*) of drawing out children's natural tendencies (*xing*) relies on parental figures to allow, even promote, children's attachment to them. Clinical psychologist Gordon Neufeld and physician Gabor Maté (2004) describe attachment as the "pursuit and preservation of proximity, of closeness and connection: physically, behaviorally, emotionally, and psychologically" (p. 17) that is required for an infant's survival and "what makes a family a family." Attachment is a force like gravity or compasses pointing north, they suggest, that need not be consciously understood in order to work. Physically, attachment is a force of attraction that "holds the particles of an atom together and binds the planets in orbit around the sun. It gives the universe its shape" (p. 16). Psychologically, attachment to parents in a child's early years is particularly critical to a person's development and relationships with others. The authors refer to this development as a natural emergence of maturity through attachment as "nature's blueprint." To interpret *ming* (what *tian* commands) as a person's configured genetic expression shaped by prenatal experiences from which *xing* (natural tendencies) emerge need not be viewed from an essentialist perspective that suggests people are in passive relation to nature. To see people as embodied, instead, emphasizes the constant motion of bodies including the movements of the atoms that constitute the cells that generate our organs, which continually churn to keep us alive. People are accumulations of atoms whose engagements generate broader events than the particles themselves. From the perspective of how a young child develops emotionally, natural and human contexts are related if one considers humans literally a part of *tian* and vice versa. To see people as part of *tian* resonates with a processual orientation that suggests people emerge from ongoing contexts.

In fact, how parents promote attachment with their young children influences their children's future relationships. Clinical psychologist and social worker Erica Komisar (2017) who wrote *Being There: Why Prioritizing Motherhood in the First Three Years Matters*, makes the point that the relationship between a primary caretaker and an infant are of essential importance especially in the first three years of life. Referencing John Bowlby's attachment theory, Komisar writes, "When the child is confident of his mother as a secure and safe base he is free to explore the environment. The sensitive responsiveness of his mother determines the quality of the attachment bond and the beliefs about what to expect from relationships and from himself" (p. 56). Komisar suggests that it is through children's attachment to their parents and mothers in particular that they learn what it means to be cared for and loved, "It is important that a baby be able to depend on his mother and can express that need. Dependency is an essential bridge to healthy separation and critical for intimate love. This 'internal working model' is a baby's model for all relationships in the future" (p. 57). The attachment young children have with their parents provides a pattern for the quality of relationships they have as adults. In short, it is how parents relate with their young children that initially shape their children's processes of personal cultivation, which can have resonating impacts.

Attachment theory underscores how acutely parents can influence the *xing* (natural tendencies) of their children by suggesting that the ability to emotionally regulate occurs through attaching to primary caretakers. Children need their emotional needs met as much as their physical needs. In fact, how parents promote attachment has a neurological impact. In particular, stronger attachments with primary caregivers result in the formation of larger hippocampuses, the part of the brain involved in aspects like learning, memory, and emotional regulation.

The level of parental attachment impacts children's ability to achieve emotional security, read social cues, and closely relate with others: "The ability to regulate our emotions means we can be angry without losing our temper, can experience sadness without getting depressed, and can be happy without becoming manic. Resilience is the ability to return to a regulated emotional state after being excited or upset" (p. 76). The development of emotional maturity here sounds remarkably similar to the notion equilibrium as described in the *Zhongyong*, chapter 1: "The moment at which joy and anger, grief and pleasure, have yet to arise is called a nascent equilibrium (*zhong*); once the emotions have arisen, that they are all brought into proper focus (*zhong*) is called harmony (*he*). This notion of equilibrium and focus (*zhong*) is the great root of the world; harmony then is the advancing of the proper way (*dadao*) in the world" (Ames & Hall, 2001, p. 89).

The process of attachment between parents and children, however, often happens unconsciously. Parents help their children pursue a developmental pathway of *dao*, or as Ames and Hall put it of "becoming consummately and authoritatively human" through a process of attachment without realizing attachment often operates without our consciousness. In fact, it is when attachment breaks down that awareness is required to address it, "As long as attachments are working, we can afford to simply follow our instincts—automatically and without thought. When attachments are out of order, our instincts will be, too" (Neufeld and Maté, 2004, p. 17). By instincts, the authors refer to how babies have the capacity and interest to learn and move toward emotional maturity and how most parents naturally seek to act in ways that foster their children's growth. The authors point out that that only a "thin layer" of the human brain is devoted to conscious thinking, while the larger part is devoted to "the psychological dynamics that serve attachment" (p. 18). While humans share the attachment instinct with other animals that rear their young, it is only humans, as far as we know, that can become conscious of this process.

The *Zhongyong* suggests parent and child relationships can be a valuable context for personal cultivation. Recent neuroscience research points out that parents necessarily shape the process of the development of emotional maturity for their young children. Perhaps the role of a "wise parent," then, could be envisioned as a way to become more conscious of the role of attachment as a process of helping their children pursue *dao* or way-make toward cultivating harmony amongst relationships. The deliberateness of developing an approach to become aware of and foster attachment may be regarded as an intention to deliberately educate (*jiao*) their young children. Given that until the age of twelve, a child's neural speed is half of that of an adult's (Lillard & Jessen, 2003), this suggests that the education (*jiao)* needed to support *dao* relies heavily on the parent with regard to cultivating children's emotional maturation process. In other words, a person's personal cultivation at a young age largely relies on one's parents and may be considered the responsibility of a parent. However, the responsibility of education (*jiao*) in the context of personal cultivation shifts as a child grows older. And what may be required of later personal cultivation is a reflective reckoning or remembering of how we were parented. Engaging a process perspective draws attention to the shift in responsibility for personal cultivation (from parents to children developing maturity) by emphasizing the importance of taking a long-term view of life and learning.

A Process Orientation Harmonizes

If people are what they do, then how they treat others says volumes about who they are. One aspect of a Confucian relationality is a process orientation. A process orientation situates life as changing and necessarily contingent. The *Zhongyong* engages a process orientation when it situates relationships as the ongoing contexts for personal cultivation for the purposes of harmonizing relationships. Harmonizing relationships requires that people develop an ability to emotionally regulate to engage others with thoughtful propriety. I mention again lines from the *Zhongyong*, chapter 1, which discuss how important the development of emotional capacity is in relation-ing with others and generating the contexts in which people live: "The moment at which joy and anger, grief and pleasure, have yet to arise is called a nascent equilibrium (*zhong*); once the emotions have arisen, that they are all brought into proper focus (*zhong*) is called harmony (*he*). This notion of equilibrium and focus (*zhong*) is the great root of the world; harmony then is the advancing of the proper way (*dadao*) in the world" (Ames & Hall, 2001, p. 89). The development of emotional maturity is a critical undertaking of personal cultivation because it influences how people feel about and engage others. Engaging a process orientation, which features the ability to take a long-term perspective of life, contextualizes personal cultivation by foregrounding the importance of genuine regard for others, characterizes notions of hierarchy as constituted by changing roles and reciprocity, and insinuates the extensive and productive nature of relating.

For those seeking to become exemplary, according to the *Zhongyong*, the ability to regulate emotions generates harmony in the world. Personal cultivation, then, is a process one undertakes to strive to harmonize relationships. To personally cultivate in order to create balance and harmony does not simply imply that people succumb to other's wishes in a passive way to "keep peace." Rather, it suggests that people who wish to live ethically should relate with others with attentive propriety, integrity, and earnestness. Harmony is not meant to imply similarity but emerges through engaging tension and difference in deliberate ways. Textual examples of harmony relate it to food or music (Ames, 2011, p. 275). Harmony, Ames points out, entails a process of different elements coming together to create something that is more enriched than the elements on their own. For example, harmony in music does not emerge from all instruments playing the same note or random different notes at the same time; it requires that musicians play notes attending to specific and varied notes as well as the space of the moments between. It is through attention to difference and change of multiple sounds that harmony emerges. It is ongoing thoughtful action and response that occurs in an ongoing way. Similarly with the making of food, the creation of harmony involves a deliberate mixing of textures and flavors to create something more than the ingredients themselves. For instance, a person may find it difficult to ingest a large amount of salt on its own. But a bit of salt added to a dish made from various ingredients can draw out their flavors in surprising ways. Chefs and musicians become so masterfully attuned to their ingredients and instruments that they can create imaginative configurations that astound the senses.

For those seeking to become exemplary, according to the *Zhongyong*, a process of personal cultivation includes the development of emotional maturity, which encourages people to act reflectively. To "bring into proper focus (*zhong*)" a person's emotions generates harmony in a processual world because the process influences one's actions. What is required is not copying other's behaviors; it is about doing the hard work to get in touch with one's feelings that emerge from experiences, creating coherency between one's thinking and feelings, which encourages one to try to understand others and respond to them in reflectively deliberate ways. A process of personal cultivation from a processual perspective emerges necessarily through relationships and through attending to our daily relation-ings with others. This means that people who seek to become exemplary are challenged to continually attune to their own actions, feelings, and responses to others at every moment because it is our activities that inform the texture and robustness of our lives. The *Zhongyong* makes a case for how important it is to develop the capacity to manage one's emotions and goes even further to say that it is this capacity that generates the contexts in which people live when it suggests that "harmony then is the advancing of the proper way (*dadao*) in the world" (p. 89).

Situating people and our relation-ing from a temporally ongoing perspective foregrounds the importance of relating informed by genuine regard for others. This notion becomes clear in the way the qualities of exemplary leaders in the *Zhongyong* are often described in terms of how others might perceive or respond to them. Leaders do not hold or claim others' deference as a personal state. The qualities of wise leaders cannot exist as essences, but are connected, not only to how others might perceive them, but more specifically how they perform the work of governance, which could itself be considered a form of intra-action:

> Only those of utmost sagacity in the world:
> have the perspicacity and quickness of mind needed to oversee the empire;
> have the tolerance and flexibility needed to win them the forbearance of others;
> have the energy and fortitude needed to maintain their grasp;
> have the poise and impeccability needed to command respect;
> have the culture and discernment needed to be discriminating. (p. 112)

The qualities mentioned—perspicacity and quickness of mind, tolerance, flexibility, energy, fortitude, poise, impeccability, culture, and discernment—are directly related to the activities of engaging particular roles that necessarily involve others. Rather than essential traits, these qualities require and emerge from engagement with others. For instance, one would benefit from acting with insight and flexibility to more successfully facilitate the numerous responsibilities of governance, which necessarily involve communication with many people. The development of tolerance, flexibility, poise, and impeccability are needed not for authoritarian purposes, but to "persuade"; such qualities are necessary "to win the forbearance of others."

When regard for others is viewed as primary, this implies that relationships (and by implication, relation-ing) matter most. Exemplary leaders are not simply trying to persuade those they govern to accept their leadership; they genuinely place relationships with people foremost when they consider governing approaches. The importance of regard for others becomes even more evident when parents are substituted for the descriptions of sagacious leaders given that relationships between parents and children are also a way forward in the world. Sagacious parents require insight and quickness of mind to contribute to the developing maturity of a child and the energy and courage to maintain the relationship in times of difficulty. What subbing in parents for leaders illustrates is the importance of the quality of relating, one that emerges not through force but through respectful regard. This means putting the relationship and relation-ing first even when this may be the most difficult. Neufeld and Maté (2004) point out that children do not grant adults authority to parent them because they are adults or because the adults love them or have their interests in mind. A child must want to be parented: "parenthood is above all a relationship, not a skill to be acquired. Attachment is not a behavior to be learned but a connection to be sought" (p. 55).

The role of genuine regard is particularly important in the context of parents and children especially when parents play such an important role in the personal cultivation of their children. A process-oriented perspective of parenting encourages taking a long-term view of children's development. Parenting generally involves the constant work of trying, in part, to keep young children safe, for instance, from ingesting something that might be a choking hazard and to accustom them to behaving in particular socially expected ways, such as sharing toys with siblings and greeting friends upon meeting. While much of parenting may be preoccupied with these types of behavior-related activities, taking a long view of the relationship between parents and children means parents must attend to the impact of how they relate with their children when addressing behavior and conduct. This means that parents must strive to help their children feel positively regarded even when they find their conduct most challenging because children foremost register and experience their parents' tone and behavior rather than intentions. Neufeld and Maté (2004) point out that much advice about parenting often offers techniques about how to manage children's immediate behavior, but what gets missed is that focusing on cultivating the relation-ing between parents and children is what matters most overall, implying that how they relate matters. The relation-ing and relationship are inseparable.

If children do not positively feel regarded by their parents, this will take a toll on their emotional development. If children sense that because of their behavior they are not valued by their caretakers, this may lead them to emotionally shut down. This threatens the attachment they have with those who are trying to parent them and may lead to even more challenging conduct. "It is when things are the roughest that we should be holding on to our children the most firmly. Then they, in turn, can hold on to us" (p. 197). Trying to parent or teach lessons when upset, the authors warn, may lead to children feeling anxiety about how their parents view them. When children do not feel valued, the feeling undermines their instincts to please their parents, which damages the relationship. The impact of children's anxiety about their relationships with their parents limits children's emotional and maturational development. By "holding on to our children," the authors suggest, it is important to reassure children about their unconditional acceptance by expressing a genuinely warm and caring attitude even when addressing behavior. In this way, parents contribute to the emotional maturational process of children in the long term by supporting the attachment relationship between parents and children. This is important because parental nurturing is required to help a child develop the capacity to emotionally regulate.

The importance of genuine regard in relationships challenges assumptions of normative notions of hierarchy. Because a process-oriented view of relationships highlights the importance of regard in relation-ing, it makes notions of hierarchy more fluid. Li-Hsiang Lisa Rosenlee (2006) suggests that while a Confucian tradition does engage a social hierarchy, Rosenlee emphasizes that the nature of relationships should be mutually responsive. For instance, children are generally expected to observe a socially normative notion of deference to their parents. However, this does not mean that parents have absolute authority, "There is no such thing as right without obligation" in Confucian ethics (p. 157). Rosenlee also points out that social positioning often is not fixed and that it changes throughout people's lives; for instance, children grow up, may become leaders, spouses, in-laws, parents, and grandparents: "One is neither definitely socially inferior nor superior, and each relation is premised on complementarity and reciprocity instead of domination and submission" (p. 158). To engage a process orientation is to take into account a longer-term view of change as part of people's emerging contexts and lives. In the context of relationships between parents and children, as children grow older their roles and responsibilities change to the extent that they may become parents to their own children (and as a reader of an earlier version of the manuscript pointed out, perhaps parents to their own parents). In particular, engaging a process orientation suggests the value of considering personal cultivation through a lens of change and shifting responsibility; people's roles emerge and change through relation.

The notion that hierarchical roles are not normatively fixed extends to a process-oriented approach to view reverence of ancestors. For example, in chapters 17 to 20, the *Zhongyong* mentions that Confucius identified people such as Shun; Kings Wen, Tai, Ji, and Wu; and Duke Zhou as models not only of their time but also to those who followed because they constructed relationships with their ancestors through ritual. In chapter 19, Confucius identifies King Wu and the Duke of Zhou as filial exemplars who honored "the purposes of one's predecessors" and strove to maintain their ways (Ames & Hall, 2001, p. 98). Sor-hoon Tan (2003) cautions that Chinese notions of hierarchy of ancestors and ancestor worship in a religious sense is quite distinct from that of a Judeo-Christian medieval religion from which the English word "hierarchy" is associated; Tan warns that the term carries with it a religious Judeo-Christian connotation: a "hierarch is a priest that rules over rites and implies a ranking where the 'Creator' is envisioned as separate from the 'created hierarchy' " (p. 99). Such an order could presumably not change unless the "Creator" changes it. On the other hand, remembering and honoring ancestors through the performance of rituals and reference to them in a hierarchical way from a Confucian tradition is not thought of as an external activity to worship a divine being but rather is a continuation of the roles ancestors played in relation to their family members when they were alive. Tan points out that the view of the cosmos from a processual orientation is not one of a fixed transcendency but rather is what Tan calls self-generating and self-sustaining: "Without the same associations of transcendence, inflexibility of social stratification and persistence of inequalities are contingent rather than theologically or metaphysically necessary" (p. 100).

More broadly, engaging a process orientation highlights the notion that it is through people's actions and relations that we construct the contexts in which we live. Ames and Hall (2001) describe people in a processual world as foci in a changing field. This perspective "presumes a world constituted by an interactive field of processes and events in which there are no final elements, only shifting 'foci' in the phenomenal field, each of which focuses the entire field from its finite perspective" (p. 7). In other words, people's networks of relationships are generated through engagement to insinuate a broader contextual and connected field. People are part of the same connected field that continually changes because it is constituted by their constant movement in a similar way to how configurations of atoms and molecules constantly move to construct our bodies and environments. This changing field is both physical and psychological, implying that form and function are entwined. A physical configuration refers to the atoms constantly moving that construct our bodies and environments. At the same time, the psychological configuration is inseparable in that it is our neurological development and bodies that make it possible for us to act and experience. It is these patterns of configurations of the physical—naturally moving atoms and molecules—and of the psychological—including cultural and social contexts—that are mutually entailing and changing.

A process orientation highlights the accumulations of people's actions and relations by situating them from a long-term perspective. When people are considered focal events or "foci," their movements contribute to the construction of a contextual field that informs aspects of natural, social, and cultural phenomena. People's actions are productive in the way that *tian* is productive, from chapter 26, "Now the firmament (*tian*) is just an accumulation of light, but given its boundlessness, the sun, moon, stars, and constellations are all woven through it, and all things are covered by it" (p. 107). What emerges from this framing of a natural context of *tian* is how its activity ("an accumulation of light") generates the context for other events. This "accumulation" does not seem intentional or even directed; it emerges because of its "event" nature. The way of *tian* then is effortless growth and "accumulations." While it may be impossible to conceive of the extensiveness of an intra-active field that changes and how people form an intimate part, people can at the same time influence the networks that constitute the field and through them the field itself through reflective and attentive actions. This implies that how people engage others and respond in every moment has contextual implications in the short and long term.

A process orientation situates life as changing and necessarily contingent. It suggests the value of considering personal cultivation toward harmonizing relationships through a lens of shifting responsibility. Engaging this perspective is to take into account a longer-term view of change, which suggests the importance, for those seeking to become exemplary, of cultivating genuine regard for others. Regard for others and a view that people's roles may change through time suggests attempting to view hierarchical constructs as fluid rather than fixed and highlights the importance of mutual responsiveness. More broadly, engaging a process orientation contributes to the notion that personal cultivation is extensive because it suggests that it is through people's activities that they construct the ongoing contexts, including the roles that people perform, in which they live. A process orientation also situates people, then, as events.

Framing People as Events

If people are who they are because of what they do, then this suggests people's particularities emerge from their specific actions. A concept of Confucian relationality that engages a process-orientation perspective of life suggests that people live in mutuality. In other words, people are necessarily constituted by others through our relation-ing, implying people cannot exist as "individuals." A normative notion of individual assumes that people can be characterized as abstractions—that people have personalities that belong to them, which set them apart from others. However, a process-oriented view of the world implies that it is through their specific actions and experiences in the context of relationships that their particularities as people continually emerge. This perspective situates people not as abstractions but as specifically embodied. A process orientation supports the view of people as particular events that are shaped by their actions and relationships.

To view people as living in mutuality through our relationships foregrounds the notion that people are events. A general notion of the term "events" suggests that they are occurrences that take place within a specific time frame and spatial context. For instance, a grandmother's birthday party is an event where family and friends gather together to celebrate. The event itself might be a dinner party that happens at a particular day, time, and place. But when taking into consideration what makes that particular event an event, it is the ongoing relationships of the people who gather, which emerge as central. In other words, the event of the birthday party itself is simply a moment, an occurrence, in the ongoing relation-ing of people, which is the more extensive event. If the more extensive event emerges from people's relation-ing, then this situates people themselves who are doing the relation-ing as ongoing events. To return to chapter 26 of the *Zhongyong*, "The way of heaven and earth can be captured in one phrase: Since events are never duplicated, their production is unfathomable" (p. 107). The text suggests that what something is ("heaven and earth") emerges from what it does—"the way." It is "the way" of natural contexts that makes them events. Similarly, for people, it is through our relation-ing that we generate the relational contexts in which we live, including perceptions of "who we are." Jane Bennett (2010) writes, "Organic and inorganic bodies, natural and cultural objects . . . *all* are affective" (p. xii). Drawing on Spinoza's notion of affect, Bennett suggests that people, places, and what might be considered material "things" have a vital force that emerges from the capacity to act upon and be responsive.

To situate people as events is to necessarily situate them as specific rather than abstract. When we think about people as specific, then we can see people, as Ames (2011) suggests, from a perspective of correlative cosmology as narratives rather than as beings or individuals. According to Ames, correlative cosmology, which informs traditional Chinese medicine's notion of the body as dynamic form and function, situates life and so-called "things" as aspects of the same reality that are inseparable. For a notion of a relational person, this means that a person's network of relationships cannot be static. There could be no relationship without relation-ing, and the relation-ing is necessarily specific and contextualized. For instance, interpersonal neurobiologist Daniel Siegel and educator Mary Hartzell (2003) suggest that parents actively sculpt their children's growing brains. "The immature brain of the child is so sensitive to social experience that adoptive parents should in fact be called the biological parents because the family experiences they create shape the biological structure of their child's brain. Being a birth parent is only one way parents biologically shape their children's lives" (p. 34). In other words, who raises a child and how a child is raised matter because parents are not abstractions to their children. Relation-ing makes people particular. In fact, everything children experience (see, smell, touch, feel) impacts how they make sense of and engage the world around them, including their relationships. "All of this takes place at the cellular level in our neurons and in the connections among our brain cells called synapses" (Siegel & Bryson, 2014, p. 42). In other words, people are necessarily embodied and shaped by our specific experiences through our relationships.

To situate people as specific events is to foreground our relationing, our actions, and our activities. Aspects of work by pragmatists George Herbert Mead (1934) and John Dewey (1957) can assist with the construction of a conception of person that suggests people and conduct are inseparable, reinforcing the notion of people as events and confluences of actions specifically contextualized. Mead (1934) provides a way to understand a notion of self not as "individual" but as necessarily relational through the suggestion that a "self" develops through time and experience because a "self" is generated through a process of active social experience. It is a cognitive framework that situates a notion of mind as socially constituted because it ascribes meaning to gestures and responses that emerge from relations with others. In other words, we are born into social mediums. As we develop, the attitudes and institutions of our communities influence us. If this is the case, then the field of a person's mind extends "as far as the social activity or apparatus of social relationships which constitutes it extends; and hence that field cannot be bounded by the skin of the individual organism to which it belongs" (p. 223). In brief, people can only exist relationally.

Dewey (1957) suggests that relationships and environments constitute people by evidence of our various habits. These habits are not simply rote actions that we half-unthinkingly take. Rather, they are persistent social functions that include people's actions in our environments and with each other. They are constituted by what we continually do, but also by our approaches to how we think. Habits are a form of what Dewey calls "active means" that influence how we act whether we are conscious of them or not. For example, Dewey points out that just because we are not walking in a particular moment does not mean that our ability to walk and the sensation of walking do not influence the way we understand distance or how we experience walking when we dream. Acts emerge before thought and habits before abilities: "Our ideas truly depend upon experience, but so do our sensations. And the experience upon which they both depend is the operation of habits—originally of instincts" (p. 32). Ideas can only emerge from habits or "demands for certain kinds of activity" (p. 26). Habits, then, are mediums that serve as filters that shape our perceptions and thoughts. People are not discrete from others because from birth we are exposed to others' habits through our families, which shape our individualities including notions of a "self." Just as the activity of walking implicates relation between person and environment, for the ability to walk entails not only movement of our legs but also involves the ground we walk on, so it is the same, for instance, for our ideas of propriety and our actual conduct. We are born into families and existing systems of organization that give actions meaning. Our social environments situate us as necessarily intradependent.

Both Mead and Dewey reject the notion that people can be isolated individuals or souls but suggest that activity and conduct are primary to determinations about who we are, what we think and believe. In other words, we construct our "identities" performatively. If we consider that meaning continually emerges through engagement in a process of gesture and response because of the ongoing influence of our habits, then our actions contribute to the construction of who we are in every moment rather than situate us as having essentialist qualities.

When people are situated as specific rather than abstract, then people can be viewed as constituted by networks of relationships. Relationships, then, from a processual orientation, are not simply had; they are constructed through engagement; people, then, are specific events and narratives that enmesh. At people's early ages, their parents and environments actively shape their neurological development, which includes their social and physical development. This suggests that people live in mutuality because how people act in every moment has both a short-term influence on those with whom they relate and also a longer-term influence shaping people's systems of meaning including attitudes, notions of identities, and the contexts of our lives. A view that people live in mutuality supports the notion that personal cultivation is extensive because it contextualizes personal growth as emerging through relation.

Personal Cultivation Emerges Through Relationship

If people are constituted by relationships, then personal cultivation emerges through them. A concept of Confucian relationality situates personal cultivation as extensive because it influences not only the person undertaking the process but also those whom a person engages. To attend to how people engage others on a daily basis to harmonize relationships, people need to try to understand others' experiences. In *Zhongyong*, chapter 13, the text suggests that genuine regard for others requires in part the capacity to imagine oneself in the place of others. "Putting oneself in the place of others (*shu*) and doing one's best on their behalf (*zhong*) does not stray far from the proper way. 'Do not treat others as you yourself would not wish to be treated'" (Ames & Hall, 2001, p. 94). "To put oneself in the place of others" challenges those who seek to become exemplary to not immediately judge others' actions or words from one's own perspective but rather requires one to engage an attentively inquiring perspective that seeks to thoughtfully consider why some might act in the way that they do. "To put oneself in the place of others" implies that one needs to try to feel what others might be feeling. It is through reflectively considering why they might feel what they do that one can then genuinely do "one's best on their behalf."

One way to seek to understand the experience of others is to become attuned to one's own feelings and emotional experiences. The *Zhongyong* identifies the importance of attitude in the following lines from chapter 20: "The Master said, 'Being fond of learning is close to acting wisely (*zhi*); advancing on the way with enthusiasm is close to acting authoritatively (*ren*) and having a sense of shame is close to acting with courage (*yong*). Those who realize these three realize how to cultivate their persons . . .'" (p. 102). While "wisdom, authoritative conduct, and courage" are, as mentioned earlier, the methods of "excelling in character" (from chapter 20, p. 102), it is important to note that how one engages these methods is critical. To be "fond" of learning, to advance on the way with "enthusiasm," and having a "sense of shame" are emotional characteristics, which complement and are entwined with engaging the three methods of the "way forward." To genuinely undertake a process of personal cultivation, then, the text suggests that people need to do more than act the part of exemplary person in a behavioral sense. People need to express their conduct with genuine feeling, and this implies trying to understand and respond to others in part by seeking to understand their own feelings.

To attune to their feelings, reflection is key. People have the intuitive potential to reflectively learn and the resources to live in harmonious ways, but this requires effort to realize: "What *tian* commands (*ming*) is called natural tendencies (*xing*); drawing out these natural tendencies is called the proper way (*dao*); improving upon this way is called education (*jiao*)" (p. 89). This notion of education could be considered a process of personal cultivation that requires people to be continually mindful of and attentive to how they engage others. This means that they must learn about how people behave and consider their actions not simply through mimicry of others' behaviors or acting upon immediate emotional responses but by striving to act in thoughtful ways. In chapter

13, the text references the *Book of Songs* and states, "In hewing an axe handle—the model is not far away" (p. 94). The passage continues, "But in grasping one axe handle to hew another, if one never looks directly at the axe handle in one's hand, the handles still seem far apart" (p. 94). In seeking to become exemplary through harmonizing relationships, people might turn to social expectations about conduct for guidance. However, without undertaking the reflective activity of turning to look and study the axe handle in use, people may not notice the ramifications of their actions. To act with integrity requires more than outwardly expressing what might be considered socially appropriate behaviors in particular contexts. It is through reflective inquiry that they might understand and feel the ramifications of behaviors and act with this in mind. Reflective inquiry encourages the development of coherence between thinking and feeling that makes the way for thoughtful action and response to others. It is through reflection that people might be able to develop the capacity to try to imagine what others might feel—although this is no easy task, as I touch upon later.

To better understand others, reflectively inquiring about people's own feelings is critical, and opportunities emerge for this through their relationships. While it is through everyday engagements that people are challenged to reflectively attend to their conduct, it is taking on the responsibility for our relation-ing with others that can provide a valuable opportunity for us to personally cultivate. To return to considering a parent and child relationship, for example, suggests that for parents to encourage attachment in their children, they have to be open to attending to their own feelings and reactions to their children's behaviors. Children need to attach to their parents to develop emotional maturity. It is through parents providing unconditional regard to and acceptance of a child through embodying a caring attitude even in moments when a child's behavior is most challenging that encourages a child to feel emotionally safe. When provided the caring context in the form of a safe relationship with parents, a child's emotional maturity will emerge on its own—it is not something parents need to forcefully teach. To provide a safe relationship, parents will often need to personally cultivate too. Neufeld and Maté (2004) write, "It is not our children's fault that they are born uncivilized, immature; that their impulses rule them or that they fall short of our expectations. The discipline for parents is to work only in the context of connection" (p. 215). For parents, it is valuable to realize that it is through attachment that children pay attention and that parents must work on themselves to encourage this. More to the point, the authors write, "our ability to manage a child effectively is very much an outcome of our capacity to manage ourselves . . ." (p. 215).

How parents relate to their children impacts the process of personal cultivation in children, and the reverse is true as well—parents' relationships with their children offers opportunities for the parents to personally cultivate. It is a process that is mutually entailing; the more parents personally cultivate through their relation-ing with their children, the more this impacts the emotional maturation process of the child. Parents are provided an opportunity to personally cultivate from assisting in the emotional maturational process of a child because young children can behave unpredictably and emotionally, which can elicit strong feelings and responses at times from parents. It is through seeking to understand these responses that parents can reflectively engage children rather than acting in automatic ways. One way to frame these responses is as bodily sensations. Siegel and Hartzell (2003) suggest that people's internal subjective experiences are filled with "surges of energy and information processing in our minds" (p. 225), which take the form of feelings and sensations. These feelings and sensations constitute the basis of primary emotions, which are intrawoven with meaning-making processes. In other words, bodily sensations influence how people make conscious sense of the world. The authors write, ". . . sensations are a rich untapped source of insight and wisdom. Coherent self-knowledge may depend upon our becoming more sensitive to and aware of our internal states and the sensations that accompany them" (p. 226).

Young children's behaviors can easily provoke parental feelings. For instance, when my then one-year-old daughter gleefully ran toward a leftover rain puddle at the start of a walk one morning ready to splash in it, this triggered my anxious response to want to keep her from doing it. After I urged her to not jump in and even tried to guide her away from it by holding her hand when she protested, I wondered when we continued on our walk why I had such an automatic response. Maybe I feared that her shoes and feet would get wet and that this would not allow us to proceed with our walk. This is reasonable, but why did I respond emotionally—why did my heart beat more quickly, why did I feel anxious? So what if her shoes became wet for a short time? Maybe she would not mind it, and she certainly was not in danger. We could go home and change her shoes and socks; maybe she would learn from the experience of stepping in a puddle especially because children learn through play; we did not have to go on a walk, we could simply embrace the moment of playing in the puddle. The more I thought about it, the more I wondered if this might have been a way my parents responded to my stepping in a puddle as a young child.

Parent's feelings evoked by the behavior of their children may be a mystery to parents but upon reflection may offer insights into how they were raised themselves. While I did not have a conscious memory of such an experience, when I reflected on the possibility that my parents responded to me in the same way I initially responded to my daughter, I could understand such a reaction given that I had a younger sister when I was a toddler my daughter's age. I can imagine that my parents with young children to care for would have wanted me to stay clear of a puddle because it would take more work to change my shoes, or jumping in a puddle might sidetrack us from going where we were going. More broadly, reflecting on the moment with my daughter helped me consider what it might have been like for my parents raising my siblings and me, the kind of expectations they had and the way they may have engaged me as a young child. This reflection in turn allowed me to react less emotionally to my daughter the next time a similar situation happened. I learned to assess the moment; did we need to go somewhere? Could we change our plans? Would it be difficult to change her shoes? More often than not, I would remember to put her rain boots on if it had rained the night before and enjoy watching her laughing as she splashed in a puddle. More notably, the reflection also helped me to attune to her reaction, to ask what she might feel if I responded by stopping her play. The initial emotion need not lead to an automatic response; I was able to better gauge my daughter's activity and her response to my request after becoming aware of and reflecting on my emotion. Even during moments when I wanted her to avoid a puddle, I found I could communicate this in a less abrupt way by redirecting her or finding a different way to approach the situation.

Parental feelings triggered by children, if reflected on, may provide occasions for parents to further their own emotional development. If the ages from 0 to 5 years are the most important time for the development of maturity and this impacts people's future relationships, then it is valuable for adults who are interested in personally cultivating to reflect on those early years of their lives. But the difficulty is that people may not have the capacity to remember those years consciously simply because they were still physically developing at that time. For many, it may be simply impossible to explicitly "remember" how their parents raised them. But parenting children offers one opportunity to do this because when parents raise children, they have automatic feelings and responses to their behavior that may offer some indicators of how their parents raised them. When caring for children, children's behavior "triggers" responses in their parents that provide an opportunity to parents to personally cultivate. In fact, this opportunity for parents to make sense of their lives is valuable for continuing adult development of emotional maturity. Siegel and Hartzell (2003) suggest, ". . . the most powerful predictor of a child's attachment is the coherence of the parent's life narrative [, which] allows us to understand how to strengthen our child's attachment to us. We are not destined to repeat the patterns of the past because we can earn our security as an adult by making sense of our life experiences" (p. 248).

To make sense of our lives through reflecting on feelings that emerge through our relationships is one way that enables us to more thoughtfully engage others. The *Zhongyong*, as mentioned earlier, states, "Wisdom, authoritative conduct, and courage—these are the three methods of excelling in character." It is through reflection on our relation-ing, though, that one understands what it means to be wise. These three methods of excelling in character must be practiced, and the practice emerges through our relation-ing. This practice likely requires effort and attention. When people's actions directly influence the quality of their lives, attitudes and cognitive processes that inform their actions, such as mindfulness, generating intentions and choices, only have meaning when contextualized relationally. These processes can be critical approaches that people can use to improve our relationships with others, and they mainly emerge with practice through their relation-ing.

The reflection required to increasingly understand people's feelings in order to become exemplary in their conduct with others is difficult. For Confucius, living well necessitates attention and deep reflective work. Throughout the *Zhongyong*, there are lamentations about how challenging it is to be exemplary. For example, distinctions are made between exemplary persons and petty persons, and the text references numerous comments attributed to Confucius about those who quit trying to be exemplary (see chapters 2, 4, 7, 9, 11, and 14). Notably, in chapter 13, Confucius even admits that he cannot achieve his own expectations regarding living properly when he points out that he is not able to be a son to his father in the ways that he would expect of his own son, or to treat a friend in the way Confucius himself would wish to be treated by others. That said, Confucius suggests it is important to make a continual effort. In chapter 13, Confucius is to have said, "Where in everyday moral conduct and in everyday attention to proper speech I am lacking in some respect, I must make every effort to attend to this" (p. 94). The notion of living properly in relation to others through living harmoniously, while it is not out of reach for people, is not easy to do because it requires people to do the work of attending to how one relates with others continually. Opportunities abound daily, if only people were to realize this and make use of them. From chapter 4: "Everyone eats and drinks, but those with real discrimination are rare indeed" (p. 90). While living reflectively could be considered mundane, it is work that requires ongoing and serious attention:

> Study the way broadly, ask about it in detail, reflect on it carefully, analyze it clearly, and advance on it with earnest. When there is something that one has yet to study or that, having studied it, has yet to master, do not stop; where there is something that one has yet to ask about or that, having asked about it, has yet to understand, do not stop; where there is something that one has yet to reflect upon or that, having reflected on it, has yet to grasp, do not stop; where there is something one has yet to analyze or that, having analyzed it, is still not clear about, do not stop; where there is the proper way that one has not yet advanced on or that, having advanced on it, has yet to do so with earnestness, do not stop.
>
> While others can accomplish this with just a single try, I will try a hundred times; while others can accomplish this with just ten tries, I will try a thousand times. If in the end people are able to advance on this way, even the dull are sure to become bright; even the weak are sure to become strong. (p. 104)

A process of personal cultivation through reflectively inquiring about feelings as they emerge from engaging others is accessible and relevant to all in part because it can be pursued as part of people's everyday lives, but it requires an inordinate amount of effort. What makes becoming exemplary difficult is not only the ability to envision what proper conduct might look like; it is the actual reflective work it takes to persistently achieve it in every moment. It is important because it allows people to attempt to "put ourselves in the place of others." By learning about why they feel what they do, people may be able to relate more to others via trying to imagine what they might feel. While it is not likely that anyone can wholly understand others or even oneself, the inquiring process encourages the development of the capacity to empathize with and recognize that others feel differently than we do.

A concept of Confucian relationality engages a process-oriented view of the world to situate people as living in mutuality. Because people's actions matter foremost, it situates a process of personal cultivation as emerging through people's relation-ing. For instance, the *Zhongyong* implies that parents contribute to the construction of their familial contexts through their actions, which radially influence their children's future relationships and various other contexts. At the same time, it also suggests that personal cultivation or "ways forward" emerge through many types of relationships, which involve using similar methods ("wisdom, authoritative conduct, and courage") that emerge through relationships and require practice. Wise people need not engage others with loud voices or actions. By undertaking the difficult work of reflectively cohering and integrating their feelings and thoughts in order to reflect in part on their own experiences, they can try to put themselves in the place of others. This allows them to act and respond with genuine regard and care even when others' conduct may be challenging. These actions not only influence those one engages but also can have an extensive impact by shaping the broader relational contexts in which people live. In the next several chapters, I engage a concept of Confucian relationality to explore some aspects of the context of higher education, including how faculty are situated by universities, the value of faculty collegiality, and teaching as an opportunity for personal cultivation.

PART 2

UNIVERSITIES

TOWARD SHARING RESPONSIBILITY

Chapter 3

The Tenure Expectations Paradox

In the first part of the book, I focused on developing a concept of Confucian relationality and provided some background of the Confucian tradition by exploring the role of commentary in shaping it. In the next few chapters, I use the concept to engage several aspects of contemporary higher educational phenomena. I begin in this chapter by exploring the expression of a product orientation in institutional orienting documents at a case study institution and how it situates multiple faculty roles as separate and competing. A product focus of instructional faculty roles creates a paradox for faculty who are expected by institutions to master the craft of teaching to foster global citizens; at the same time, faculty members find through their pursuit of tenure status that institutional prestige relies largely on publications of their research work. Instead of viewing faculty roles as separate and competing, engaging a Confucian relationality examines the value of viewing the roles as cohesive through a focus on the endeavoring of those undertaking faculty activities.

While a market-oriented paradigm normatively situates faculty members in economic terms as producers and their roles as separate, a Confucian relationality emphasizes the aspectual and ongoing nature of faculty activities in higher educational institutions. University institutional documents often express a product orientation through how they seek to direct and evaluate faculty activities in the arenas of research, teaching, and institutional and community service. Strategic directions and tenure and promotion guidelines, for instance, focus on the products of faculty activities in ways that situate faculty roles as separate from each other.

When faculty roles are viewed as separate, it is easy to view them as competing, given the limited time and energy of faculty members.

Engaging a Confucian relationality suggests that a focus on the action of faculty work brings to the forefront the importance of how faculty members feel about their roles in a cohering way. When the world is viewed from a process perspective as changing, harmonizing relationships is viewed as an important aspect of personal cultivation because relationships are considered mutually entailing so reflection on experiences can influence attitudes that in turn influence people's activities and intra-actions. To consider the importance of how faculty members regard their work because it shapes how they engage their roles draws attention to the ongoing nature of faculty work. Faculty activity when viewed as continually emergent contributes to the construction of university contexts in accumulatory and ongoing ways. At the same time, engaging these contexts in turn also informs faculty activities. To focus, then, on the ongoing activity of faculty work is to situate faculty members' roles as aspectual because the activities cannot be viewed as separate from those undertaking them. This emphasis on the ongoing nature of faculty work can assist with assessing and navigating product-oriented tensions that emerge from institutional documents.

When institutional documents send misaligned messages about institutional values, faculty members may face tension regarding how to expend limited time and energy. Universities' attempts to direct faculty activities influence the experiences of faculty. For instance, institutional documents emerge when committees often constituted by administrators and faculty members strive to articulate the aims and guidelines of institutional activities. Their purpose is to seek to shape the direction of the university by directing, to some extent, the activities of their colleagues. For faculty members, how they interpret these institutional documents can impact their experiences as faculty members and influence their regard toward their activities. Because faculty activities contribute to the construction of university contexts, institutional documents that seek to direct faculty attention are important to take a closer look at because they indicate how universities envision the roles of their faculty members. More than an act of public relations, documents like strategic directions, mission statements, and tenure guidelines reflect dominant institutional paradigms that require faculty members' attention.

Documents that seek to direct and evaluate faculty activities, such as tenure and promotion guidelines, convey institutional authority. While faculty members have choices regarding how they construct their dossiers, they are pressured to attend to the tenure and promotion guidelines as closely as possible because the process of evaluation of the dossiers determines the viability of their academic futures at particular institutions. As a result, the guideline expectations must be "valued" by faculty members who seek tenure and promotion and impact their activities. To clarify, I read value not primarily in an abstract cognitive moral sense, but with regard to those institutional educational expectations that require attention and responsive activity from participants. In other words, what is valued becomes valuable because of attention paid to it by participants of a system (faculty, staff, and students) in a functional way and not because it has some essential or inherent importance. For instance, a product orientation tends to frame aspects of educational constructs in terms of a language of measurement. As a result, more easily quantifiable aspects attract more attention simply because they are more measurable, not because they are necessarily more valuable (Biesta, 2010).

Institutional directives in documents convey a paradoxical message to faculty members when they emphasize the importance of faculty teaching in the pursuit of cultivating educated citizens and yet also discuss the preeminent value of faculty research. For instance, higher educational institution mission statements often state goals of fostering ethical citizens, which foreground the importance of faculty teaching. The University of Michigan (n.d.) mission statement published on the institution's website suggests that it seeks to develop "leaders and citizens who will challenge the present and enrich the future." It does this to "serve the people of Michigan and the world through preeminence in creating, communicating, preserving and applying knowledge, art, and academic values." Stanford University's (2018) website states that its goals are to "prepare students to think broadly and critically and to contribute to the world, and to use Stanford's strengths to benefit the region, country, and world." Even small liberal arts colleges sound the same focus of developing thoughtful citizens. Vassar College's (n.d.) mission statement states, "The College makes possible an education that promotes analytical, informed, and independent thinking and sound judgment; encourages articulate expression; and nurtures intellectual curiosity, creativity, respectful debate and engaged citizenship." These statements, with their emphasis on the development of critical thinkers and ethical global citizens, imply the preeminent importance of faculty teaching because it is faculty members who facilitate courses and develop curriculum that directly engage and evaluate students. The statements suggest that it is faculty members who are institutionally tasked and responsible in large part for cultivating intellectually curious global citizens.

While higher educational mission statements infer the primary importance of faculty teaching, at the same time the increased modeling of universities as businesses tends to emphasize the value of research when it situates faculty members as producers. A product-oriented perspective views faculty roles as separate, even competing, activities in part because it frames faculty contributions in terms of market-oriented goals and metrics. In other words, a product orientation relies on a provision of evidence through measurement as a method to show contributions, which is considered important for hiring and for promotion. Vassar College (2019), for instance, "seeks to recruit a faculty of the highest quality. It looks for certain measures of competence, including achievement and potential in the following areas: teaching, scholarly work or artistic activities, and service to the college" (p. 100). At the University of Michigan (1954), the tenure and promotion guidelines state, "To warrant recommendation for initial appointment, candidates must have given evidence either here or elsewhere of their ability to handle satisfactorily the duties of the positions in question."

The mission statements articulate the need for faculty to provide "evidence" of their contributions. From a product perspective, the prioritizing of the value of evidence is the same for the various faculty roles. What it does not consider is what qualifies as evidence for each role. Because faculty roles are viewed as separate, how do committees compare the evidence from each? Can the evidence be measured and evaluated in a standardized way? Teaching is a relational activity whose success in part relies on student achievement, which makes the development of standardized measures difficult. When it comes to the various roles of instructional faculty members, the arena that lends itself most easily to the provision of evidence through scholarly publications would be research. At Stanford University (2019), this predilection for the foremost value of research is stated up front: "For recommendations of reappointment or promotion of a member of the Stanford faculty to tenure status, the department or school is required to present evidence that the candidate's overall performance justifies the award of tenure, including evidence that the candidate has achieved true distinction in scholarship." While the institution does mention the value of teaching in relation to scholarship, the achievement of tenure requires success in the production of research foremost.

The product-oriented paradox that emerges from the juxtaposition of institutional statements and documents is related to the importance of teaching through the expectation of cultivating ethical global citizens and the value of research distinction. A crux of the paradox is that processes such as teaching that are directly relational and contextual tend to be more difficult to collect evidence for in standardized and measurable ways because so much of teaching depends on how faculty and students relate. Teaching requires faculty members to adapt to some extent to their students, their subject experience level, and learning styles, among others. At the same time, a normative notion of success in teaching in part depends on students' commitment to achievement in courses, which may vary for extensive reasons depending on past experiences with subject areas, the current states of their lives, and their attitudes about and motivation for taking particular courses.

When institutional statements discuss the goals of cultivating ethical global citizens, they insinuate the importance of faculty teaching. However, when tenure requirements focus on the provision of evidence to determine faculty contributions, they foreground the value of research. Because a system of peer review has largely been established as part of the publishing process, it is easier for tenure and promotion committees to evaluate evidence of research production in standardized ways. Institutional goals of developing ethical global citizens then are undermined in part by product-oriented tenure requirements for instructional faculty who feel pressure to focus more on publishing to achieve tenure or promotion.

In this chapter, I take a closer look at the product-oriented paradox at one institution. I examine the University of Hawai'i's Strategic Directions document (see Appendix A) and consider how its external publicly articulated goals (strategic directions) align with the internal institutional expectations for a major part of its employ (tenure and promotion guidelines for instructional faculty [Appendix B]). The focus on one case example encourages a more in-depth inquiry than an overview of many institutions. Because so many higher educational institutions face the same market-oriented pressures, the challenges of one institution will be similar to some extent to others. While a strategic directions document is carefully constructed by faculty and administrative leaders and vetted by various committees to serve as a guiding text for institutional directions over a period of time, tenure and promotion criteria and guidelines articulate the conditions for faculty members' employment. The guidelines are just as important and revelatory because faculty reward systems reflect institutional and administrator predilections (for example, increased scholarly output) or their concerns (not enough scholarly output) (Gardner & Veliz, 2014). Those who are perceived to meet the desire for what is normatively valued are rewarded with tenure and promotion, while those who do not may have their applications denied and as a result may have to seek employment elsewhere. While the documents address different audiences for different purposes, when considered together, their resonances can be viewed as reinforcing institutional normative paradigms. At the same time, perceived disjuncture provides an opportunity for inquiry.

To examine the product-oriented paradox, I engage a concept of Confucian relationality. I do this by using aspects of the concept to inspire inquiry. For instance, the concept suggests that people's activities matter foremost because they influence how people relate with others and construct the contexts in which we live. This leads me to ask, how are people framed by the documents? A Confucian relationality engages a process orientation that considers the world as changing. This leads me to consider, when reading the documents, where are discussions of the processes mentioned to achieve stated goals? To view a world as changing is also to consider how events are located in time and space. This leads me to ask what the longer-term implications are about the goals and guidelines mentioned in the documents.

The concept of a Confucian relationality makes the paradox visible in part by showing the limits of a product-orientated paradigm and inferring what it leaves out. In particular, the framing of faculty members as producers insinuates the separation of the different types of faculty activities. This leads to a simplified view of learning as training as opposed to a more enriching notion of learning. It also leads to a devaluing of teaching because it suggests that evidence of faculty contributions needs to be measured in some way. Engaging a concept of Confucian relationality challenges a product-oriented notion of faculty as producers because it shows where relational processes already exist, for instance, in faculty tenure and promotion evaluations. Engaging a Confucian relationality assists with seeing the connection between processes and outcomes, encouraging a broader view of envisioning the ongoing nature of faculty work. This situates faculty roles as inseparable because it considers them as emerging from faculty ongoing inquiry and learning.

The paradox created between the importance of teaching indicated by institutional expectations to cultivate ethical global citizens and the importance of research distinction are important to dwell upon because they influence how faculty regard and approach their activities. This in turn may have a radial impact on those they engage in their various activities. If value emerges in part from attention, then it follows that value can change if attention shifts. That attention has a kind of agency resonates with Ingold's (2018) argument that the purpose of education, rather than a transmission of information or the development of critical reasoning, should be the development of attention. It is through refinement of attention, which includes developing responsiveness to environment, that influences how people correspond with each other, thereby enriching relation.

To put it another way, attending is a form of experience from which people learn and that influences what people do. Rather than overlooking the product-oriented paradox that emerges from institutional directives, engaging a Confucian relational orientation invites inquiry about the normative expectations and pressures faculty members face in ways that disrupt their impact by illuminating the tensions that emerge in the documents when institutions rely on a product orientation to frame complex processes and roles that resist delineation. It also provides a way to address the paradox when it envisions faculty activities as aspectual from the perspective that they are ongoing endeavors.

Product Paradigm Stresses Efficiency

Engaging a Confucian relationality makes visible the product-oriented tension that emerges from institutions that ask faculty to prioritize the cultivation of wise citizens and the production of research at the same time. It does this in part because it raises questions about "how" events emerge (processes) rather than "what" might be perceived as constituting them (products). By focusing on the processes, a tension emerges in part because the processes of teaching and research are too often normatively narrowly situated in institutional documents in terms of product-oriented goals. A product or market orientation tends to emphasize outcomes over processes, envisions the world as measurable, and people as separate. A product orientation frames faculty roles largely from the perspective of what they produce. This perspective insinuates that the products faculty members generate are separate from each other. Because faculty time is limited, this perspective can set these goals in competition with each other. Situating faculty "products" as separate and in competition with each other reflects the expression of an extensive market paradigm that values efficiency foremost.

To explore how a broader product-oriented paradigm is expressed in a university context, it is useful to take a closer look at how it is reflected in two guiding institutional documents. The University of Hawai'i's Strategic Directions document (Appendix A) seeks to provide a guide to institutional priorities for six years "to achieve the outcomes" directed by the Board of Regents, a group that oversees the institution for the state. How it expresses a product-oriented paradigm is valuable to track because it shapes the broader context, preoccupations, and practices of the university. The "Criteria and Guidelines for Faculty Tenure/Promotion Application" document (Appendix B) details the criteria required for dossier construction. It requests that faculty submit evidence of excellence in teaching, research, and service for their tenure and promotion applications. Engaging a Confucian relationality can assist with identifying the challenges of using a product paradigm in an institutional context as reflected by the documents and how a product focus deemphasizes some faculty roles such as teaching.

The Strategic Directions document expresses a product-oriented paradigm in multiple ways. For instance, it details the institutional goals through a business plan format and language. The university's office of the vice chancellor for academic affairs published the 10-page document on its webpage to accord with a timeline for the Western Association of Schools and Colleges (WASC) reaccreditation process. Representatives of various university governance groups, including faculty, staff, and students, formed the 16-person Strategic Planning Committee to vet and measure the progress of the development of the priorities. The introductory section of the document lists the core values of the institution as academic rigor and excellence, integrity and service, aloha and respect. These core values could be framed as process oriented in that they describe attitudes and approaches to activities.

However, the body of the document displays a different focus. It describes four product-oriented strategic directions/goals, each accompanied by a paragraph-long description followed by a number of so-called "action strategies" and bulleted "tactic" points. Each goal description closes with a "productivity and efficiency measures" section constituted by a list of progress indicators. The majority of the document describes the four institutional goals using market-oriented language, which expresses a sense of efficiency that bolsters the linear structure of the document. For instance, the first words of each tactic read like the descriptive active verbs used in business parlance with the use of words such as "integrate," "develop," "support," "improve," and "create." The structure of the document reinforces a product orientation in that the outcomes—action-result trajectories—are prioritized over inquiry about the complexity of processes. For instance, the list of action strategies and bullet-pointed "tactics" that follow each goal, closing with a productivity and efficiency measures section, describes specific progress measures to evaluate productivity. The specific measures that close each section emphasize productivity, implying causal connections among the various sections.

In the Strategic Directions document, the product-oriented paradigm frames the purpose of the institution in economic terms. Economic concerns orient the strategic directions, and this is evident in the content of the university's goals, which situates the university, to some extent, as a job creator and preparer of the workforce for the state. A sentence from a description of the first goal indicates how the institution situates people: "An educated labor force and engaged citizenry are essential in today's global, knowledge-based economy." The goal aims to prepare students perceived to be low income and from underserved regions to succeed in "the workforce and their communities," suggesting that to attract such students to the institution and ensure they graduate are ways to increase what it refers to as "educational capital." It frames students foremost as laborers and the educational institution as primarily offering paths to students to gain better employment. The second goal in the document directs the university to "create more high quality jobs" to "diversify" the state's economy. The description states that the creation of an "economic sector" related to research and innovation is something that the university, as part of the state community, has a responsibility to undertake. The first two goals situate the university in economic terms more broadly as a workforce creator as well as a contributor to the development of an industry of research and innovation that would create jobs and prepare people for employment.

A product-oriented paradigm prioritizes efficiency as a method to support the goals. To aid in the development of the workforce and research innovation, the third and fourth goals of the document describe how the university will support faculty to prepare workers and create jobs. Goal three involves modernization of facilities and the campus environment to provide spaces conducive to educational and faculty research activities.

The fourth goal supports the development and use of "efficient" and "cost-effective" practices to ensure institutional financial viability and sustainability. Support for the development of a labor force is envisioned, in this goal, as best realized through the creation of a "high performance mission-driven system," which is accountable and transparent. Such a system, the document states, achieves "higher performance" by helping students find various ways to enter the process of schooling, streamlining administrative support, making more efficient use of facilities, and using better so-called "metrics" to account for efficient productivity.

The product-oriented notion of efficiency is a method that is envisioned as organizationally extensive. The document of strategic directions emphasizes the extensiveness of a product orientation when it discusses the importance of operating the university foremost as an "efficient" system. Notably, while the fourth goal of the document expresses an institutional commitment to seek financial sustainability and viability through the fostering of accountability and transparency in administrative operations, it has a broad reach. While the position of being fourth implies by its sequencing that it has lesser importance than the other goals, the impact of the high-performance mission-driven system initiative addresses the operations and management of the institution overall. This goal is unique from the others because it suggests a method by which to orient institutional function. It also suggests that efficiency needs to be a critical consideration for people who constitute the institution. The strategic goals when considered together generate an image of an institution that uses business practices to operate an efficient system that will maximize the creation of jobs for the state and prepare its workers. Faculty, staff, and students are largely situated as "producers" or "products" in this endeavor.

In particular, the product orientation of the document situates faculty members in economic terms as producers. Implicit in the first two goals of the document is that faculty member activities are critical for the institution to achieve these goals. It is faculty members who are the workforce generators because they are the forefront of engaging students in the classrooms. Also, the university relies on faculty members to be the producers of research and innovation that are meant to diversify the state's economy and create high-quality jobs. Faculty member activities are implicitly framed in economic terms from the perspective of a product paradigm. That said, the document does not explicitly state who is supposed to realize these goals. Even though a one-page matrix that accompanies the Strategic Directions document identifies loosely defined "planning and implementation task forces" and "work groups" to initiate each goal, goal actualization relies in large part on the faculty who directly engage students, create curriculum, and use the classrooms. While various institutional entities may have their own interpretations of the strategic goals, it is faculty across the board who would ultimately be expected to maximize classroom space usage, to align curricula with community and workforce needs, and to "integrate entrepreneurship and innovation . . . for students across the system."

I want to point out that there is some resistance. In a letter to the co-chairs of the research campus's strategic directions committee, the chair of the committee on academic policy and planning, which is part of the faculty senate, noted the importance for the administration to recognize the centrality of faculty to institutional endeavors and suggested the need for increased support for faculty and students to "achieve excellence" in terms of academic quality in addition to attempts to actualize the more practical goals of retention and graduation. The chair wrote, "By supporting faculty we do not necessarily mean financial support, although that would be nice, and do not mean artificial workshops to tell faculty how they should teach, but changing the climate of the university so that there is a general sense of the key role of faculty, as well as their inclusion in key decision-making on all of these matters."

The "Criteria and Guidelines for Faculty Tenure/Promotion Application" document also expresses a similarly product-oriented paradigm to some extent. It does so through its request that faculty members provide evidence of their contributions. Although the language of the document is not as business focused as the strategic direction goals, the framing of faculty members as producers is reflected in the institution's tenure and promotion guidelines, which express a product-oriented value of efficiency through the request for evidence of faculty contributions. The "Criteria and Guidelines for Faculty Tenure/Promotion Application" document made available on the university's "Tenure, Promotion, and Contract Renewal" webpage provides criteria and specific instructions for dossier construction that detail the expectations for evidence of excellence in teaching, research, and service activities. The guidelines suggest that provision of "evidence" is critical. Accomplishments should be documented "with as much objective evidence as possible," and letters from colleagues and students should "evaluate specific contributions or achievements rather than those which simply express support for your case." In addition, expectations include a request to applicants to follow formatting requirements, a statement of endeavors, and other specifics with regard to providing supporting materials.

The request for evidence in the tenure and promotion guidelines document situates faculty activities in separate categories. The criteria for instructional faculty members' tenure and promotion evaluations includes four points detailed in two pages:

1) The university must have a need for a faculty member with the particular qualifications of the applicant.

2) A demonstration of "a high level of competence as a teacher" is necessary.

3) Scholarly achievement in comparison with peers in one's discipline.

4) Service activities in the profession and general community.

The listing of the categories in numerical order from two to four suggests that faculty activities are separate from each other for evaluatory purposes. The criteria, with their largely product-oriented focus, positions faculty members as producers of teaching, research, and service.

While the Strategic Directions document describes a product paradigm in detail in part through its delineation of institutional goals that situate university faculty members as producers of a workforce and of research innovations, the tenure and promotion guidelines echo a product orientation through its reliance on persuasive quantifiable evidence to determine faculty contributions. Both documents focus on outcomes in a way that foregrounds efficiency as a method to situate institutional function. The emphasis on efficiency emerges most clearly in the belief in the system's capacity to adequately measure institutional and faculty achievements. However, the product focus relies on various assumptions about people, contexts, and processes, which have broader implications for how institutions situate learning and teaching.

Abstraction Decontextualizes

Engaging a Confucian relationality raises questions about the broader challenges of situating people from a product orientation. For instance, the framework shows the limitations of using a product perspective to frame university goals when it raises questions about the roles of contexts and the processes of achieving the stated goals in the Strategic Directions document. While a product-oriented paradigm situates faculty and students from an efficient product-oriented perspective as producers and products, this notion assumes that people's actions are rational, controllable, and quantifiable. For example, goal one of the Strategic Directions document seeks to increase the participation and graduation rates of students within higher educational institutions, and the tactic under the first action strategy states, "engage K–12 students and their parents statewide early and often to promote and encourage them to prepare for college." But initiatives designed to reach out to "engage K–12 students" to "promote and encourage them to prepare for college" could have varied outcomes that may not at all be efficient or effective. An additional snag is that the goal seems to assume that to engage students to prepare them for college would necessarily correlate with an increased number of degrees and certificates, the corresponding productivity and efficiency measure. This assumption leaves out the consideration of other factors (sociocultural, financial, and family commitments, among others) that may deter students from preparing for or attending college. To consider that people cannot be completely situated as products, that people's contextual behaviors are complex and difficult to measure and predict, raises questions about the assumed correlations between the various stated goals, their action strategies, tactics, and productivity and efficiency measures.

Engaging a Confucian relationality raises questions about the specific contexts of goal achievement. A product-oriented paradigm prioritizes measurement yet decontextualizes through abstraction. While the document of strategic directions attempts to convey an explicit image of the institution as very much product oriented, the language even given its attempts to appear confident and clear can at the same time be quite vague. A Confucian relational perspective features a process orientation, which situates events in the world as ongoing and specific. This suggests that all activities are necessarily contextual, a notion that sets into relief the abstractness of the strategic goals. Even under some gentle questioning, words that intend to assist in the activity of situating aspects of educational endeavors in quantifiable terms become hard to understand in part because they are largely decontextualized. For example, the first action strategy of the fourth goal is to employ best practices in management, administration, and operations. One of the listed tactics is to "create effective and efficient organizational structures that leverage the advantages of centralization and decentralization to maximize efficiency and responsiveness to internal and external stakeholders." Yet what do the words "leverage" and "efficiency" mean in the stated context? What assumptions are being made about specific contexts and whether a committee or a person in a leadership position would be most suited to making decisions about them? When connecting the stated action strategies and tactics with their implied productivity and efficiency measures, I find they do not quite align. For instance, when considering the relation between the productivity and efficiency measures that are part of that same section, I am left to wonder whether "Education and related expenditures per completion" or "FTE Students/FTE Executive/Managerial ratios," identified as a bullet-pointed measures, are the intended focal connection. Questions emerge about what it means to "create effective and efficient organizational structures" and for what purposes? Who determines whether an organizational structure is effective and efficient? What is the implicit expectation of faculty to engage these goals? Although the language strives to give the impression of confidence and specificity, questions emerge about the details of realizing the strategic goals when looking closely at the document. As a result, the intended meaning of the product-oriented yet decontextualized tactics becomes less clear.

Engaging a Confucian relationality raises questions about the processes required for goal achievement. Because the concept emphasizes action over being, it infers the notion that events change. In the context of the document, the concept raises questions about the ability of an institution to realize its stated goals and the resources it intends to use to support them. Given that alignment of the broad goals with action strategies and the productivity and efficiency measures would require a great deal of resource to realize, the question of whether the institution is in a position to commit to the processes required to achieve such goals is a genuine one. To what extent is it possible for the institutional system to achieve the goals of increasing graduation rates for low-income students, diversify the state's economy by leading development of a $1 billion innovation in research education and training, modernize facilities, and implement a high-performance system based on best business practices in six years? Upon inquiry, the limits of a product-oriented framework's purview and mindset become clear. I suggest that not only is the perspective problematic, but the needed resources, energy, and research required to actualize each production-oriented goal could be quite overwhelming. While each goal is not impossible to actualize, to support the processes to realize them in terms of their productivity and efficiency measures would require considerable resources and attention.

In short, engaging a concept of Confucian relationality shows that some expressions of a product-oriented paradigm within the document tend to be hollowly aspirational because they leave out discussion about how the institution intends to realize the product-oriented strategic direction goals in terms of resources and responsibility. For instance, an initiative to engage students and their parents to promote preparation for college is no small undertaking if seriously considered. In alignment with the logic of a product orientation, extensive research would be needed to study and quantify how best to engage students and parents and what kinds of sustained promotion would be most effective. Additional and specific action strategies would need to be generated and followed up on; progress measures would need to be set and data collected to ensure progress was made. Who would undertake these tasks? While the strategic directions use a product paradigm to frame institutional goals, they leave out discussions about the specific people, contexts, and processes required to achieve them.

What About Teaching?

A product-oriented paradigm, which determines the value of faculty member contributions in terms of measurement, deemphasizes teaching. For instance, in the tenure guidelines document, because the categories of the products of faculty contributions are separate, they may be perceived as in competition with each other. Because a product orientation determines faculty contributions in terms of evidence, it emphasizes the importance of research production. For instance, while the criteria for evaluation are noted numerically (one could from consideration of the sequence argue there is a slight indication of the importance of each criterion), there is no direct articulation about how faculty should scale or compare the criteria with each other.

But there is some indirect implication. While the bibliography/research section is sequenced after teaching and before service expectations in the tenure and promotion guidelines, the length of the description of the section implies its primary value. With regard to evaluating faculty research contributions, the format includes the directive to separate published works, conference presentations, and manuscripts into at least 14 categories, including books of original scholarship, chapters in books, edited volumes, textbooks, and articles in international or national referred journals, among others. Within each category, the guidelines note that the list of works should be sequenced with the most recent first. Also, for coauthored works, the guidelines suggest that applicants describe the extent of their contributions. The level of detail the guidelines require, expressed through the delineation of very specific categories, implies the importance of research publications to dossiers.

The request for evidence of teaching contributions, by comparison, is limited in detail. According to the tenure and promotion guidelines, the bibliography section "provides an invaluable objective record of your scholarly activity." However, it is much more difficult to describe teaching contributions, although the guidelines request it: "you must have documented evidence of your teaching ability and of your contributions to the curriculum." The guidelines state the importance of providing evidence of teaching contributions: "Evidence of progress over the years in the scope, depth and effectiveness of your teaching may be helpful to reviewers in evaluating your maturity as an instructor." While the Criteria and Guidelines for Faculty Tenure/Promotion Application document seeks to frame teaching in a similarly product-oriented fashion as it does with research, it struggles to do so with the same élan. The guidelines state that

> In all cases, the evidence should include summaries of student evaluations, how your classes contribute to programmatic and institutional learning outcomes, or other objective assessments of a significant sample of the course taught during the probationary period.

Demonstration of competence is a key concern, and teaching evaluations serve as the major evidence of teaching quality: "Teaching ability is usually documented by means of teaching evaluations. These should reflect a representative sample of all of the courses you have taught in recent years." Additionally, the guidelines request other product-oriented evidence of teaching competence through the notation of teaching awards, discussion of documented evidence of "teaching ability," and "contributions to the curriculum" including materials from courses that one has created or modified. The guidelines also request that applicants list "innovations in teaching or teacher training" such as textbook development or creation of educational materials.

I should mention that while I suggest that the tenure and promotion guidelines foreground a product orientation that weights research publications, and anecdotes from faculty support this, the university's assistant vice chancellor of academic personnel in an informal phone conversation with me about this research stated something different—that teaching quality and scholarly achievement (research contributions) should be weighted equally for the purposes of evaluating instructional faculty tenure/promotion applications. This shows that there is some tension between an administrator's intentions and the predominant way faculty members interpret such guidelines more broadly.

While the tenure and promotion guidelines seek to request evidence of teaching contributions from a product paradigm perspective, they are difficult to describe in standardized product-oriented ways. Teaching quality simply put is hard to measure in part because it is relationally complex, requiring faculty to respond in varied ways to students. What counts as evidence from a product perspective may not adequately describe quality teaching. Scholarship regarding teaching evaluations, for instance, shows a disjuncture between the intended purposes of the evaluations and what they actually describe (Germain & Scandura, 2005; Ozcan, 2013). In other words, teaching evaluations have less to do with understanding teaching quality than students' past schooling experiences, their own perceived performance in classes, and the quality of engagements they have with their peers. Teaching evaluations also reflect students' race and gender biases. Gender bias plays a role in how students evaluate female instructors, especially junior faculty (Mengel, Sauermann, & Zölitz, 2019). The study that involves analysis of almost 20,000 evaluations at one university found that women faculty members systematically received lower evaluations than their male colleagues. Male students rated female instructors 21% of a standard deviation worse than male faculty, and female students rated them about 8% of a standard deviation lower than that of male instructors. Another study found that students' racial biases make their way into how they perceive the quality of teaching instruction. For instance, instructors with Asian last names often received lower ratings of teaching quality, expressing a broader ideological exclusion at work (Subtirelu, 2015). These types of systematic biases have profound implications for the career progressions for some faculty members.

The teaching evaluations may also have little to do with consideration of whether faculty members sought to promote the core values stated in the Strategic Directions document or, for that matter, whether they tried to prepare students to be workers or educated citizens. Given how inadequate teaching evaluations are for evaluating teaching, how should faculty provide evidence not only for the teaching that occurs in the classroom but also the quality of mentoring that happens outside it in measurable ways? How might faculty quantify the value of meeting with students outside class to go over their papers or talk about their schooling experiences or respond to their varied questions? While faculty members seeking tenure could write a detailed narrative or tally up the hours spent mentoring, such "evidence" might still be inadequate to show the quality of their engagement with students in measurable and standardized ways.

While faculty members' contributions with regard to creating curriculum and modifying materials from classes are important, these activities may have only an indirect influence on the development of teaching practices and provide limited acknowledgement of the energy needed to undertake teaching-related aspects such as mentoring. As mentioned previously, the evidence requested for the teaching section of dossiers is quite subjective, especially in comparison with the specificity of the bibliography section intended to evaluate research contributions. While some institutions have introduced innovative ways to evaluate teaching, such as the construction of teaching portfolios for tenure and promotion purposes, such initiatives often have a limited impact on faculty members, motivation to improve teaching, if there is no additional institutional support for teaching and mentorship (Liston, Hansman, Kenney, & Breton, 1998). To clarify, I do not suggest that there should be a rigorous peer-review process for evaluating teaching. Teaching is hard to evaluate because it is a process that involves engagement between faculty and students inside and outside classroom spaces. Rather than try to continue on the path of emphasizing outcomes, for example, such as evaluation of faculty members by correlating student test scores with teaching quality or other such product-oriented measures, administrators and faculty members need to ask initially how adequate a culture of measurement suits the activity of evaluation of teaching and other difficult-to-measure aspects of institutional educational function. They may then consider how to develop a broader institutional culture that values teaching.

While the intention of those who created the tenure and promotions guidelines document may not have been to situate evidence of publications as more valuable than evidence of teaching, it ends up having such an impact in part because it contributes to the construction of a product-oriented culture of measurement that prioritizes measurable outcomes. As a consequence, a product orientation situates faculty members not only as producers but as producers of research foremost. The guidelines discuss product-oriented objective expectations for both research and teaching, yet the sophistication of processes required to determine the evidence between the two differs. The difference is evident in part by looking at the amount of space each section takes up in the guidelines. The description of the bibliography section and preferred formatting details take up one full single-spaced page, while the section on teaching uses slightly over one-third of a page. The broader point is that in terms of a product orientation, the research bibliography section can be situated easily from such a perspective because it is already product oriented.

A product orientation can have profound implications for aspects of institutional function. While public higher educational institutions may feel pressure from the public and politicians to justify their activities for request-for-funding purposes and address the strategic direction goals toward these stakeholders, the deployment of a product-oriented paradigm influences how faculty and students situate learning and informs their activities. It also has ramifications for institutional support for the development of the craft of teaching. The product-oriented paradigm expressed within institutional documents situates learning as training, which contributes to a deemphasis of the importance of teaching. A view of learning as training narrows the outcomes of learning to those that are preconceived. It implies learning has a particular productive purpose. Outcomes that emerge from the experience of participating in classes that do not align with intended purposes are viewed as peripheral. For faculty members, to view learning as training suggests faculty should prioritize "teaching to the test" to seek particular outcomes rather than encourage student exploration and critical thinking, which may involve far messier processes. I want to clarify that I do not discount the value of administrators and faculty collaboratively discussing the directions of an institution.

In fact, this type of process is extremely valuable to institutional function because it is a move that recognizes the disciplinary power of institutions and the intention to express such power responsibly. Guidelines, even if abstract or unrealistic, can be useful from an institutional perspective in that they provide some notion of direction that can influence the activities of participants of an institution. Higher educational institutions also do not operate as isolated entities but are part of a complex societal, political, and economic field that influences how they choose to construct their identities through public documents. But the focus here is to inquire about how institutional documents reflect broader paradoxical expectations reflecting a product paradigmatic orientation that faculty members are challenged to navigate when compelled to address multiple institutional expectations through their activities. Dwelling on this leads to inquiry about how a product paradigm deemphasizes teaching and prioritizes research at the same time institutions tout the importance of the cultivation of global educated citizens. Engaging a Confucian relationality offers a way to address the paradox by calling attention to aspects of the documents overshadowed by a product paradigm.

Addressing the Paradox

One way to address the paradox is to make visible the processes that generate educational endeavors. To see institutional complexity motivates inquiry about possible ways forward and directions for change. Engaging a Confucian relationality, for instance, draws attention to the processes involved in assessing faculty activities and encourages acknowledging the complex tensions among various institutional expectations of faculty, including those that support a product orientation. Identifying disjunctures and misalignments and dwelling on them provide a way to critically inquire about university directions. The act of inquiry may embolden faculty members to reflectively navigate how they make use of their time and to address the paradox of being asked to prioritize teaching and research.

Engaging a Confucian relationality draws attention to processes like the peer-review process of academic journals and book publishers, which tenure and promotion review committees rely on to determine the quality of faculty research contributions. Reputable journals and presses ask multiple reviewers familiar with the subject of a submitted work, often with author-identifying information removed, to evaluate it. The process can at times take years because it may involve requests for revision before a journal or press accepts and publishes a manuscript. Scholars view the process of peer review as established and rigorous and generally agree that while it not a perfect one, it is adequate to determine the quality of research contributions in various fields for the purpose of tenure and promotion application reviews. Tenure and promotion committees rely on the peer-review process to vet research, and this allows them to more easily evaluate faculty research contributions in quantifiable terms.

However, committees may find it more difficult to evaluate teaching contributions in a similar standardized way because there is no comparable peer-review process for teaching. Teaching activities do not lend themselves to being easily or accurately quantified. As a result, research may be weighted more than teaching by committees simply because they can easily rely on the peer-review processes of journals and publishers to determine the quality of faculty members' research for the purpose of comparison with others'. To make visible the important role of the peer-review process is to show that tenure and review evaluations rely on far more complex processes to be able to operate in a product-oriented way.

Engaging a Confucian relationality also draws attention to how the tenure and promotion evaluation process itself is quite subjective. While a product paradigm that values efficiency would infer the importance of evaluatory objectivity to more easily compare faculty member "products" for the purposes of comparison, the tenure and promotion guidelines describe an evaluatory process that is largely dependent on those who constitute the review committees to make contextual determinations regarding the value of an applicant's scholarly work. For instance, the guideline's first criterion for tenure and promotion is that "the university must have a need for a faculty member with the particular qualifications of the applicant." The guidelines, for instance, do not elaborate by delineating how committees might go about identifying whether there is a need for an applicant's particular qualifications, but the first criterion implies that the institution reserves the right to make a decision about a faculty member's application in a way that has nothing to do with the applicant's contributions.

Also, while the guidelines clearly request evidence for faculty contributions, at the same time they suggest that what constitutes evidence in part relies on the subjective view of others. For instance, the guidelines request that letters of written assessments seek to demonstrate "a level of scholarly achievement appropriate to the rank at which tenure is sought in comparison with peers active in the same discipline." The letters themselves emerge from more complex collegial relationships. While a letter itself might be perceived as physical evidence, the content is largely subjective depending in part on the strength of the relationship between the letter writer and the subject of the letter. I want to point out that departments also have their own tenure and promotion guidelines and criteria, which are drafted and reviewed by their faculty and may indicate metrics (for example, number of publications). Often the criteria are interpreted and based on the guidelines drafted by the board of regents and faculty union.

In fact, the tenure and promotion guidelines openly declare the subjectivity of the evaluation process. The tenure application section states: "The tenure/promotion application is the means by which you convince those involved in the review process of your achievements and ability." Put another way, the university expects faculty members to not only show evidence that they are productive but that the evidence should be persuasive, suggesting that assessment of one's productivity is largely left up to the committee evaluating the dossier. The process of evaluation itself is ambiguous. The instruction section states:

> The general reasons for granting tenure are that the University has concluded that you are and will continue to be a productive and valuable member of your department, school/college, and campus, that your pattern of continuing professional growth is positive, and that the University anticipates a long-term need for your professional specialty and services. This is a matter of judgment, and there may be honest differences of opinion based on fair and thorough consideration of the evidence.

This statement suggests that tenure/promotion decisions are normatively made and in part dependent on how committee members evaluate and "judge" the "evidence." The tenure and promotion guidelines do not (perhaps cannot) describe specific "productivity and efficiency" measures as in the Strategic Directions document. For instance, one stated measure in the Strategic Directions document is the aim to increase the percentage of working-age adults with degrees to 55% by 2025. While such a statement of a specific quantifiable goal eclipses questions regarding the importance of the quality of education that those students receive, the naming of a specific number suggests there is some way to evaluate the success of such an endeavor. Tenure and promotion evaluation processes, on the other hand, cannot be objective in a similar way because a process of "judgment" relies on the views of others. While the university situates faculty largely as producers, the productivity and efficiency measures—in the business lingo employed to describe the strategic directions—used to determine faculty contributions are even vaguer in the tenure and promotion criteria and guidelines, leaving review committees to interpret them. Because the guidelines normatively weight publications, it is likely the committee will do so as well, although the specifics of various interpretations may be somewhat arbitrary depending on the experiences and beliefs of the committee members.

The uncertainty of the evaluation process is exacerbated in part because unquantifiable aspects of the promotion process do not mean that they are any less important. For example, faculty members cannot underestimate the importance of the quality of collegial relationships and the role they play, although not easily visible, as part of the tenure and promotion process. While committee members are expected to recuse themselves if they know the applicants they will be evaluating, colleagues such as department chairs and personnel committee members are expected to make "written assessments of your strengths and weaknesses . . ." The quality of applicants' collegial relationships could influence their co-faculty assessments. Foregrounding relationships from a process-oriented view of the world imply that a tenure and promotion evaluation process is necessarily subjective.

Engaging a Confucian relational perspective emphasizes the process-oriented aspects of the tenure and promotion evaluation procedure, implying a provocative disjuncture from product-oriented expectations. It draws attention to how review committees rely on the peer-review process of journals and presses to quantify faculty research contributions and incorporate process-oriented aspects such as letters detailing faculty research contributions and reputation to evaluate faculty. It suggests the evaluation process itself is subjective. For instance, while the guidelines detail a product-oriented request for evidence of a faculty member's contributions and achievements for tenure consideration, at the same time the document also suggests that committees must use their judgment to determine the quality of contributions, a process-oriented focus. One way to address the tension for faculty between focusing on teaching and research is to see the processes involved in the tenure and promotion evaluation procedure that exist in addition to the product-oriented expectations for dossier construction. To see the tensions more clearly provides moments for inquiry that has implications for how faculty members navigate institutional expectations and reflect on their own.

Engage the Core Values

Engaging a Confucian relationality can assist with noticing the resources within university documents to address institutional tension regarding faculty activities. One way to address the broader paradox is to see faculty roles as inseparable. Engaging a Confucian relationality draws attention to the significance of an institution's process-oriented aspects by emphasizing the importance of people's activities. A product paradigm, for instance, would emphasize, in aphoristic terms, activity as a means to an end. With a focus on the end product, this suggests that the means should be as efficient as possible. With a focus on end products, faculty activities of teaching, research, and service are viewed as separate endeavors. A Confucian relationality, on the other hand, emphasizes the means itself. This implies attending to the importance of how people undertake what they do. Rather than efficiency, a process-oriented perspective values the quality and richness of activities. The concept implies that what naturally emerges are by-products to some extent from attending to the quality of the means. To focus on the means situates faculty roles as inseparable because it is the means—the approaches, processes, and attitudes—that unite them through the experiences of faculty members. To envision this perspective of faculty roles as inseparable need not be imposed. Rather, engaging a Confucian relational perspective draws attention to the resources in the university context itself, more specifically within the institutional guidelines that support this view.

To consider the process-oriented aspects of institutions is to draw attention in part to the role of an institution's core values. A product-oriented paradigm expressed in institutional documents tends to overshadow a process-oriented notion of their specified core values as touched upon earlier. For instance, while the Strategic Directions document pays lip service to the institution's core values of academic rigor and excellence, integrity and service, aloha and respect, it does not actively explore the implications of emphasizing them. Besides the mention of the core values in the introduction section of the document, they are not directly referred to again, nor does the document articulate their connections to the stated goals, action strategies, and tactics. How are readers supposed to understand how the generation of revenue from land assets and the reduction of costs support the development of academic rigor? How important is a particular goal in consideration to others, and what is the level of detail and commitment expected from such an initiative?

The strategic directions goals do not mention how the core values might be institutionally realized. Rather, the action strategies and tactics that follow each goal generally correlate with the notion of creating an "educated workforce," not how to achieve academic excellence or wise citizens. One possible reason that the document leaves the core values largely untouched is that the product orientation it engages insinuates the difficulty of measuring the relational (integrity and respect) and, for instance, outcomes of the development of the craft of teaching (academic rigor and excellence). To commit to developing these core values more fully might mean an inevitable reckoning with the goal of molding the university into a high-performance, mission-driven system committed to accountability and managing costs.

To emphasize the expression of the institution's core values not only supports the notion of fostering educated global citizens but also generates a way to situate faculty activities as inseparable. Engaging a Confucian relationality suggests that an institution's core values could be situated as a form of "*dao*" ("way-making") within a particular university context because they suggest an approach to undertaking educational activities. While a product orientation foregrounds "efficiency" as a way forward, a process orientation might foreground the core values of academic rigor and excellence, integrity and service, aloha and respect, as ways forward.

When an institution's core values are considered in relation to different faculty roles, they suggest that "How one advances along the way is one and the same" (*Zhongyong*, chapter 20, Ames and Hall, 2001, p. 102.) In other words, just as different types of relationships (kin and political roles) provide contexts that engage the same methods (wisdom, authoritative conduct, and courage) for personal cultivation, different faculty roles are characterized through how they approach engaging these roles and not necessarily by their perceived "products." Research, teaching, and service, then, rather than perceived as separate from a product perspective, are envisioned as inseparable and ongoing processes from a Confucian relational perspective through how faculty engage these roles.

To situate the core values as an approach to or way-making of faculty activities is to focus on the "means" of faculty activities. In other words, the core values could be situated as a method of engaging activities. For instance, to situate faculty members as striving for academic rigor and integrity in research suggests that they are constantly experimenting with ideas, pushing the boundaries of their fields to develop new ways of knowing. A normative notion of experiment involves engaging in a process of observation, prediction, and testing in order to explore ideas. It suggests that those who undertake the process must at some level be open to the unexpected. In other words, the product of experimentation may not always be clear. To experiment in imaginative ways suggests that faculty must adopt the position of openness to continually learning. Learning then is not a fixed state but rather implies a continual endeavoring, a way to approach how faculty undertake their activities. Appeals for academic rigor and excellence can relate to all aspects of faculty work including teaching; similarly, values of respect and integrity apply to any activity faculty undertake. Focusing on processes suggests the importance of continually learning from the experiences and implies that outcomes may be unpredictable. Focusing on the means rather than the products in the spirit of experiment and learning may influence attitudes in which faculty may undertake their activities. Rather than efficiency, the spirit of experiment implies the value of exploration, process, and imagination. To emphasize an institution's core values provides a way for faculty members to envision their activities as coherently related and encourages them to develop their own pathways to navigate institutional tensions.

While the Strategic Directions document mentions the core values in passing, the guidelines for tenure and promotion perhaps inadvertently come closer to articulating one way to express them by framing faculty members as learning. Engaging a Confucian relational perspective draws attention to the part of the tenure and promotion guidelines that suggest it is important for faculty members to develop the capacity for experimentation through attention to all of their faculty roles. This notion of faculty continual endeavoring further highlights the tension between situating faculty as producers through the request for evidence of contributions and the more process-oriented and ambiguous aspects of the evaluation process, which try to situate a faculty member's contributions contextually. In particular, one line stands out. The tenure and promotion guidelines state that review committees seek to confirm that a faculty member's "pattern of continuing professional growth is positive." In other words, the line implies that, rather than simply producers, faculty members must always be learners.

In brief, the core values of academic rigor and excellence, integrity and service, aloha and respect, resonate with envisioning a faculty member as continually learning. The type of learning that expresses the core values likely would involve developing the capacity for imaginative and experimental thinking about varied experiences and in different contexts. That faculty peers determine the value of contributions implies there is no fixed point of success; rather, faculty must continually strive to achieve excellence and rigor in whatever they do. While faculty members are expected to delineate their contributions into specific categories, the ambiguity of the evaluation process itself suggests there is room to consider their activities relationally, to consider them aspectually. To situate faculty as learning frames the activities of teaching, research, and service in overlapping and ongoing ways. Faculty members, then, are not simply producers. From a Confucian relational perspective, they engage the roles of teachers, researchers, and providers of community and institutional service coterminously by being learners foremost.

Engaging a Confucian relationality not only suggests the limits of a product orientation but also provides a way to see the value of those aspects of the educational system that foreground relationship without a need to quantify it. For instance, an institution may seek to acknowledge the value of support for teaching, rather than solely relying on establishing measurable goals that seek to describe quality teaching, by creating the conditions for discussions about teaching that foster a culture that values teaching within departments and the university more broadly. How institutions support discussions about the value of teaching may vary depending on their specific contexts but could include acknowledging that developing the craft of teaching requires faculty time, effort, and robust institutional support. By taking responsibility for creating the conditions for seriously supporting learning about teaching, administrators may rely less on attempts to measure the outcomes of teaching as a sole approach to determine quality. Furthermore, engaging a Confucian relational perspective recognizes the importance of outcomes *and* the educational processes that exist as part of institutions. It can assist with the characterization of the value of relationships in educational function, offering a valuable approach to complicate the shape of institutional directions. To suggest that a process-oriented framework lays bare the limits of a product-oriented one is not to suggest that such a framework needs to be imposed. Rather, engaging a Confucian relational framework contributes to the acknowledgment of the complexity of a university institution that currently exists. Relationships, contexts, judgments, and processes *already play* important roles in university function.

Faculty members can address institutional tension regarding their activities in part by noticing the tension and also the resources in the university context itself that can be engaged to mitigate it. For instance, while a product-oriented framework seeks to situate institutional expectations of faculty activities as separate and in economic terms, engaging a Confucian relationality implies their intraconnectedness and their relational aspects. This view resonates with the core values mentioned in passing in the Strategic Directions document, which bypass categorical delineation. A process-oriented perspective situates faculty member experiences, their attitudes and approaches to what they do, as valuable because it situates faculty members as continually endeavoring, a notion that further emphasizes the aspectual nature of their activities. A process-oriented framework like a Confucian relationality that accedes this, then, can contribute to a revaluation of the importance of relationships in education institutional endeavors by drawing attention to those existing aspects of institutions that emphasize this. While engaging a Confucian relationality makes visible the dominance of a product-oriented paradigm that informs institutional guiding documents like the Strategic Directions and tenure and promotion guidelines, it also provides an opportunity to focus attention on some process-oriented aspects of university contexts like faculty collegiality.

Chapter 4

Foregrounding Collegiality

In this chapter, I use a concept of Confucian relationality to explore how the development of collegiality in faculty learning communities can influence faculty attitudes and encourages reflection on faculty activities. Tony Becher (1989) in the book *Academic Tribes and Territories: Intellectual Enquiry and the Cultures of Disciplines* draws from interviews with hundreds of academics across disciplines to identify what Becher calls inner and outer circles of professional acquaintance. While the outer circles can number in the hundreds, including "the distant intellectual relatives and passing professional friends" that faculty members might encounter at conferences and on email lists, among others, inner circles may number between six and twelve people. Becher writes that the collegial bonds of the inner circles of critical friends are closer and stronger than the outer circles in that they are cultivated with people faculty might turn to for advice or support during "times of intellectual adversity" or wish to assist in turn as they engage their faculty roles. Collegiality, in other words, in terms of the development of critical friendships with colleagues can be valuable toward enriching faculty experiences and navigating institutional engagement.

The development of collegial relationships in outer and inner circles generally flies under the radar at an institutional level in part because the relationships often occur informally, and as a result, their value may be easily overlooked. Cooperation and conversation to some extent is often assumed in research contexts. While the writing of research and artistic endeavors themselves often require solitary concentration, at the same time connecting with colleagues about a shared area of interest is an embedded part of the academic research and publication process. Most academic books, for instance, have lengthy acknowledgement sections to identify those who contributed ideas. The relevance of research is often a consideration of journals, presses, and conferences when deciding what to publish and feature, which means that authors must situate their work in conversation with and in the context of others' research. With regard to sharing teaching-related experiences or ideas, colleagues may feel more isolated. Faculty members generally facilitate their own courses as sole central authority figures responsible for designing curriculum, determining evaluation processes, and directly engaging students. No matter what type of context, a product-oriented institutional perspective generally overlooks the value of faculty collegiality because it may simply be viewed as a means to achieve particular end products (research publications, positive teaching evaluations) and not something institutions necessarily need to support.

While the value of collegiality may be more broadly overlooked at the university level, it is openly discussed as a part of research about faculty learning communities. Generally topic or cohort focused, participants and facilitators in learning communities strive to create contexts conducive to risk taking where faculty members feel comfortable sharing their teaching experiences and questions; in fact, the communities need to feel trustworthy and noncompetitive to encourage participants to reflect on their experiences together (Glowacki-Dudka & Brown, 2008; Limbrick & Knight, 2005; Ward & Selvester, 2012; Yayli, 2012). While garnering attention by some researchers, the development of collegiality in faculty or professional learning communities is often viewed from a product-oriented perspective as an effective method to share teaching innovations. This narrow focus on learning teaching approaches as sought-after outcomes places less emphasis on the significant participant commitment and effort required to develop collegiality and also tends to deemphasize participant differences. Engaging a concept of Confucian relationality shows that while faculty collegiality in the research is often situated as a means to an end (to encourage the development of the craft of teaching), it could also be viewed as a valuable achievement in itself that enriches faculty experiences and collaborative learning.

To engage a Confucian relationality suggests the value of supporting the development of collegial relationships as part of forums like faculty learning communities because they enrich faculty experiences more broadly. For instance, researchers describe these learning communities as collegial, often interdisciplinary groups of faculty and staff who want to collaboratively address a broad range of student needs by learning about varied teaching approaches (Ward & Selvester, 2012). The collegiality university-affiliated faculty learning communities foster is characteristically located in between Becher's notions of outer and inner circles in terms of closeness, although it tends to be more deliberately cultivated. The groups, through open discussion about teaching and academic experiences, seek to encourage the building of trust among faculty participants. Faculty learning communities prioritize the cultivation of collegiality by attending to the enrichment of faculty experiences.

A Confucian relationality, which situates faculty members foremost as learners, also suggests the value of collegial relationships in learning communities to support imaginative collaborative learning. Engaging the concept, which envisions people as necessarily intradependent, suggests that learning through relating to others offers a creative way to develop familiarity with particular teaching innovations through reflective and experimental thinking about teaching. The relationships of those involved that emerge become enriched and can extend to influence various academic communities in unpredictable ways. From this perspective, how researchers situate the development of collegiality in university-affiliated learning communities requires reevaluation.

In this chapter, I engage a concept of Confucian relationality to examine three studies about university-affiliated learning communities to consider how the development of collegiality in the research can be situated as a process and a valuable achievement that recognizes the effort participants must expend to create the conditions to generate it. Engaging the concept increases the visibility of how the quality of engagement among participants, including commitment and reciprocity, contributes to enriching networks of relationships in ways that extend beyond the contexts of particular learning communities. It recognizes that the development of collegiality in learning communities requires time and effort. In particular, instead of theoretically framing the learning communities as communities of practice, which reflects a product-oriented perspective, a more suitable frame would be collaboratives of intellectual play, drawing from developmental psychologist Peter Gray's (2013) research about the educative and imaginative force of fostering a playful mindset.

Engaging a Confucian relationality provides an opportunity to discuss the importance of supporting the enrichment of faculty experiences. It does this in part by inspiring inquiry about what is overlooked in product-oriented views of faculty learning communities and the way the development of collegiality is normatively situated in research about them. While institutions may relegate interdisciplinary supportive pedagogical spaces narrowly as faculty development, a Confucian relationality emphasizes the significance of quality intra-actions and envisions the potential for the development of collegiality to strengthen relations among people within university communities more broadly. The concept also broadens notions of the value of collegiality from a narrow product-oriented one to include those outcomes that may be unexpected or difficult to quantify.

While a focus on several articles about learning communities may seem limited to discussing a complex and broad topic like faculty collegiality, I remind readers that the broader project here is in part to consider how engaging a concept of Confucian relationality leads to inquiry about specific aspects of higher education practices. To focus attention on a specific topic encourages more in-depth analysis. As the project functions as an inquiry, I hope this chapter provides possible directions that future research about collegiality may take given that the value of the development of collegiality is generally overlooked as a part of higher education institutions and thus warrants increasing attention.

Enriching faculty experiences through developing collegiality is one way for faculty to navigate the product-oriented tension among institutional expectations. From the perspective of a Confucian relationality, people live in mutuality, and this means that those who seek to become exemplary are challenged to continually attune feelingly to their actions because their activities inform the texture and robustness of their lives. As a result, harmonizing relationships does not mean that people passively succumb to other's wishes; instead generating balance occurs by engaging differences deliberately by cultivating the attitudes of attentive propriety, integrity, and earnestness. For faculty members, this means a valuable way to enrich faculty experiences is through developing collegial relationships. While instructional faculty members who seek tenure and promotion cannot completely lose sight of tenure guidelines, emphasizing supporting the quality of their experiences endeavoring in faculty roles can be cohering. Focusing on the process of engaging their roles and letting go to some extent of a notion of measurable outcomes can lead to making reflective and even satisfying choices about how to expend time and energy.

More Than a Method

The product-oriented perspective of the three articles discussed in this chapter regarding university-affiliated faculty learning communities finds expression in how the authors determined success based on whether they perceived the purposes set out at the start of the research to have been realized. This type of focus narrows the type of outcomes researchers might view as valuable. Part of the reason this is the case is that the articles position learning communities as an effective method to pursue the realization of particular goals. They consider the development of collegiality in particular as an expectation and method rather than a valuable achievement. While this product-oriented approach is not in and of itself problematic, it does overlook the value of the development of collegiality and its unpredictable and more extensive impacts.

The three articles link the value of learning communities as a method with the particular purpose of sharing teaching approaches with faculty. While the teaching practices they address differ, they express a product-oriented perspective through their preconceived notions of outcomes. For instance, Andrew Furco and Barbara Moely, authors of "Using Learning Communities to Build Faculty Support for Pedagogical Innovation: A Multi-Campus Study," published in the *Journal of Higher Education*, explore how faculty learning communities were created to promote the institutionalization of service-learning initiatives, an approach to teaching that integrates community service with academic work (Furco & Moely, 2012). They reported the findings of their three-year grant-funded study that included eight campuses across the United States. The authors suggest that faculty often resist teaching innovations because they may not understand an innovation's goals or its practices or feel that it competes with their personal teaching approaches and even curbs their academic freedom. They also suggest that the creation of learning community seminars that spanned a time frame of eight to ten weeks on the campuses addressed these issues because it provided a structure and conditions for participants to learn about service learning in ways that contributed to the participants' professional growth.

In "An Exploration Into Inquiry-Based Learning by a Multidisciplinary Group of Higher Education Faculty," published in the journal *Higher Education*, Daniela Friedman, Tena Crews, Juan Caicedo, John Besley, Justin Weinberg, and Miriam Freeman wrote about their experiences as part of a grant-funded faculty learning community of six that was created to explore inquiry-based learning—an approach to develop students' critical thinking skills (Friedman et al., 2010). The purpose of the community was to explore ways in which university faculty could integrate inquiry-based research methods into their teaching. The authors hoped that through the discovery of how inquiry-based methods support student learning, they would revise their classroom curricula and prepare themselves to teach courses about inquiry fundamentals. Over the period of a summer, faculty participants were expected to meet together six times, design their own courses that engaged students in inquiry, learn about practices that supported inquiry, and make campus-wide presentations about inquiry-based teaching. The majority of the paper discusses how each interdisciplinary member of the group implemented the approach in their classroom contexts.

Finally, in "Faculty Learning Communities: Improving Teaching in Higher Education," published in *Educational Studies*, Hsuying Ward and Paula Selvester (2012) describe a learning community at a medium-sized university supported by a two-year grant that introduces faculty to universal design for learning—an approach to teaching that uses technology to make course content accessible for students in multiple ways. The purpose of the development of a faculty learning community was to introduce universal design for learning practices to help faculty use instructional technology within the universal design framework and to assist faculty in developing related projects that could be published to support the compilation of tenure and promotion portfolios. Faculty members met twice a month for an hour and a half and, in the second year, broke into two groups of between five and seven participants to accommodate varied schedules. The authors found that participation in a faculty learning community before and throughout a semester could help faculty members construct content and make adjustments to the use of universal design learning approaches in their curriculums.

The articles about university-affiliated faculty learning communities describe attempts to familiarize faculty with particular pedagogical practices like service learning, inquiry-based teaching, and universal design for learning through the development of collegiality as part of faculty learning communities. This product-oriented view situates the development of collegiality as part of "communities" as an efficient approach for faculty to learn about different teaching practices. One implication of this type of product focus is that its emphasis on achieving preconceived goals tends to overlook participant differences and experiences.

Unexpected Value

A concept of communities of practice is often used as a product-oriented theoretical frame for faculty learning communities that overlooks participant differences to construct identities based on practices linked to achieving particular outcomes. Researchers use the concept of communities of practice in relation to learning communities to emphasize the importance of learning with peers for the purposes of increasing professional knowledge and enhancing student learning (see Glowacki-Dudka & Brown, 2008; Vescio, Ross, & Adams, 2008). However, a troubling aspect of this product-oriented and identity-based way to learn specific teaching practices is that the focus on outcomes as preeminently valuable tends to minimize the varied experiences of participants.

A concept of communities of practice expresses its product orientation when it links the value of particular practices directly to preconceived outcomes. Social anthropologist Jean Lave and social theorist Etienne Wenger (1991) characterize communities of practice such as workplaces or specific professions as spaces where relations are formed through collective learning as part of specific contexts that generate meaningful patterns of activity. A concept of communities of practice developed in part from a theory of situated learning, which suggests that contexts shape learning (Lave, 1988; Lave & Wenger, 1991). However, perhaps because they mainly focused on particular workplace contexts to conduct their research, it is important to point out that the practices the authors observed employees undertaking emerged for particular purposes. Employees developed practices that sought to support realization of the goals of their employers. To identify groups with regard to their practices emphasizes a view of learning as social and contextual but also product oriented because to focus on outcomes to characterize practices determines what activities have value.

The linkage between practices and goals suggests that activities of communities that yield particular outcomes are viewed as more valuable than others. Lave and Wenger's focus on practices as a way to characterize particular groups implies the importance of group goals. For instance, the construction of specific outcomes influences perceptions of the value of particular practices. If specific goals orient practice, then those activities deemed to contribute to the achievement of those goals may be seen as valued. A tailor-in-training, for example, might engage in interaction with other tailors to learn how to produce accurate cuts of fabric. Such a practice would be considered valuable because it helps tailors create clothing. While the concept suggests learning is ongoing, it also implies practices emerge from an interest in achieving perceived material goals, such as the generation of particular outcomes. Wenger (1998) articulates the importance of the relationship between practice and outcome when he writes, "No matter what their official job description may be, they create a practice to do what needs to be done" (p. 6). Those practices viewed to most efficiently produce what "needs to be done" are likely to be considered more valuable than others that may not be viewed in this way.

In a community of practice where product-oriented activities are viewed as valuable because they lead to particular outcomes, the focus on mastery of practices is related to the construction of participants' identities within the communities. For instance, participants are identified as "newcomers" and "masters (newer ones and older ones)" (Lave & Wenger, 1991). They are identified primarily in relation to their experience within a group and more specifically how familiar they are with a group's practices. This implies that the learning that occurs from participation within communities of practice is largely connected to learning the practices of a particular community, which become referents: "learning occurs through centripetal participation in the learning curriculum of the ambient community" (p. 100). "Centripetal participation" means that the extent to which newcomers understand tailoring, for instance, like tailor apprentices, shapes their identities as part of their communities. An apprentice becomes a tailor and "master" within a community by learning the practices of the profession. The link between identity and the practices of a profession generates a notion of experience as valued largely in relation to the mastery of the practices.

In a product-oriented notion of a community of practice, the emphasis on participants' relations to practices suggests identity construction is in part a cognitive act. Wenger (1998) suggests that because people participate in multiple communities, a "reconciliation" of identities needs to occur. From this perspective, identities need to be cognitively constructed: "maintenance of an identity across boundaries requires work and, moreover, that the work of integrating our various forms of participation is not just a secondary process . . . it is at the core of what it means to be a person" (Wenger, p. 160). Wenger considers such work a "private achievement" that implies people can reconcile numerous identities consciously, and that they must do this independently from others. This view of identity formation as abstractly private situates people as deeply autonomous from others. It implies that people can enter or leave communities as "individuals."

The emphasis on identifying communities in a product-oriented way based on their practices and people's perceived identities tends to minimize the varied experiences of a group's participants. While participants' activities can shape the practices that emerge from a community, the experiences that may not be viewed as relevant to preconceived notions of the goals of particular communities are theoretically considered less valuable. In other words, this is not to say that this conception seeks to erase differences between people, but to identify a group based on its practices can have the impact of overlooking people's differences, raising questions about issues related to group inclusiveness.

Lynn Fendler (2006), for instance, explores how the discourse of community especially in educational contexts and research can have an exclusionary impact. By undertaking a critical review of the term from a historical perspective, Fendler suggests that while educational literature understands the term "community" to mean "shared values, unified purpose, and/or common beliefs" (p. 303) and by implication practices, the use of the concept of community without careful consideration of its assumptions may exclude diversity and perpetuate norms of those who are privileged (p. 304). Fendler points out that it is important to be aware of the implications a notion of community has for its participants especially in contexts where people are perceived, for instance, to have different levels of institutional authority.

The concept of communities of practice where the practices define the communities to the extent that they are linked to particular outcomes and a notion of faculty learning communities have marked distinctions. For instance, the two types of communities have varying temporal characteristics. While workplace communities of practice like tailoring use practices that may have been established through years, the practices of semester- or year-long faculty learning communities may not be as developed. Also, because the practices of some faculty learning communities seek to encourage quality engagement among voluntary participants, they are responsive to participants' interests. As a result, the practices of faculty learning communities may rapidly change, making it difficult to construct extensive community-based identities based on them.

Another difference between the two concepts in regard to situating learning communities is that their specific products may be difficult to measure. While learning communities may be used to convey new teaching approaches, no matter how well participants understand a particular teaching approach, there is no guarantee that its use will have the same impact on every class and student. Faculty members approach teaching differently, and how they use specific teaching innovations will also vary. More broadly, what a concept of communities of practice may miss is the value of unexpected outcomes. For instance, in learning communities the development of collegiality might actually foster more than the intended outcomes in ways that are unimagined. The potential of learning communities to generate future collaborations may be overshadowed by the focus on whether or not faculty have learned about particular teaching innovations. A Confucian relationality, on the other hand, makes increasingly visible the importance of the development of collegiality in faculty learning communities toward higher education contexts and the value of focusing on processes more than outcomes.

Generating Collaborative Space

Rather than situating the development of collegiality mainly as a means to an end for faculty to learn teaching practices, a Confucian relationality inspires situating faculty learning communities more so as collaboratives of intellectual play. The term play used here refers to "a state of mind that promotes imagination" (Gray, 2013, p. 152). Peter Gray (2013) draws from developmental psychological research to suggest that contexts that induce a playful state of mind uninhibited by evaluation or rewards promote learning, creativity, and problem solving. To extend this notion to learning communities suggests that turning attention to enriching the quality of experience of participation through the development of collegiality generates the space for imaginative intellectual collaborative learning. The collaborations often yield engaged learning about teaching and also return varied outcomes that may not be preconceived. A Confucian relational focus on process rather than outcomes relies on differences among participants of a group to enrich experiences.

To frame faculty learning communities as collaboratives of intellectual play suggests that making the effort to develop collegiality among participants creates the conditions to generate imaginative attitudes with regard to learning about teaching. Use of the term collaborative emphasizes intra-action as a unifying register rather than normative notions of identity. Gray points out that while the use of the word play in part often refers to how children are self-motivated to learn and practice survival and social skills, to look more closely at the characteristics of play implies it has to do more with mental attitude and motivation rather than specific behaviors that are relevant to people of any age. For instance, two people might be engaged in a similar task, but one may be playing imaginatively and the other not (Gray gives the examples of typing on a computer and throwing a ball). The way to tell the two apart is to look more closely at the details that reveal why they are doing what they are doing and how they feel about it. For adults, reference to a playful attitude need not refer to activities in a zero-sum way but can combine with other motives and attitudes related to adult responsibilities. This suggests that while faculty may choose to participate in learning communities to learn about teaching approaches because teaching is part of their employment obligations, the context of the learning community can also shape participants' attitudes and experiences with regard to how they approach the learning.

The development of collegiality in learning communities contributes to fostering learning about teaching as intellectual play because it enriches the experience of participation. Valuing the experience of participation resonates with Gray's characterizations of play as necessarily motivated by means more than ends, as guided by mental rules, and as fostering imaginative learning. When achieving a goal becomes a primary focus, people generally seek to achieve it as efficiently as possible. However, Gray suggests that undertaking an activity with a playful attitude suggests that the activity itself is undertaken for its own sake in an intrinsically motivated way rather than simply as an extrinsically motivated means to an end. In other words, the activity itself is so rewarding that the outcomes are considered secondary to the process itself. This does not mean to suggest that play does not have goals but rather that the goals are considered an intrinsic part of the experience rather than an extrinsic reward.

Enriching the experience of participation in an activity involves generating the conditions for developing a playful state of mind in part via structure. Gray suggests that playful activities are guided by mental rules. Rather than freedom in the context of "anything goes," play actually requires that participants expend quite a bit of conscious effort to attend to particular guidelines. Much of the enjoyable and creative parts of play, according to Gray, result paradoxically from creating and willingly following rules. Following guidelines especially when play involves others suggests that people must come to agreement on guidelines and adjust them on occasion. This means that people must at times put aside their personal preferences for the sake of the play to some extent because to engage in play also implies a willingness to accommodate others' perspectives for the sake of fairness. It seems paradoxical, but playing by the rules is what makes play enjoyable.

Emphasizing the experience of participation fosters a playful state of mind that creates the conditions for imaginative learning. Play takes place in a real physical world and is often about it but at the same time is to some extent removed from it. Gray provides the examples of how architects and scientists make use of their imaginations to design and hypothesize. Architects design houses by engaging their imaginations to visualize houses, imagining how people might use them, considering how they might be situated in particular landscapes, envisioning how the sun would come through windows of the houses at different times of the day and season, and asking what types of aesthetics might best suit the houses and their clients' preferences. Before becoming real houses, architects build pretend ones in their minds and on paper. Similarly, scientists generate hypotheses to explain facts by going beyond them when they plan experiments. Play, Gray points out, is about engaging the human capacity to consider abstractly and hypothetically by imagining situations that have not been experienced and logically thinking about them.

When activity is not focused on producing particular outcomes in response to external demands, the work of play is not experienced as negative pressure. A non-stressed state of mind is important for generating the conditions of play according to Gray (2013) because it makes space for an alert and active mindset necessary for play to occur. To participate in play requires an active and alert mindset because it requires people to think about what they are doing to engage the guidelines of play rather than passively absorbing information from the environment or responding in habitual ways. Because a person at play is focused on enriching the experience of the process rather than focusing on outcomes, the mind is not distracted by fear of failure.

In fact, a positive, playful, and unafraid frame of mind promotes imaginative learning as an inadvertent outcome. Gray references research by Barbara Fredrickson to suggest that positive emotions broaden perceptions and thinking that may encourage, for instance, curiosity, novel configuring of ideas, and ways of behaving that initiate the development of new thinking and skills. Negative emotions, on the other hand, tend to narrow perspective and direct thoughts to address the source of distress. The experience of distress interferes with creativity, learning, and reflection because it activates an autonomic arousal system that is expressed by a response to tasks with a sudden increased amount of physical energy accompanied by a narrow focus on achieving goals to alleviate the stress as quickly as possible. Evolutionarily, researchers theorize that strong negative emotions that indicate stress, such as fear and anger, emerged to address emergency situations. As a result, stressful situations are not ideal occasions for engaging new ways of thinking or behaving because people tend to respond to these types of situations with coping methods that are habitual.

Rather than situating the development of collegiality mainly as a means to an end for faculty to learn teaching practices, a Confucian relationality inspires situating faculty learning communities more so as collaboratives of intellectual play. Learning communities that seek to prioritize the development of collegiality generate the space for imaginative intellectual collaborative learning. The development of collegiality emerges from a willingness of participants and facilitators to take seriously the experience of participation in learning communities. By focusing on the experience rather than solely the outcomes, engaging general guidelines to cultivate the learning communities space, and generating a context in which participants feel comfortable speaking with each other in a nonjudgmental way creates the conditions for a relaxed and attentive state of mind that encourages collaborative learning about teaching through the development of faculty collegiality.

Taking Experiences Seriously

While the authors of the three articles about learning communities situate the development of collegiality as a method to achieve the goal of learning teaching practices, engaging a Confucian relational perspective suggests that the development of collegiality is a process that should be viewed as just as important, if not more so, as the preconceived goals. The focus on the development of collegiality suggests a process that attends to enriching the quality of people's experiences without being distracted by concern for achieving particular outcomes. In learning communities, the development of collegiality encouraged faculty to engage an intellectual playful mindset to reflect on their classrooms and teaching. Through the generation of a collaborative and collegial space, faculty members were able to actively take the time to think through the use of new teaching approaches removed from the actual pressure of teaching and facilitating courses. Rather than seeing the development of collegiality mainly as a means to an end to develop particular teaching approaches, a Confucian relationality situates the value of attending to enriching the quality of participants' experiences that paradoxically leads to multiple valuable outcomes.

The development of collegiality in learning communities emerged in part through the support of dynamic communication. In the Furco and Moely (2012) article, the authors describe their learning communities as topic-based cohorts that facilitators set up to be voluntary, interdisciplinary, structured, goal oriented, safe, and supportive. Facilitators sought to develop collegiality through dynamic communication in part through the validation of participants' perspectives about student learning and, at the same time, by challenging participants to learn about a teaching approach with which they were unfamiliar. They encouraged participants to "discuss issues and questions about teaching openly and in confidence" (p. 133) by making the time for this type of discussion. A process of dynamic communication, facilitators suggest, both generated a supportive environment and encouraged collaborative and open discussions about teaching. This process provides an example of how learning communities strive to attend to participant experiences rather than focus solely on outcomes.

The development of collegiality also generated a supportive environment in part by inviting participants to engage in collaborative, process-oriented, open-ended activities that did not seek to judge others' thinking, which reflected a focus on activities that were centered on the means rather than the ends. For instance, while Friedman et al. (2010) described how their group initially worked to collectively define inquiry-based learning to create what could be thought of as a safe and open environment by means of their process-oriented activities. For instance, one of the first activities the group undertook was a process the authors called "brainwriting." Each person anonymously wrote down a definition of "inquiry-based learning" on a piece of paper, and the papers were passed around to others who would write comments, edit, and ask questions about each definition. The group then discussed the process and collectively constructed a working definition of an inquiry-based teaching approach. This activity shows how participants sought to create a context where people felt comfortable to share their perspectives and reflect on them with others. It also models an experience-based approach to teaching that shows what inquiry-based learning looks like through inviting participants to engage in it rather than being told the definition of the term, for instance, in a lecture presentation. In brief, the open-ended nonjudgmental activities encouraged participants to take risks of sharing their thinking with others in an intrinsically motivated way that contributed to enriching participant experiences in the learning communities.

The broader conditions it took to encourage participants to develop collegiality included the fact that participants voluntarily chose to participate in the learning communities and felt self-directed to some extent with regard to their willingness to participate in the group activities. Gray (2013) points out that when people choose to participate in an activity and have some say in shaping it, they tend to engage with more effort and fully than when compelled by others. The effort and care it took to generate the conditions and circumstances for the development of collegiality enriched faculty member's experiences of participating in the groups. Rather than taking an efficient route of sharing information about particular teaching practices in a didactic way, facilitators instead encouraged the development of collegiality by generating supportive learning environments.

The development of genuine collegiality in learning communities depended on the willingness of participants to follow guidelines of engagement of the proposed activities. To return to the example mentioned earlier about the group engaging in a brainstorming activity that invited participants to share their ideas, its success relied on participants' willingness to make an effort to respond to such requests. The development of collegiality in the learning communities included, for instance, creating meeting norms to cultivate a tone of respect among participants. Ward and Selvester (2012) describe the introduction of learning community meeting norms to encourage "efficient group work to allow the processes of critique, self-reflection and self-disclosure to take place" that would "facilitate a positive environment in which to take risks" (p. 115). The norms the authors identify include (1) openness to improvement; (2) trust and respect; (3) a foundation in the knowledge and skills of teaching; (4) willingness to offer and accept supportive and constructive feedback; and (5) shared commitment to teaching and learning. Ward and Selvester note that "Building trust and ensuring bonding are critical for a successful FLC. The elements of 'openness,' 'trust and respect,' 'willingness to help' and 'accepting criticism,' when put into practice, require a lot of care on the part of the facilitators" (p. 116).

To ask voluntary participants to follow and engage learning community structures was no small request of faculty, especially when it came to making time and space for meetings. While participants were aware of the time commitments prior to participating in the communities, they also had the choice to drop out of the communities if they chose to. But because the development of collegiality the communities engendered was engaging and felt worthwhile, faculty members were motivated to participate and create respectful contexts in which they felt they could speak openly about their experiences and share their ideas. As a result, the facilitators of the faculty learning communities included plans for multiple meetings with the expectation that participants would attend as many as their schedules allowed. Ward and Selvester (2012) mention that their faculty learning community met twice a month for an hour and a half; Furco and Moely (2012) set up the expectation that groups would meet for an 8- to 10-week seminar; and Friedman et al. (2010) met seven times, mostly in person and twice online. The meetings provided participants with the space for engaging others. The expectation to meet regularly implicitly confirmed that the development of respect, openness, and reciprocity required time and a level of commitment to cultivate.

While the three articles discuss the development of collegiality among participants as part of the facilitation of faculty learning communities, they also implied that such expectations do not happen magically or automatically but instead made use of guidelines and structures to make time for the cultivation of dynamic communication, for instance. In other words, the development of collegiality requires work, suggesting that it cannot be taken for granted or assumed. The development of collegiality in the learning communities was not something imposed, but rather its value had to be agreed on to some extent by participants. While a group may agree to adopt norms for engagement, the continual realization of the norms required attention and effort and contributed to the development of a supportive context.

Imagining to Learn

Descriptions of how facilitators of the learning communities sought to develop collegiality among faculty participants also draw attention to the circumstances that fostered imagination. Because faculty members were willing to follow the guidelines of the learning communities, the collaborative contexts became forums for imaginative thinking and learning. For faculty members participating in learning communities, the collegial forums offered occasions to learn through intellectual play by imagining how particular teaching approaches might work in the classes they taught. For instance, Ward and Selvester (2012) mention that participants would start their meetings with what they called the "critical friends protocol," which invites faculty members to share their syllabuses with others, discuss the objectives, and reflect on their effectiveness. Others would then offer constructive feedback or ask questions with a universal design for learning framework in mind to encourage reflection about how to revise the syllabuses. Sharing their syllabuses and discussing their classes in detail with other faculty members meant bringing their teaching, their students, and the content of the courses they taught to bear in their imaginations to some extent. The reflection that emerged from this imagining combined with feedback or questions about incorporation of design for learning approaches to their classes by others likely further enriched their imagining.

Similarly in Friedman et al. (2010), "elaborate discussions" (p. 767) took place in which faculty members exchanged ideas about how they would incorporate inquiry-based learning into their specific class plans. To exchange ideas in this way required to some extent imagining how this learning approach might play out in different ways in their actual classes. Hearing about how others planned to use this approach likely contributed to generating new ideas and questions about how to use the approach in their own classes. Hearing about differing perspectives may have inspired inquiry that fostered a paradox mindset in which reflection on tensions spurs creativity (Liu, Xu, & Zhang, 2019). It also likely inspired an interest to return to the classroom to see if actual use of the teaching practices would yield similar results to what they imagined.

The notion that the development of collegiality supported the imaginations of participants not only was reflected in the way they discussed trying out teaching practices in their classes but also extended to the shaping of the learning communities themselves. For instance, Furco and Moely (2012) reported that group members invited leaders of community organizations to join the learning community meetings to contribute to discussions about service learning. The development of collegiality encouraged participants to imagine the value and possibility of inviting community leaders they personally knew to attend learning community sessions with their colleagues. It encouraged them to take action to make it happen—to vet the possibility with the colleagues, to discuss the potential gathering with community leaders, and to find a time for the leaders to come, among other details necessary to realize an imagined idea.

Facilitators of the learning communities sought to enrich the quality of participant experiences by generating structures to feature the development of collegiality. This occurred through the use of open-ended activities to foster conversations, sharing of ideas, and reflections on teaching. The learning communities created the conditions for the development of positive emotions, which encouraged curiosity and intellectual collaborative play that returned enriched outcomes without needing to focus directly on trying to achieve them.

Open-ended activities made the space of learning communities feel supportive to generate new thinking without fear of failure. For instance, asking faculty members to share thoughts about inquiry-based learning in writing means they can provide no wrong answers. The open-ended question welcomes multiple perspectives and responses. Open-ended activities generate inquiries that encourage faculty participants to experiment with and explore ideas. Consider the more didactic approach of facilitators providing a definition of "inquiry-based learning." The provision of a ready-made definition would imply there is a right and wrong answer that could be evaluated. Participant time and effort might be spent trying to understand the definition to "get it right"; there might be less interest, then, in developing one's own notion of the concept. This notion of needing to "get it right" might extend to faculty using a particular approach in the classroom and focusing more on how others might use it rather than considering how to tailor the approach to their own particular contexts. This is not to say that a definition could not be provided at some point, but it might have a more meaningful impact if given after participants had a chance to devise and reflect on their own.

The collegiality developed by the faculty members became manifest in part through the shaping of the learning community itself in ways the facilitators might not have even imagined. Collegiality encouraged faculty to participate in the structuring and activities of the learning communities themselves. The development of collegiality helped participants imagine the use of various teaching approaches in their classrooms and also to feel invested in the experience of the learning community and contribute to it beyond what might be normatively required. And the emphasis on the development of collegiality returned more unpredictable outcomes.

Beyond Measurable Outcomes

To view the development of collegiality in learning communities as having primary importance upends notions of valued outcomes. Perhaps paradoxically, the emphasis on the quality of experiences returned outcomes beyond the expected. In other words, when outcomes are viewed as secondary to processes, then outcomes and their value need not be predetermined. When the value of the development of collegiality is viewed not simply in service of promoting the learning of new teaching approaches but as a valuable process and outcome itself, then the varied outcomes linked to supporting the collegiality emerge as valuable too, like the development of collegial networks post-learning community contexts. Loosening the link between processes and outcomes broadens a notion of the value of outcomes.

The articles about faculty learning communities actually revealed that there were multiple outcomes that could be perceived as valuable if the development of collegiality was viewed as a process *and* important outcome as well. The authors of the articles allude to how collegial relationships fostered new courses, promoted engagement beyond the group, and resulted in the development of collegial networks. For faculty learning communities, an emphasis on the development of collegiality through collaborative and playful learning influenced participants' actions beyond the contexts of the communities. For instance, new courses emerged from collaborations of a learning community—Friedman et al. (2010) imply the importance of collegiality when they describe how some participants—faculty from the fields of journalism, philosophy, and public health—developed a new course outside the context of the faculty learning community. The collegiality developed through participation in the learning community, the article implies, contributed to the collaborative construction of a new course that otherwise would not have existed.

Another implication of a process focus that situates outcomes as secondary is that outcomes need not be situated in competition with each other. This suggests that even those outcomes considered normatively minor might also be meaningful to some. For instance, Ward and Selvester (2012) note almost in an offhand manner that all the participants to whom they sent their post-faculty learning community surveys responded. The authors mused about why this was the case: "We believe this was due to the collegiality that had grown over the time we worked together" (Ward & Selvester, 2012, p. 118). While the authors did not dwell on the remarkable notion that everyone may have responded to their survey because of the influence of collegiality, they provided a glimpse of the strength of collegiality to encourage activity outside the specific context of a faculty learning community in ways that can be unpredictable. While this might be viewed as a minor outcome from a product-oriented focus of learning teaching approaches, from the perspective of the authors this is an outcome that supported their research and benefited readers of the research too. Notions of value can differ for different people and need not have a fixed universal value.

Another implication of the easing of an evaluatory frame of outcomes is that outcomes can be viewed as valuable in ongoing and unpredictable ways. Without a need to quantify outcomes or evaluate them in order to find them meaningful, an emphasis on process suggests that outcomes may return value in surprising ways. For instance, the development of collegiality in learning communities built collegial networks that continued beyond the specific context of the communities themselves. Ward and Selvester (2012) found that while many appreciated the chance to practice and learn about technology and particular computer programs as part of a universal design approach, some also appreciated the importance of developing both a collegial network and, as one participant put it, a "community of peers to troubleshoot with" (Ward & Selvester, 2012, p. 118). To have a community of peers to troubleshoot with suggests that conversations among the colleagues of the learning community might continue past the actual context of the learning community itself. The notion that participating in a learning community might help cultivate future engagements could be envisioned as a valuable outcome for participants and for the university context more broadly. Viewing the building of collegial networks as a valued outcome reminds researchers and faculty that the development of collegiality generates the potential for future undetermined outcomes.

The focus on enriching processes and experiences broadens notions of which outcomes are valued. The varied outcomes that emerge need not be compared in competitive and evaluative ways. When outcomes are viewed as secondary, there is no need to predetermine outcomes in more than a general way to indicate a direction. The issue with fixing an outcome in a product-oriented way is the narrow perspective of value that comes with it. The value of varied outcomes might be missed simply because they did not look like the outcomes initially sought. Varied outcomes are by-products of a focus on the process of engagement. As by-products, they can have value for different people at different times. For learning communities, this suggests that the development of collegiality could return outcomes in unpredictable and ongoing ways that need not be fixed.

To be able to view outcomes as secondary to the processes of participating in learning communities also meant that participants could learn about teaching through reflectively and rigorously imagining the use of new teaching approaches in their classrooms in a low-pressure way. "Play," Gray (2013) writes, "serves the serious purpose of education, but the player is not deliberately educating himself or herself" (p. 154). Rather than seeking external approval for actions, performing well during play is an intrinsic goal where failure has no serious consequences. The development of collegiality made space for experimental thinking that fostered collaborative learning about teaching approaches in part because the development of collegiality helped participants develop positive states of mind where they felt comfortable sharing their perspectives about classrooms and teaching. To exercise the capacity to learn in an intellectually playful and imaginative context occurred because participants could focus on the process of engaging others and learning together without needing to worry about the success or evaluation of outcomes.

Developing Inner Circles

While the authors of the articles did not linger on the influence of collegial relationships beyond the contexts of the learning communities, engaging a Confucian relationality suggests the potential value of unpredictable occurrences that emerge from the relation-ing. The concept situates the development of collegiality as having an influence not only on the participants of faculty learning communities but also on the broader communities of which they are a part. For faculty members, their participation in the learning communities may have helped some colleagues move from outer circles of professional acquaintances that Becher references to a supportive inner circle of critical friends.

The point here is not to deemphasize the success of faculty learning communities attempting to introduce teaching innovations: The authors have achieved what they set out to do. The articles make a convincing case for how university-affiliated faculty learning communities can be effective methods for introducing teaching approaches to faculty in higher education institutions. The authors suggest that, in particular, the development of collegiality fosters a dynamic that encourages collaborative learning, engaged conversation, and reflection that support the craft of teaching. In fact, the implications of these articles, when considered together, should compel those university administrators interested in exploring ways to support this form of instructional development to take heed of their effectiveness.

But the focus, rather, has been to consider from a Confucian relational view how learning communities' work to support imaginative collaborative learning through the development of collegiality in particular has a more extensive value to university communities than the articles might explicitly indicate. To engage a Confucian relationality to consider research about faculty learning communities suggests that existing scholarship already includes some discussion about the development of collegiality that could conceivably warrant more attention than it receives situated in a product-oriented way as a method to achieve a goal; a Confucian relational view emphasizes the value of dwelling on the significance of the processual aspects of the development of collegiality mentioned in the research.

The development of collegiality that yielded positive emotions and space for intellectual play returned enriched outcomes in surprising ways. Because participants could focus fully on the experience of the learning community's activities and not have to worry about outcomes, the outcomes that did emerge were more diverse than researchers might have initially considered. If the focus on outcomes in learning communities is viewed as secondary to the value of enriching faculty experiences, then notions of value can be situated more expansively. When the development of collegiality in learning communities is viewed not only in service of promoting a way of teaching but as valuable itself, then those difficult-to-quantify outcomes linked to enriching collegiality emerge as valuable too.

Chapter 5

Responsive Pedagogy

A normative institutional perspective supports the predominating neoliberal product orientation that frames teaching as a separate activity of faculty work that offers less prestige than publishing research. From this perspective, teaching has less prestige than research because a product-oriented insistence on linking value to the measurability of outcomes sets up a competitive dynamic among various faculty roles, which distracts from a broader consideration of their value to university participants and contexts. Because research is more easily measured in terms of publications than the outcomes of teaching, the value of teaching becomes normatively minimized as well and so do university interest and support for the development of the craft of teaching.

A Confucian relationality, as I have been discussing, offers a different perspective. In this chapter, I engage a concept of Confucian relationality to draw attention to the relational aspects and value of educator and media scholar Elizabeth Ellsworth's work on pedagogy. Ellsworth's research about how classroom experiences challenge normative assumptions about teaching provides an insightful example of how relationally complex and broadly valuable teaching can be to university communities. Furthermore, this exploration provides a context for discussing the way a concept of Confucian relationality can be used to critically inquire about other theoretical constructs such as poststructural feminism, with which it shares similarities.

One historical reason faculty prestige tends to emerge from research rather than teaching is the influence of a German model of the university that prioritizes research development. Throughout the mid- to late 19th century, Americans who went for short trainings and courses in Europe returned to influence the development of universities in the United States. Specifically, ten thousand Americans studied in Germany between 1815 and 1914 (Marsden, 1994). Their visions of American universities featured the notion that the pursuit of academic freedom without interference by government could best be achieved through the use of the scientific method. This vision reflected in part a predominant feeling that intellectuals should seek to develop knowledge for its own sake and the belief that specialized research could solve practical problems (Glyer & Weeks, 1998).

Professionalization based on research productivity and ideals such as the importance of the pursuit of knowledge generated a growing scholar community that became socially mobile (O'Boyle, 1983; Glyer & Weeks, 1998). Prestige and status became aligned with research productivity, and as a result these normative beliefs influenced the structures of universities and became reflected in promotion requirements, salary structures, and governance/administrative lines, among others. As areas of research became more specialized and research productivity became a marker of expertise, the bureaucracy of the university also became more complex as more departments were created.

While the emphasis on the production of specialized research at universities highlights the importance of graduate education as a way to prepare and certify future scholars in the United States as in the German university model, universities today are expected to educate undergraduates too. Undergraduate course experiences can dissuade or persuade students from pursuit of further study in particular disciplines and even shape how they perceive subjects as relevant to their lives post–formal education. How faculty members approach teaching can have a pronounced impact directly on student experiences, their classroom activities, and their lives. But while doctoral studies focus on preparing faculty to conduct research, there often is less preparation for faculty to teach. As a result, new faculty members are largely expected to learn about teaching as part of their employment as instructional faculty.

Engaging a concept of Confucian relationality, on the other hand, suggests that teaching is undervalued for its capacity to enrich university contexts. While it suggests the value of all aspects of faculty work and views them as unified in terms of faculty endeavoring, teaching in particular is important because it foregrounds relation. Because a Confucian relationality positions faculty in part as expert learners, reflective pedagogical research can provide a resource to generate inquiry about teaching for instructional faculty of any discipline. Rather than relegate reflective pedagogical research to the field of educational studies, engaging the concept suggests its value and relevance to all those who teach no matter the discipline.

Elizabeth Ellsworth came to educational studies as an assistant professor in the 1980s after completion of graduate work in film studies and endeavored to use a humanities research approach to explore theorizations about pedagogy in part through intensive reflective inquiry about teaching. Ellsworth (1997) embarked on a field largely dominated by social science research approaches with the hope that engaging a humanities perspective could "change—unfix—our theorizing and practice as educators" (p. 11). A professor emerita of the School of Media Studies at The New School, Ellsworth's recent work involved the exploration of public pedagogy through aesthetic experience through media arts collaborations. As Ellsworth's professional trajectory shifted throughout her career, she continued to strive to inquire about the complexities of pedagogy through teaching practice and research.

Ellsworth explored the relational complexity of teaching by examining pedagogical constructs. In her book *Teaching Positions: Difference, Pedagogy, and the Power of Address*, Ellsworth (1997) argues the notion that envisioning teaching as direct transmission of information is problematic because faculty cannot know how their students will perceive what they say. Complicating this notion is that faculty member assumptions about students inform the way they speak to them. Rather than rely on assumptions about students, Ellsworth suggests that a better approach to communication would be to see it in terms of conversation asking the question "how will I respond?" rather than "did you get it?" This shift in perspective from student to faculty response in regard to conversation destabilizes the roles of teacher and student by emphasizing the partialness of all perspectives.

The early focus of this chapter explores how a Confucian relationality situates aspects of Ellsworth's reflective pedagogical research as process oriented. Emphasizing the process aspects of her explorations of teaching through engaging a Confucian relationality encourages recognizing the value of these explorations in a way that is not framed in terms of measurable outcomes. Then, because Ellsworth's reflective pedagogical research is largely process oriented, I suggest that her responsiveness to students provides an example of personal cultivation that has an extensive influence on her students, colleagues, and field. The latter part of the chapter examines how the concept of a Confucian relationality can be engaged to frame Ellsworth's work in juxtaposition with other theoretical frameworks in complementary and challenging ways. In particular, the concept of a Confucian relationality can be used to destabilize assumptions about frameworks that share similarities with it like a poststructural feminist one. It does this in part by raising questions about the implications of envisioning people as necessarily intradependent rather than individuals in particular theoretical contexts. When juxtaposed with a poststructural feminist framework to situate Ellsworth's work, the concept of a Confucian relationality serves as a point of inquiry that enriches both frameworks.

Reading reflective pedagogical research like Ellsworth's from a Confucian relational framework reinforces the notion that complex relationships constitute contemporary educational contexts. While the value of some university aspects that foreground the relational like teaching tend to be overlooked by a product orientation, the concept draws attention to them and emphasizes their importance. Practically, for faculty, engaging a Confucian relational perspective might even lead to greater job satisfaction when it comes to thinking about teaching. For instance, Ellsworth suggests that to react with engaged surprise rather than dismay when realizing that at some moments students hear something different than what faculty intended to say may lead to opportunities for inquiry. From a Confucian relational perspective, these opportunities for inquiry lend themselves to enriching relation, thereby potentially influencing how faculty members feel about and their experiences teaching.

More broadly, engaging a Confucian relational concept emphasizes the importance of faculty teaching in university contexts in extensive and unpredictable ways. It emphasizes the value of supporting relationships that already exist as part of university contexts. Engaging the concept as a contemporary educational resource shows the complexity of educational contexts by drawing attention to the value of the processes and relationships that are overshadowed by a product-oriented ethos that links value with quantifiable measures.

Unlearning Positions of Privilege

Engaging a Confucian relationality encourages viewing aspects of Ellsworth's explorations about teaching as process oriented in nature. A process-oriented view of teaching and of the development of pedagogy emphasizes the notion that the activities involve relation. A focus on the relational aspects of the activities emphasizes a contextual nature of engagement that is necessarily specific and changing. As a result, envisioning teaching as process oriented suggests participants of classrooms engage each other intradependently. Attending to the quality of relationships that emerge from classroom contexts, then, can generate the conditions for mutual growth of all participants. To situate aspects of Ellsworth's research from a Confucian relational perspective draws attention and discussion about its broad value without a need to rely on measurable outcomes.

Ellsworth (1997) provides an example of a process-oriented view of teaching by situating pedagogy as contextually responsive. To foreground responsivity in teaching, Ellsworth suggests that relation must be considered foremost when she suggests faculty need to come to terms with the notion that teaching is impossible if it is viewed reductively as a transmission of information through direct communication. Teaching is impossible from this perspective because there is no guarantee that another will hear a speaker's intended meaning.

Finding a notion of pedagogy as information transmission problematic, Ellsworth reinforces a focus on teaching as necessarily involving relation when she undertakes a broader challenge to, as she frames it, "unlearn" positions of privilege. When teaching is seen as a transmission of information, then it de facto privileges faculty perspectives because faculty are perceived especially from a product orientation as experts who convey information. Pedagogy from a product perspective takes on a didactic tenor in which a "return of difference" in understanding generally implies some fault of the student, for instance, of not listening with effort or "correctly." Acknowledging privilege complicates normative notions of pedagogy: "I am trying to unsettle received definitions of pedagogy by multiplying the ways in which I am able to act on and in the university both as the Inappropriate/d Other and as the privileged speaking/making subject trying to unlearn that privilege" (Ellsworth, 1989/2013, p. 210).

Rather than make assumptions about what one is supposed to know and do as a teacher, Ellsworth describes a view of responsive pedagogy that considers disjuncture between listeners and speakers as providing opportunities for inquiry. Ellsworth points out that there is often some dissonance between a speaker's intention and a hearer's understanding. A process orientation suggests that moving toward enriching relationships involves engaging differences. Disjunctures between expected and actual responses to questions help participants locate their own assumptions and encourage further inquiry.

Ellsworth's theoretical explorations about responsive pedagogy consider the importance of participant experiences when they position the classroom as a space in which all participants can learn from each other. To view teaching as responsive insinuates that all knowledges are partial in nature and that conversation necessitate an openness to the unexpected that may emerge. This suggests that speaking and listening with regard to teaching and learning may best be situated as conversation instead of dialogue. To view conversation as ongoing and changing generates a destabilization of normative notions of teacher and student roles that assume a fixed structural relationship. A process-oriented notion of responsive pedagogy reflects an intention to unlearn because it leads to the destabilization of normative roles within classrooms, implying that classroom positionalities are not fixed but necessarily contingent.

PEDAGOGY AS CONTINUAL ADDRESS

Ellsworth (1997) suggests that one aspect of responsive pedagogy is its continually performative nature, which is informed by ongoing modes of address. The conception of a "mode of address" emerges from film and media studies, which suggest that how people convey stories are influenced by whom they imagine their audiences to be—the way they say something reflects in part how they imagine others will perceive it. Similarly in a classroom, the assumptions teachers may have about students impact how they address them. Ellsworth asks, "How do teachers make a difference in power, knowledge, and desire, not only by *what* they teach, but by *how* they *address* students?" (p. 8). With this question, Ellsworth insinuates pedagogy is performative in that it must continually be enacted. It does not exist as a fixed or essential activity but one that continually becomes what it is through engagement. Although pedagogical modes of address can be difficult to trace, they emerge in the expression of a powerful intention to shape another's experiences, responses, and even identities.

Pedagogy is performative in part because it is social. Ellsworth describes pedagogy as an intensive "social relationship" (p. 6): "It gets right in there—in your brain, your body, your heart, in your sense of self, of the world, of others, and of possibilities and impossibilities in all those realms" (p. 6). It reflects social roles in tangled and not always visible ways. For instance, our relationships are shaped not only by what we say but our expectations of how others will respond. As a result, pedagogy is socially performative because what happens in the classroom is always "inaugural." Teachers cannot control how and what their students hear, so the impact of their teaching practice can be unpredictable.

> Our "practices of everyday life" are inaugural, they are not re-presentations of already achieved and decided Truths. Our improvisations are performative, they are culture-in-the-making. All the pregiven norms and prescriptions called up by the question, How will you respond are both enacted *and reworked* in my response. There is a performative aspect to any response I give, and that prevents my response from being an answer, from being settled. (p. 137)

For Ellsworth, the performativity of pedagogy is implicitly relational because it foregrounds response in engagement. How people respond is influenced by how they perceive they will be heard or what they imagine others to be conveying. The focus on responsiveness is to consider engagement as meaning making in process.

When pedagogy is viewed as an ongoing performative process, then the activity of "pedagogy-izing" cannot be neutral. Ellsworth implies that while teaching attempts are informed by intentions, expectations, assumptions, and desires, they are always in a state of becoming something that cannot really ever be realized in any fixed or final way. While faculty may try to convey class content for a particular audience, it is impossible to completely know their students or themselves. Ellsworth writes, "I never 'am' the 'who' that a pedagogical address thinks I am. But then again, I never am the who that *I* think I am either" (p. 8). All participants speak from partial perspectives.

People's experiences and beliefs inform what and how they hear in unpredictable ways. Ellsworth points out that "pedagogy is much messier and a more inconclusive affair than the vast majority of our educational theories and practices make it out to be" (p. 8). In fact, Ellsworth suggests that the relationship between teacher and student is a paradox that is impossible to resolve, in part because the outcomes of our modes of address can be unpredictable. Even when pedagogy is perceived to be successful, it is not necessarily replicable; it "cannot be copied, sold, or exchanged—it's 'worthless' to the economy of educational accountability" (p. 17). Pedagogy cannot be fixed because it involves relation. For instance, the same class plan may resonate differently with one group of students than with another. Because the impact of modes of addresses can be impossible to control, there is always the potential for disjuncture between what is said or heard because of differing expectations, perspectives, and experiences of those in a classroom even during what might be considered normative "successful" communication. Ellsworth situates pedagogy as an event that emerges from engagement rather than "a representation of something else 'over there'" (p. 16). The activity of attempted communication that emerges from classroom contexts will always be processual because it is relational.

While a product-oriented view of pedagogy may suggest that the outcomes of teaching practices are (or should be) largely predetermined, a Confucian relational view of Ellsworth's views of pedagogy suggests pedagogy is a becoming that emerges from intra-action among people. Because faculty members teach using modes of address, which take into account imagined responses of listeners, they cannot always know how their pedagogical approaches will be received. This focus on pedagogy as continual address rather than a fixed notion of practice implicates teaching as necessarily relational. This process-oriented view situates classroom participants as people who perform the roles of teacher and student through their engagement, roles that have meaning in part because they must be continually enacted.

Rupturing the Dialogue Mirror

Ellsworth (1997) elaborates on a process-oriented view of responsive pedagogy through exploring the difference between the terms communicative and analytic dialogue. Ellsworth suggests that "communicative dialogue" is what educators often assume normative "successful" communication looks like, which implies that learning occurs when people speak and listen with "absolute representation" as a goal reflecting a product-oriented notion of teaching as transmission of information. In other words, when one person speaks to another, it is assumed that the words used should directly convey a particular idea. Perceived successful communication occurs when a listener hears the speaker's deliberate intention, whereas any misunderstanding has a negative inflection. "Analytic dialogue," on the other hand, does not assume or expect complete understanding but instead foregrounds the question "How will I respond?" (p. 136). To situate dialogue as open in this way suggests that dissonance in a conversation has the potential to generate richness in communication and relationship. This framing of dialogue as conversation resonates with a concept of a Confucian relationality that suggests that communication thrives on difference rather than similarity.

Ellsworth points out that critical pedagogists often rely on the use of dialogue to teach. Dialogue is given a mystical role in educational settings because it is assumed to be capable of everything from "construction of knowledge, to solving problems, to ensuring democracy, to constituting collaboration . . ." (p. 49). But it is also a practice that has emerged from particular social, historical, and political constructs influenced by networks of power, knowledge, and desire. Without consideration of the modes of address, which are influenced by culture and power that inform notions of dialogue, Ellsworth warns that it is difficult to see limitations of a dialogical construct: "What can't be subverted by the dialogical process is communicative dialogue itself. What can't be subverted by dialectical thinking is dialectical thinking itself" (pp. 147–148). In other words, Ellsworth suggests there is an unquestioned assumption that the dialogical process can be used, for example, toward a libratory endpoint.

This view of a dialogical mode of communication often assumed in teaching is reinforced by what Ellsworth calls "communicative dialogue," a process in which the speaker expects to achieve conscious reflective understanding in the listener—"did you get it?"—before the listener can respond to a speaker's views. With communicative dialogue, the emphasis is largely on the conveyance of a speaker's intentions; there is an assumption that views can differ only once there is mutual rational understanding. The structure of the address of communicative dialogue strives to generate a sense of cohesiveness, which ideally allows for people to consciously reflect together by sharing their thoughts. This sharing then encourages participants to broaden or change their perspectives by adding on to each other's perspectives. This results in what Ellsworth calls a "mirrored" understanding that is "repetitive." The structure of communicative dialogue suggests that any difference can be referenced consciously, and it is this structure that intends to keep out "the unmeant, the unknowable, the excessive, the irrational, the unspeakable, the unhearable, the forgotten, the ignored, the despised" (p. 95). It is a structure and expectation that attempts to fix perspectives and implies that people can fully understand other's perspectives.

But, Ellsworth asks, what if a listener does not understand the conscious intention of a speaker? How can communicative dialogue be transformative if it is restricted by conscious discourse? Ellsworth points out that the expectation that everyone in a class should participate in a dialogue that expects mutual understanding before the offering of different views is coercive because it requires participation. One who does not understand is excluded and viewed as a disruption of the continuity of a dialogue through the breaking of the "rules of reciprocity, commitment, and participation—the rules of continuity" (p. 108).

Ellsworth suggests that teaching is impossible especially if one understands it as a matter of transmission of information because faculty cannot know how their students understand or perceive what they say. It is likely that an instructor's modes of address will misfire at times. Rather than overlook the implications that students may not understand a teacher's conscious intention, faculty should instead acknowledge, even embrace, this possibility. The recognition of the impossibility of teaching generates possibility because it creates an opportunity for the development of multiple and creative modes of address: "Instead of trying to manage and control a relation that is uncontrollable, we might ask, What might we learn from ways of teaching that are predicated, paradoxically, on the impossibility of teaching?" (p. 9). If faculty see teaching as a "paradoxical relation" (p. 16), then it increases the chances that teaching can be transformative. Working through paradox can be generative in that it turns up creative responses that can encourage one to question one's own assumptions and practices. Such a view of teaching also contributes to the richness of engagement in the classroom because it encourages participants to be increasingly attentive and responsive to each other.

Rather than the focus on the speaker intention of "communicative dialogue," Ellsworth suggests that "analytic dialogue" with its focus on listener experiences may be a more useful construct to envision engagement in classrooms because it foregrounds participant responsiveness. It recognizes the value of seeing an ongoing exchange of roles—of speakers as listeners and listeners as speakers. Analytic dialogue emphasizes the listening aspect of engagement with an intent to be open to differing perspectives; a focus on "analysis" provides a way for participants to reflectively engage that allows for numerous responses and differences more akin to a conversation. This approach to engagement opens instead of shuts down or excludes because it takes as an assumption that "we are both empowered and condemned to meaning-making. We cannot

not communicate. We cannot *not* respond to the events and stories that in-form us. Even not responding is a response—it has its consequences for myself and for others" (p. 136).

Response is an embedded part of engagement that shapes participant experiences. Ellsworth suggests that the question "How will I respond?" acknowledges the importance of response because it is not threatened by disruption or performativity because it "insists on the consequences of difference" (p. 137). By difference, I take it that Ellsworth means that modes of address can be received in varied and unpredictable ways. To ask "how will I respond?" allows for multiple understandings because it is a question that does not assume a shared agreement of what has been said. The question suggests that even if one does not hear something said in the way a speaker intended in the classroom, one can still engage in constructive ways that encourage inquiry.

Ellsworth orients the activity of analytic or conversational communication within a classroom as necessarily relational because the focus on the responses to questions insinuates the importance of engagement that fosters learning. It is from the return of differences in response to questions that people learn. The focus on responses is not threatened by discontinuity because within the context of a conversation, learning happens when assumptions have been questioned and initial thoughts have changed: "it happens when 'self-reflection' describes an ellipse, rather than a circle" (p. 147). Learning occurs not when notions of knowledge are transmitted from one person to another but when the questions asked become displaced by responses that may be unexpected, disrupting the initial context/thoughts from which the questions emerged. In other words, to seek answers to questions generates a return or response that shakes up the points of observation that initially informed the questions. This perspective recognizes the complexity of modes of address in the classroom in ways that situate not only students as learning from classroom conversations in unpredictable ways but faculty members too.

While a product-oriented view of teaching, which prioritizes efficiency and outcomes, largely assumes that successful communication between teacher and students is a direct transmission of information, a Confucian relational view situates it as an opportunity for experimental improvisation. Put another way, Ingold (2018) suggests that "real problems" do not have solutions. Time is required to experiment not so much as a scientist might in a lab by retesting a procedure, but as an intuitive journey: "It is prospective rather than retroactive, improvisatory rather than prescriptive, speculative rather than confirmatory. The patience of experimentation, in this sense, lies in the dynamics of attention, and in the endurance of waiting" (p. 41). To speak without assurance or expectation that another will understand one's intention, to focus on responding, situates communication as poetry. Ingold suggests that if teaching emphasizes attentiveness and responsiveness, then the goal is making poetry together, "wondering and wandering" for transformative purposes rather than a narrow focus on explication. Pedagogy, from engaging a Confucian relational view of Ellsworth's theorizations, positions classroom participants as mutually, contingently inquiring.

"WHO AM I 'AS' TEACHER?"

A Confucian relational concept suggests that because people live in mutuality, it is valuable to situate people's roles as changing and continually constructed through how people engage each other. This perspective situates people as necessarily learning from each other. Extending this notion to the classroom, the notion that all participants in a class learn complicates normative ideas of teacher and student. Ellsworth destabilizes normative notions of teachers and students by framing them as positionalities rather than fixed. Positionality is a term that suggests that aspects of identity, such as gender and race among others, are relationally constructed (Alcoff, 1988). With regard to the classroom, the positions of teacher and student, rather than essential, are contingent: One would not have meaning without the other. People's positionalities, which are shaped by their specific contexts, suggest that all participants in a classroom always have partial knowledges. And it is acknowledgment of partialness on the part of all participants in the classroom that challenges what may be perceived to be a teacher/student binary:

> Am I a teacher or a student? Who am I "as" teacher, who are you as student, what do I do as teacher, what do I want from you as student? The terms teacher and student urge me to choose among the many answers currently circulating and competing for these questions. (Ellsworth, 1997, p. 141)

Ellsworth ends up considering that a teacher is both teacher and student, and that students are both students and teachers: "this new concept of the 'teacher-student' must never be constituted as a third (additive) term, because we must continue troubling every definition of teacher-student that is arrived at" (Ellsworth, p. 141). If teaching is performative, then the activity of teaching includes the ongoing cultural production of notions of teaching and learning.

Ellsworth suggests that to destabilize the roles of teacher and student does not privilege notions of student or position student as teacher but functions to continually question what it means to teach and what it means to be a student: "Rewriting the teacher-student relation this way means refusing to let the question of the teacher-student relation be settled. It means working in and through the oscillating space of difference between teacher and student as positions within a structure of relations" (p. 140). In the 2005 book *Places of Learning: Media, Architecture, Pedagogy*, Ellsworth elaborates on this movement with regard to pedagogy through the suggestion that teaching should be more about "thinking" rather than "complying." In particular, Ellsworth points out that learning is an action that involves bodies, emotions, experiences, place, and time, among others (p. 55). So speaking and listening are not straightforward processes but involve activity with what Ellsworth calls people's "mind/body/brain" systems. Ellsworth suggests that spaces or events designed to be pedagogical can create contexts to support learning. In other words, to teach does not imply that one can directly control how or what another learns, but the intention to teach can influence others' experiences in ways that are unpredictable. To teach is not to impose but is to participate in what Ellsworth calls "interrelation."

Pedagogical spaces, while they cannot dictate learning, can seek to engage a person in ways that challenge one to reconsider or amend what one thinks one knows. For instance, intentionally constructed spaces—Ellsworth provides examples of memorials and museums—try to generate experience through engaging people's bodies and emotions within a particular time and place. The emphasis here is on attempts to communicate and to construct experiences without the guarantee that one can do so. To situate teaching as an attempt to address others in a way that can return unpredictable responses implies that the meaning of the roles of student and teacher cannot become fixed because the roles only emerge through engagement. Notions that they are or can be fixed are illusory. At the same time, the notion that teaching is an attempt to address others also suggests that while one may not control what and how someone hears, one can potentially influence a person's experiences.

For Ellsworth, to unsettle meaning with regard to student and teacher roles does not imply that people should give up trying to ask about the meaning of the roles or dismiss the idea of roles altogether. Rather, the act of unsettlement that emerges from inquiry serves as a constant reminder that people should continually inquire about what they think they know. This inquiry will then inform how people engage each other. And disjuncture becomes an occasion for productive inquiry.

In reading Ellsworth's discussion of pedagogy, the immediacy and relevance of a relational perspective drawn from a Confucian tradition for contemporary educational constructs become clear. Ellsworth's work provides a language and context that can contribute to an ongoing conversation about what a Confucian relational framework means and how it can function in contemporary settings. Ellsworth's explorations of responsive pedagogy, of dialogue as conversation and analytic rather than communicative, and of the importance of destabilizing roles of teacher and student by situating all participants in the classroom as learning, highlight a process-oriented perspective of classroom contexts that implies engagement is intra-active.

From Personal Cultivation to Critique

Ellsworth generates process-oriented descriptions of pedagogy in her research in part from experience teaching in the classroom. Ellsworth's research suggests that while the classroom is often normatively situated as a place focused on student learning, it is also a place for faculty growth as well. Put another way, if people's roles and relationships constitute who they are and inform what they do, then for faculty members the classroom is also a potential forum for personal cultivation. Teaching and learning are not separate endeavors but one and the same (Ames, 2016). A faculty member who strives to be exemplary could be positioned, as Ames states, as "the most advanced learner in the classroom." While faculty members generally have quite some leeway to design curriculum and need not necessarily accommodate student perspectives, Ellsworth chose to relentlessly inquire about pedagogical assumptions that emerged when teaching, her efforts echoing Confucius's sentiment of hard work in *Zhongyong*, "if others try ten times, I will try a thousand times" (Ames & Hall, 2001).

While reflective pedagogical research like Ellsworth's may be normatively situated as part of the field of educational studies, engaging a Confucian relational framework to read it emphasizes the notion that aspects that foreground the relational constitute contemporary educational constructs more broadly and the value of considering their implications for university contexts. Personal cultivation emerges through engaging others that include attention to others' responses, responding and adapting as a result, and being willing to question one's own assumptions and work at it unrelentingly. Ellsworth engages a process of personal cultivation from a Confucian relational perspective by seriously attending to student responses to her pedagogical approaches.

When people are viewed as living in mutuality, then undertaking a process of personal cultivation has an extensive impact. While a product-oriented notion of personal cultivation might envision the process largely as focusing on perceived benefits for the person undertaking it, a Confucian relational notion of it extends beyond to enrich relations in ways that are unexpected. For instance, Ellsworth's reflective work influences the experiences of participants of Ellsworth's classroom, Ellsworth's colleagues, and extends to offering a critique of some aspects of critical pedagogy, which assume that faculty can create a safe classroom space to empower students to speak.

Ellsworth expresses an interest to learn from students when she noticed how students responded to her pedagogical intentions. Ellsworth's essay (1989/2013) "Why Doesn't This Feel Empowering? Working Through the Repressive Myths of Critical Pedagogy" describes the experience of teaching a course using a critical pedagogic approach that attempts to encourage students to challenge oppressive normative sociopolitical and cultural constructs through inquiry. While Ellsworth tried to construct the classroom space in a curriculum and instruction course called "Media and Anti-Racist Pedagogies" as a safe one to encourage students to speak with power and equal opportunity, she found the efforts backfired when students did not perceive they could speak in safety. Ellsworth noticed that encouraging students to speak and develop their voices for the purposes of empowerment ended up instead being oppressive, and that Ellsworth and the students became what Ellsworth calls "vehicles of repression." Ellsworth found that the use of the language of critical pedagogy such as "empowerment" and "dialogue" proved to be "repressive myths that perpetuate relations of domination" (p. 188). Ellsworth found that students, rather than feeling emboldened to speak, did not always voice their thoughts because they felt that if they did, they might be misunderstood, say too much, or feel vulnerable, among other reasons.

Not only did Ellsworth notice how students reacted, but she also sought to learn more about why there was a gap between her pedagogical intentions and student reactions. In the essay, Ellsworth suggests that the abstract use of the language of critical methods without historical context and acknowledgement of particular political positions can be problematic. In other words, Ellsworth implies that the content of what one teaches and how it is taught cannot be separate. The way something is taught in part constitutes the "what" that is taught. To further complicate her attempts to use critical pedagogy, Ellsworth points out that the validity of people's narratives or, as Ellsworth describes it, "words spoken for survival" or as "a reality check for survival" (p. 191), cannot be responded to as part of a rationalist debate. While such narratives and their implications can be "made problematic" (p. 194), classroom discussion is complicated by the fact that people's views are always partial and subjective. As a result, people do have particular interests and agendas that may impinge on others' perspectives despite the interest of those involved to create a safe space for equitable dialogue. Ellsworth posits that larger injustices at play in the culture make communication difficult in the classroom: "Educational researchers attempting to construct meaningful discourses about the politics of classroom practices must begin to theorize the consequences for education on the ways in which knowledge, power, and desire are mutually implicated in each other's formations and deployments" (p. 204).

Ellsworth's inquiry about student experiences in the classroom led to changing her pedagogical approaches. Ellsworth suggested that to become aware of one's own assumptions and agendas, efforts must be made to become familiar with others, which includes inquiry about what is at stake for them in their lives, their histories, and motivations. In class, Ellsworth found that this was in part made possible through the natural development of what Ellsworth called "affinity groups" that resulted from student conversations outside class. Ellsworth noticed that these informally formed groups became the building ground for coalition among various groups inside the classroom. Ellsworth welcomed these formations in class and encouraged students to work on collaborative class projects. In this way, Ellsworth adapted classroom practices and expectations in response to student reactions to her pedagogical intentions and approaches. While Ellsworth sought to understand assumptions about students, at the same time she tried to destabilize these assumptions. Through attention to the student responses to pedagogical approaches, Ellsworth considered the notion that all are working from partial perspectives whose agendas could be oppressive to others. In particular, rather than overlook the fact that faculty members cannot realize intentions to create a safe classroom space, Ellsworth acknowledged it and adapted her pedagogical approaches.

Ellsworth's willingness to relentlessly question intentions and change teaching approaches could be viewed as having an extensive impact on students. Ellsworth changed the class plan to accommodate student inclinations to speak more freely with each other in naturally formed groups outside class. Ellsworth's adaptations expressed an interest to develop reciprocity with students, a move that likely encouraged students to converse more with Ellsworth and with each other. Ellsworth's responsivity was expressed not only in a change to the curriculum but also because Ellsworth provided an example of responsive teaching. For faculty who continually strive to become better teachers through being responsive to students and through inquiry into their own pedagogical assumptions, they model for their students a process of personal cultivation. Their striving becomes something students may learn from. Students learn not simply from what faculty members may deliberately articulate or intend to convey but also from how they act and what they do.

Ellsworth's striving influenced others too. If people are viewed as intradependently networked as part of a broader field, then the personal cultivation Ellsworth undertook in the classroom had a broad influence. For instance, Ellsworth's pedagogical inquiries also impacted colleagues. In the essay, Ellsworth mentions the sharing of her course syllabus with colleagues who were like-minded. Discussions Ellsworth may have had with them about class experiences may have influenced them to consider the content of their curriculum, their pedagogical approaches, and their conversations with other faculty members in ways that are difficult to trace. Also, because Ellsworth wrote about classroom experiences in an essay, her inquiries continue to influence others in extensive and unpredictable ways.

The impact of Ellsworth's reflective pedagogical research extends to offer a critique of some aspects of the field of critical pedagogy. The field assumes that rational deliberation can be used to confront and redress racism to some extent, among other injustices, through empowering students to identify and name oppressions. But Ellsworth's classroom experience encouraged noting that theorists of critical pedagogy (she cites Giroux and McLaren [1986]; Liston and Zeichner [1987]; Shor and Friere [1987]) have not rigorously analyzed the implications of the imbalance of power between students and teachers, which tend to assume that teachers can use their authority to empower students. They imply that teachers can, through provision of the tools of rational debate and sharing what they call "subjugated histories," create an equitable classroom space that seeks to "emancipate" students even when, from her perspective, this is impossible for them. The notion that teachers can empower students through encouragement to speak their experiences and thoughts in the classroom situates teachers, Ellsworth argues, as "voyeuristic" of students because it leaves teachers' own positions, voices, and privileges uninvestigated. In other words, teachers may overlook the partialness of their own knowing and how their agendas can be oppressive to others. Ellsworth's experience of being responsive to students in the classroom ended up providing a seminal critique of critical pedagogical practices.

By observing student responses to her teaching and adapting her pedagogical approaches, Ellsworth's process of personal cultivation has an extensive impact that includes an insightful critique of a particular pedagogical approach. Roger Ames suggests that Ellsworth's critical approach to pedagogy reflects what he calls a "provisional take on practice," which underscores the need to adjust and refine theoretical structures in relation to the specifics of practice. In particular, he suggests her critique embodies *zhixing heyi* 知行合一 ("authentication in practice") and expresses Wang Yangming's notion of the reciprocity between wisdom and practice—wisdom begins practice and practice manifests wisdom (personal communication, December 28, 2016). While a neoliberal framework may overlook the value of qualitative work by educators such as Ellsworth, who strive to become more responsive teachers through theorization about the complexities of their classroom experiences, a Confucian relational orientation foregrounds it and implies its value to instructional faculty in any discipline. From a Confucian relational perspective, faculty members who choose to do the hard work of personal cultivation undertake a process that not only impacts those they engage but also extends to influence the constructs of the university institution of which they are a part in unpredictable ways.

All About Relation: Juxtaposition With Feminist Perspectives

So far I have been positioning a Confucian relationality as distinctive from a neoliberal perspective to distinguish how a process-oriented emphasis on the value of teaching differs from a product-oriented view of it. While the discussion has touched on their differences, I want to suggest that I do not mean to situate them as opposing or antithetical. Rather I consider them part of the same extensive field where exploring their differences enriches them including their relation. Differences that emerge from the juxtaposition of frameworks become potential points of inquiry that provide opportunities for further exploration. This is the case for frames that appear quite different and also for those that seem more similar than not. While I have discussed how a concept of Confucian relationality can be used to frame Ellsworth's theorizations about pedagogy, I want to point out that her work is also situated as feminist, although Ellsworth does not directly describe her work in this way; and I suggest that the frameworks need not be exclusionary. In the rest of this chapter, I explore how a Confucian relationality, especially a relational notion of person, can enrich a poststructural feminist take on Ellsworth's work.

Engagement with a framework of Confucian relationality can complement and also productively challenge other theoretical frameworks that circulate in contemporary higher educational contexts. One useful way to envision how a concept of Confucian relationality can function more broadly is to consider it as part of a processual world and to engage the concept of focus and field constructed by Roger Ames and David Hall (2001), as mentioned previously. If the world is perceived as an infinite field of interactive processes and events with foci that continually shift and whose own limited perspectives "focus" the field, then while a framework can dominate an educational institution's function as a focus, it cannot completely exclude the possibility and influence of other frameworks because it is always part of a broader field. For example, the dominating use of a neoliberal framework in an educational system cannot preclude the possibility of the construction of other frameworks that circulate or can emerge at any time. In fact, when a dominant framework is deliberately juxtaposed with others, it may even change as a result of inquiry about its assumptions.

From this perspective, the juxtaposition of a concept of a Confucian relationality with other frameworks can provoke tensions that are unpredictably productive. The activity of inquiry about the tensions of the juxtaposition of foci, like the creation of pathways between neurons in a neural network, can construct more robust connections that influence how the foci function. These provocations, rather than being dismissed or reasoned away, can be seen as a chance to illuminate assumptions and inquire about how specific frameworks might function in particular contexts.

St. Pierre (2000) describes Ellsworth as a poststructuralist feminist and educator who "is well aware of how language works to both constrain and open up the everyday lived experiences of those working in education" (p. 484). Ellsworth's description of the performativity of pedagogy and the notion of multiple knowledges resonates with feminist perspectives, and to read her work with these perspectives in mind situates her ideas as part of a feminist discourse. Rather than suggest that one framework is more adequate than another, I suggest that the feminist and Confucian relational can exist as complements that reinforce the importance of Ellsworth's work more broadly, especially in an educational system whose administrative practices and strategic directions tend to be dominated by a neoliberal orientation. The juxtaposition of the two frameworks can be useful in that it may engage questions about their assumptions and their expressions, which can in turn further inquiry about them and the relevance of Ellsworth's work more broadly. While there are numerous resonances between the two frameworks and how they might situate Ellsworth's theorizations about pedagogy, there is a key difference—the extent to which they perceive people to be intra- or interdependent.

I want to acknowledge that my approach to juxtapose the two frameworks is limited, leaving out direct discussion about power relations. I hope that my not delving into a discussion about how the deployment of particular frameworks reflects differing power constructs does not suggest that this is not an important aspect of situating the meaning of these frameworks. That said, I admit that I am approaching the juxtaposition of these frameworks in a more theoretically inquiring rather than prescriptive sense. The activity of juxtaposition, from my perspective, is that it is a process that centers on the activity of reading, which seeks to enrich the contextual field of those concepts being juxtaposed. In particular, to read two texts or concepts next to each other can destabilize my understanding of them on their own. Mismatch is expected to emerge, and rather than try to resolve this, the point is to ask what assumptions juxtaposition makes visible given that it is an activity that seeks to construct meaning from resonances and disjuncture. In other words, it is an artificial and to some extent an arbitrary construct in that I deliberately situate two concepts in conversation to enrich their relation.

While the discourses of feminism and the Confucianism from which a concept of relationality has been constructed are historically complex, nuanced, and changing, I do not presume that my discussions of them here are comprehensive or even adequate especially when compared with those researchers who specialize in these discourses. I do not suggest that by choosing these two there are not others deserving of attention. I also do not suggest that by focusing on these two that my discussion of them is any way representative or definitive. In fact, my intention here is to undertake this acknowledged limited activity with an inquiring and experimental perspective in mind, one that seeks to ask and construct what might be possible and made visible by their juxtaposition.

Feminist scholars suggest that feminism, which is a movement that has broadly been described to respond to and resist patriarchal ideology and practices, does not exist as one unitary tradition (Reinharz & Davidman, 1992; Stone, 2013). It continues to have paradigmatic shifts. For example, Black women critiqued early feminist conceptions of sisterhood as exclusive because they foregrounded Caucasian women's experiences through attempts to identify and address patriarchy (Dill, 1983/2013). In particular, Bonnie Dill (1983/2013) explains that not only did this universalist orientation overlook issues of race and class, it assumed what Dill calls a bourgeois goal of personal self-fulfillment that countered Black women's beliefs that group identity intimately shapes personal identity: "Research on kinship patterns among urban Blacks identifies the nurturant and supportive feelings existing among female kin as a key element in family stability and survival" (p. 61).

As a result of numerous critiques of early feminist movements, there has been a shift toward acknowledgement of the differences—experiences, positionalities, perspectives, and others—among people. This shift is reflected by a move away from notions of essentialism toward explorations of the contexts of people's lives and their conceptions of identity to empower underrepresented groups, promote social justice, and address oppression. In the epilogue of a book on feminism in education, Lynda Stone (2013) articulates a more recent perspective about feminism:

> Diversity through particularist feminisms is rightly valued. However particularism in feminism has also resulted in individual authors who need not and often do not identify with a feminist ideology or group. And today, this seems appropriate. The question then remains about feminist activism. The present answer is a localist orientation. This means that theorists take up and refer to specific exemplars in their writings. This means that groups of concerned citizens, feminists and non-feminists, women and men, join together to promote social justice projects that may focus on women and girls or are extensive and inclusive. Everyone can benefit. (p. 471)

A poststructuralist framework reflects this notion of particularist and inclusion-focused feminisms. Poststructuralists examine statements of truth and knowledge from the perspective that power relations have influenced them (St. Pierre, 2000). They suggest that power and knowledge have a correlative relationship. In other words, truth does not exist as some sort of external object but rather is constructed by power relations within cultural practice: "What can be said? Who can say it?" (p. 496). These questions lead to considerations of the history of particular discursive statements, and the conditions and power relations from which they emerged. To trace these statements, poststructuralist feminists often use Foucault's methods of archeology and genealogy to identify patterns of discourse that serve to marginalize women and other groups.

Ellsworth's (1997) discussions of the performativity of pedagogy and how modes of address influence engagement resonate with a poststructuralist perspective, which operates with assumptions that a word and a "thing" are not directly correlated. Words do not have essential meanings, but rather their meaning is derived from their difference or absence from other signs in language: "Meaning is generated through difference rather than through identity" (St. Pierre, 2000, p. 481). Meaning is impossible to fix because it is always delayed and questions of interest focus on how something functions, "How is it produced and what are its effects? (p. 485). The use of language itself is performative:

> We word the world. The "way it is" is not "natural." We have constructed the world as it is through language and cultural practice, and we can also deconstruct and reconstruct it.

> There are many structures that simply do not exist prior to naming and are not essential or absolute but are created and maintained every day by people. (St. Pierre, 2000, p. 483)

Ellsworth's articulation of the differences between communicative and analytic dialogue implies that the communication of conscious intent like a poststructuralist notion of meaning is always postponed because a speaker cannot know or control what a listener hears. It is the space of difference that generates further inquiry and learning.

Both a Confucian relational and a feminist framework can situate Ellsworth's work in compelling and similar ways. They are similar in their prioritization of a processual orientation and share the notion that all perspectives are partial. For feminists, the continual destabilization of knowledge frameworks situates one in a position of doubt. St. Pierre (2000) says, "the feminist poststructural critique of epistemology is one of ongoing questioning, a skepticism about the relation of women to power, truth, and knowledge—a permanent political critique that has no end" (p. 500). St. Pierre points out that at issue is not that all knowledge is "unknowable," but rather it is important to keep in mind that knowledge is partial. This awareness means people must always consider the assumptions of their knowledge constructs and beliefs. Skepticism about how meanings and truths are produced especially as derived from conceptions of rationality and power relations are important parts of the destabilization process. This means that people cannot be afraid to reflectively ask questions about their own positionality and assumptions. Both frameworks feature the importance of ongoing inquiry about intentions, actions, and responses and insinuate that personal cultivation is hard work.

But the two frameworks differ in a key aspect. While both foreground the importance of relationships and consider people to be part of a shared context, they differ with regard to extent. A feminist framework seems to be inflected with a notion of a substance-oriented perspective that suggests people are "individuals." For example, this assumption might be at work in Ellsworth's (1997) description of pedagogy as "a performance that is suspended (as in interrupted, never completed) in the space between self and other . . . between time before learning and after . . . between prevailing categories and discursive systems of thought" (p. 17). The notion that pedagogy is a suspended performance between two people seems to assume that two people can be separate from each other. Ellsworth suggests a performance is something people can be a part of or not and that they can leave it as whole persons because they are independent from each other. It insinuates that relationships exist outside each person, rather than expressing the Confucian relational notion that people are necessarily constituted by relationships and so could not exist as independent or separate from others. While Ellsworth discusses modes of address and explores how pedagogy, specifically communication, can be unpredictable and performative, she does not ask what such ideas imply about how a notion of person or self is situated.

Similarly, while feminist educator Lynda Stone (1988/2013), in the essay "Toward a Transformational Theory of Teaching," suggests that a general relational epistemology is feminist and transformational, she does not consider what this might mean for how a notion of person is constructed and the extensive impact a process of personal cultivation could have. Stone suggests that a general conception of relationality is a useful epistemological alternative to what she describes as Platonic and Rousseauian educational theories that tend to reflect dualistic beliefs and ways of knowing. It suggests that relation is what Stone calls "basic" and potentially transformative because it is located "in the realm of possibility rather than actuality" (p. 132). While Stone implies that a notion of gendered upbringings is relational in that it situates gender identity not as essentialist but informed by normative beliefs and expectations of what it means to be a man or woman, she does not push through on this idea to consider what the implications a notion of gendered upbringings means to a broader notion of self and other. In other words, Stone does not go as far as to suggest that people are necessarily constituted by others to the extent that people cannot and do not exist as individuals. But a concept of a Confucian relationality addresses this.

As discussed previously, the notion of a Confucian relational person drawn from classical Chinese philosophy suggests that people cannot be situated as separate from others:

> In Confucianism, the self is never seen as an isolated, autonomous individual whose essential qualities and intellectual capacities are bestowed from without and possessed solely within. Instead, a person is always a person situated in a social context; a person qua person is a self-in-relation. For a person without social relations is also a person without humanity. (Rosenlee, 2006, p. 39)

People are born into and live in relation. Rosenlee suggests that gender from a classical Chinese philosophical perspective has more to do with social roles than perceived traits of femininity and masculinity. A notion of woman as a gendered being emerges through the occupation and performance of different family and kinship roles. It is through action, through the roles that people enact, that there are perceived differences between genders rather than a question of capability, capacity, or essential differences. Rosenlee points out that the written character for "person" in the Chinese language is gender neutral and that specific references to gender entail the use of entirely different characters.

This is a slightly different take on gender than Stone's discussion of a notion of gendered upbringing. Stone (1988/2013) writes, "men and women develop distinct forms of self" (p. 132) because of how we are socialized and raised by our parents. She writes, "In this process, men must undergo a process of separating and distancing from a sexually different parent, their mother. Women, in contrast, remain in connected relation to her" (p. 132). While Stone suggests that the notion of differences in expectations and behaviors between genders is socially constructed in part by how parents raise their children, Stone identifies and focuses on a "sexual difference" between people as meaningful. In other words, this view of men and women as biologically sexually different implies that there is a slight essentialist notion of difference at work here, one that can be used to distinguish people from each other in a more extensive way. I am not suggesting that Stone deny that men and women are not sexually different in some ways or even more broadly that there are differences between people, but the focus on this particular distinction imbues it with an implied significance. It suggests that an identification of sexual difference, as reflected by the use of the terms "man" and "woman," indicates an embedded assumption that people are distinct selves that can be separate from others. While feminist traditions may have shifted toward the broader acknowledgement of differences among people and away from essentialist notions of identity construction, this shift may not have necessarily resulted in sustained inquiry about the implications for how a person is situated in regard to others. Engagement of a Confucian relational framework and its conception that people cannot be considered "individuals" or separate from others could be a useful way to further inquire more robustly on this topic.

One possibility of why the extent of how a person is situated by others may not be a focus from the perspectives of the feminist works mentioned is that feminism is sometimes situated, as St. Pierre (2000) describes it, as a "reverse discourse" that "circulates alongside patriarchal discourses and gains legitimacy as it works within and against their assumptions" (p. 499). This particular conception of feminism assumes that feminist discourse emerges in response to or in resistance to a more dominant patriarchal substance-oriented discourse. For instance, this notion is expressed in St. Pierre's (2000) suggestion that feminists analyze patriarchy. St. Pierre states that feminists should ask:

> How does patriarchy function in the world? Where is it to be found? How does it get produced and regulated? What are its linguistic, social, and material effects on women? How does it continue to exist? What are its differences from itself? Once these questions can be asked of the specific, local, everyday situations that oppress women, and once the working of patriarchy is made intelligible at the level of micropractice, women can begin to make different statements about their lives. Once they can locate and name the discourses and practices of patriarchy, they can begin to refuse them. (p. 486)

Feminists from this perspective are compelled to be preoccupied by exploration of the impacts of patriarchal discourse. One impact of such a focus is that the field of a reverse discourse may be delimited to an extent by the dominant discourse it seeks to explore and counter. While resistance and response to a dominant discourse may result in the development of new discourses, a dominant discourse and those that emerge as "reverse" may share or overlook some of the same assumptions, such as the notion that people are "individuals." A Confucian relational framework can help make visible such an assumption.

While both a poststructural feminist and a Confucian relational framework may adequately situate various aspects of Ellsworth's work and provide language and ways to extend theoretically understanding it, there are considerable implications that emerge from differences in how they situate a notion of persons with regard to an educational context. In particular, they may differ with regard to how they imagine the extensivity of processes such as personal cultivation. A concept of Confucian relationality as discussed in chapter 3 situates people as persons rather than individuals and as events and narratives rather than beings. In particular, it considers a person as constituted by a network of specific roles and relationships—of family, friends, and colleagues—rather than descriptive attributes or singular "beings."

From a Confucian relational perspective, personal cultivation happens relationally because it is what people do that constitutes who they are. In other words, personal cultivation in the classroom does not simply become relegated to only that context but influences the networks of people who undertake such processes more broadly. It may become manifest in how people relate with others outside the classroom in ways they may not know. This notion does not mean that people cannot be cognitively reflective for their own sake but emphasizes that reflexivity is related to what they do and how others respond.

A substance-oriented notion that people are independent from each other on the other hand suggests that development and growth are largely isolated activities. Personal cultivation in the classroom from this perspective could be seen as something that benefits the person who undertakes the process foremost. It could be seen as a self-serving undertaking rather than one that has a more extensive impact. Engagement, from a substance-oriented perspective, is seen as a choice rather than as something that constitutes us.

Stone (1988/2013) suggests that a notion of the relational as epistemological and educational ideal must be unpacked by educators. Stone writes, "I emphasize the difficulty of this task given the scarcity of descriptive examples—given the founding hegemony" (p. 132). Stone ends the essay by imploring readers to examine the implications of a relational epistemology. A framework of Confucian relationality can assist with this. But more broadly, the juxtaposition of these two frameworks can be useful in that their differences can be a source of further inquiry in varied ways. For example, the *Zhongyong* was penned more than two thousand years ago when the phenomena of extensive social institutions such as contemporary educational systems did not exist. Inquiry about how a Confucian relational framework might be used to consider Ellsworth's work provides an opportunity to consider the nuances of expressions of the framework. Consideration of Ellsworth's work from a feminist framework, which has numerous resonances to a Confucian relational one, provides a chance to ask questions about the concept of a Confucian relationality and its expression in contemporary higher educational contexts in ways that might not have occurred to me otherwise. To juxtapose these frameworks is to imply that each can enrich the other and that their juxtaposition produces meaning that is greater and more extensive than each considered on its own. Also, the resonances that emerge from the juxtaposition of these frameworks could be used to consider the limits and assumptions of a neoliberal framework. Because the emphases of the frameworks differ slightly, together they provide a wider scope of inquiry.

A framework of Confucian relationality emphasizes the importance of the cultivation of reciprocal and responsive relationships in educational institutions in part by calling attention to the reflective pedagogical work of educators such as Ellsworth. It suggests that Ellsworth's approach to inquiry about pedagogy provides in my view an example of relational personal cultivation whose influence extends beyond the classroom. Ellsworth's work is broadly relevant for faculty because her theorizations about the impossibility of direct communication have compelling implications for how faculty of any discipline might approach teaching and the development of curriculum. To dwell on the complexity of relating in the classroom from a Confucian relational perspective is not to suggest that other frameworks have no place in educational endeavors, but rather to provocate that the juxtaposition of multiple frameworks can make visible assumptions, provide opportunities to inquire about how particular frameworks may be deployed, and also enrich their discourses in mutual ways. A Confucian relationality acknowledges the partiality of all frameworks and, rather than envision this as problematic, instead encourages inquiring engagement.

Practically, what engaging a concept of Confucian relationality can do for higher educational contexts in part is to emphasize the importance of supporting the development of the craft of faculty teaching. It suggests that faculty teaching has the capacity to enrich university contexts in unpredictable ways. When teaching is viewed as a potential forum for faculty personal cultivation and faculty members are positioned in part as learners too, the impacts can be extensive. For instance, Ellsworth's reflective pedagogical research influenced student classroom experiences and inspired inquiry for colleagues and those who use critical pedagogical approaches to teach. Perception of the extensivity of impact hinges in part on the perspective of how a notion of person is situated.

When a Confucian relationality is juxtaposed with a poststructural feminist framework to situate Ellsworth's work, the concept serves as a point of inquiry that enriches both frameworks. When people are viewed as necessarily constituted by others through actions, this perspective suggests that personal cultivation influences how people engage others in nondeliberate and even imperceptible ways. At the same time, engaging a concept of Confucian relationality to consider a higher educational context provides an opportunity to explore theorizations about the concept.

In a moment when a neoliberal product orientation pressures higher educational institutions to link value to quantifiable measures, engaging the concept of Confucian relationality as a contemporary educational resource encourages attending to the value of those relational aspects of university activities such as responsive teaching that may be overlooked. The concept encourages seeing the complexity of educational contexts and the value of teaching—seeing the forest and the trees—by drawing attention to the ongoing processes and relationships that influence university activities.

Conclusion

Elizabeth Ellsworth (1997) raises the question of the importance of continual inquiry to situate pedagogy to destabilize faculty assumptions about how to address students. For faculty members, adopting a position of inquiry in relation to teaching takes form through a focus on response to students. Emphasizing response encourages faculty to reply to varied student perspectives and reactions to faculty pedagogical approaches in a reflective way. For instance, this might entail a shift in faculty response to student statements from indicating "that's not what I meant" to responding with "interesting that you see it this way, can you tell more about why?" The first response tends to situate communication as understanding in a closed loop, while the second openly inquires.

Engaging a position of genuine inquiry suggests that faculty members are open to challenging their own assumptions because it acknowledges differences and sees them as opportunities for further conversation. Orienting response as inquiry matters not only because it implies faculty member partiality but also because it signals openness to learning, to transformation through engagement. From a Confucian relational perspective, the question of response is critical. Response matters because it influences what others may do next. In a processual world, moments cannot be isolated, they are contingent. A response involves reaction, pre-action, and action—all inseparable. It is not passive but generative. Responses are agential.

The perspective of response as agential when adopting a position of inquiry more broadly can be usefully extended to frame universities as learning communities. When universities are situated as constituted by the ongoing actions and responses of people, they are positioned as open to responding through inquiry and, as a result, open to change. While institutions may feel the pressure of social and regulatory expectations to justify what they do by providing metrics as evidence of the outcomes of their activities, engaging a Confucian relational perspective suggests they can at the same time continue to inquire about the value of existing relational-focused aspects that thrive on difference. They can explore how these aspects enrich university communities. To genuinely inquire is to consider the possibility of partialness, which means university leaders are compelled to consider what is missed by the pursuit of particular agendas.

However, the pressure of a dominating neoliberal orientation on universities cannot be underestimated, especially when it is expressed through a use of product-oriented language that seeks to link contributions and evidence. The language of the market reflects a broader ethos that reflects institutional aspirations and directions. University declarations expressed in strategic direction documents, mission statements, and tenure and promotion guidelines, for instance, reflect normative institutional values that often prioritize measurable aims. The content of such documents, constructed by committees constituted by faculty and administrators, emerges to serve as a guide for institutions more broadly—how they function, what they value, and their aims. More often than not, these are described through the use of market-oriented language.

Strategic direction documents, for instance, characterize institutions in terms such as "high performance-mission driven system" and "academic enterprise" that emphasize the importance of measurable outcomes and accountability, among others, to determine institutional effectiveness. This language draws attention to those aspects of institutions that are measurable, deemphasizing aspects that are more difficult to delineate. The neoliberal pressure that universities face is expressed not only through the use of a market parlance, but also in expectations of faculty members. While tenure and promotion guidelines may not use the same market-oriented language to describe expectations of faculty that a strategic directions document does with its delineation of goals and action strategies, they still reflect a product orientation when they situate faculty roles as separate and set them in competition with each other.

Accommodating neoliberal pressure can get in the way of institutional responsiveness more broadly because it requires effort to produce evidence of contributions. Rather than focusing on achieving educational aims, administrators and faculty face pressure to consider how they would prove their achievements. A neoliberal orientation contributes to normative pressures on faculty, for instance, to prioritize publishing over teaching and service in part because it values measurable outcomes.

For instance, publications are easier to identify as a product of research than perceived outcomes of quality teaching. The focus on measurable outcomes insinuates the importance of research publications over more difficult-to-quantify activities such as teaching. It pressures faculty members to consider how to expend limited time and effort to show evidence of their contributions.

Another troubling implication that institutions face when engaging a neoliberal orientation is the pressure of determining attribution. The notion that faculty activities can be considered independently relies on situating people as separate from each other. As a consequence, a neoliberal perspective, which takes as its basic unit of focus "individuals," insinuates that each person bears clear-cut responsibilities for outcomes. This view imposes immense pressure on faculty members who are framed by a product orientation as producers—of research, teaching, and service—by suggesting that faculty work can be delineated clearly. To put the focus on faculty in this way suggests that they singularly bear the responsibility for the outcomes of these roles.

To put the issue of attribution another way, engaging a neoliberal perspective relieves universities to some extent of the responsibility, for instance, to support enriching a culture of teaching. To suggest that faculty must prove their contributions also implies that they are wholly responsible for the outcomes of their roles, a notion that overlooks that faculty roles emerge from attempting to address institutional expectations, for instance, to cultivate global citizens and strive to achieve the stated core ideals mentioned in mission statements. A neoliberal perspective absolves universities from a need to be responsive when they can simply symbolically point attributively at their faculty with requests to provide measurable evidence of their contributions for the purpose of applying for tenure and promotion.

On the other hand, a concept of Confucian relationality situates universities as responsive learning communities in which responsibility for faculty expectations are shared. In particular, when universities are framed as constituted by the intradependent activities and experiences of their participants, then it is people's shared endeavoring that coheres the communities. A concept of Confucian relationality engages a process-oriented view of universities drawn from natural phenomena that suggests that movement is constant even if imperceptible. For instance, the earth continually revolves around the sun, the cells of human bodies continually change, and people's activities continually generate their contexts.

Universities, then, emerge as a set of ongoing practices and specific contexts generated by the activities of their participants.

A concept of Confucian relationality emerges from consideration of the *Zhongyong* and the work of comparative philosophers. While normative interpretations of the text and other classical philosophical texts emerged in part from their use as content for the Chinese civil service examination process for much of the last two millennia, scholars point out that engagement with the texts can be situated as part of a dynamic, flexible tradition. The texts can be resources to productively consider contemporary contexts. In the case of higher educational institutions, a concept of relationality constructed from a classical Chinese philosophical text can be used to consider the value of those existing aspects of institutional function that support, for instance, the development of the craft of teaching through the cultivation of collegiality. Engaging a Confucian relationality foregrounds those relational aspects of educational endeavors that already exist, implying their value. Relationality situates a far more complicated view of instructional faculty expectations than a neoliberal one that seeks to view faculty roles in separate and competitive ways. It implies, instead, that all activities are intraconnected, suggesting that spending time on the cultivation of collegiality through collaboration, for instance, to support teaching can yield unexpected outcomes.

Along the same lines of historically situating the Confucian tradition as changing by emphasizing its commentarial aspect is for readers themselves to take the role of engaging the texts actively, including their translations and commentaries. One way to be an active reader is to take an interpretive approach to situating the texts and the tradition. This means adopting a process-oriented view of reading the classical texts that suggests that there can be no fixed or essentialist reading because the texts have different meanings for different people through time. A Confucian commentarial tradition, from an interpretive perspective, situates Confucianism as a dynamic philosophical tradition constituted by readings of texts that necessarily reference readers' specific locational and ontological orientations. Situating Confucianism as multivocal, then, accommodates the fragmented nature of a complex tradition, which is continually constructed by those who read and write about the texts rather than constituted by purported universal truths about the texts. Written commentary, from an interpretive perspective, generates new texts with new meanings.

A concept of Confucian relationality engages a process-oriented worldview that situates people as living in mutuality and personal cultivation, as a result, as extensive. It does not assume that measurable evidence is necessary to determine value because it engages a notion of the world as continually changing. From this perspective, people are situated as specific, intradependent, and necessarily constituted by others; how people engage is of paramount importance because it is their actions that directly influence the quality of their relationships and lives. A process of personal cultivation that foregrounds reflective inquiry can have an extensive impact because it emerges through attention directed at improving the quality of actions with others in part by trying to put oneself in the place of others. When people are viewed as ongoing events specifically located spatially and temporally, then undertaking an activity of personal cultivation has extensive impacts. Personal cultivation emerges from seeking to understand the experience of others, which then results in the capacity to attune to people's own feelings and emotional experiences. From this perspective, educational endeavors and function cannot be seen as outside or separate from people's intra-actions.

When educational institutions are viewed as constituted by the activities of their participants, then what engaging a Confucian relational concept does is draw attention to those relational aspects that influence how participants act. For instance, when institutional documents such as tenure guidelines and strategic directions from a case study university were viewed from a Confucian relational perspective, attention was drawn to envisioning faculty activities not as separate but as cohering based on their activities. This occurs in part by drawing attention to the university's stated core values such as academic rigor and research integrity and asking how they could be situated as a method of envisioning engaging faculty activities. To situate faculty members as striving for academic rigor and research integrity suggests that they are constantly experimenting with ideas and pushing the boundaries of their fields in order to develop new ways of knowing.

To engage a Confucian relational perspective is to situate a university as a responsive learning community in part because it situates the faculty who are key participants in pursuing university activities as learners too. A normative notion of experiment suggests that those who undertake the process of research and engaging in observation, prediction, and testing to explore ideas must at some level be open to the unexpected.

In other words, the products of experimentation may not always be clear. To experiment in imaginative ways suggests that faculty must adopt the position of openness to continually learning. The spirit of experiment implies the value of exploration, process, and imagination. Rather than viewing learning as a fixed state, viewing it as a continual endeavoring is a useful approach to consider how faculty undertake their activities. Emphasizing the process rather than the products of experiment and learning may influence attitudes in which faculty may undertake their activities. Viewed in this way, appeals to engage an institution's core values for academic rigor, excellence, respect, and integrity may be situated as an approach to or way-making of all faculty activities. Situating faculty as learners suggests that it is important for faculty members to develop a capacity for experimentation that is relevant to all of their faculty roles.

Engaging a Confucian relationality situates universities as learning communities in part because from a process-oriented perspective, people necessarily live in mutuality. From this perspective, people are born into particular intradependent contexts and emerge as part of them through their activities and experiences. When people are viewed as ongoing events specifically located spatially and temporally, then learning necessarily emerges through relationship. When universities are viewed as constituted by the activities of people and these activities as generating the context of the university, then it is useful to view these activities not as occurring in isolation but as necessarily contingent and involving others. Nowhere is this more clear than in research about faculty learning communities to show the potential of drawing out the value of the development of collegiality as an aspect of university communities.

When learning is viewed as necessarily emerging from engagement with others, then enriching relationships may be viewed in part as supporting learning. This is the case with research about faculty learning communities and the value of the cultivation of collegiality. University-affiliated faculty learning communities are often viewed as gatherings of interdisciplinary faculty for specific periods of time to learn about various approaches to teaching. Facilitators of these communities intentionally foster collegiality by building trust through inviting participants to engage in open-ended discussions and activities that encourage reflection on their teaching practices and experiences. By creating a noncompetitive atmosphere through the structure and expectations of the learning communities, the facilitators generate the space for imaginative intellectual collaborative learning. The collaborations often yield engaged learning about teaching and also return varied outcomes that may not be preconceived. A Confucian relational focus on process rather than outcomes that assumes people's intradependence suggests that engaging differences among participants of a learning community enriches their experiences.

While faculty may choose to participate in faculty learning communities to learn about teaching approaches because teaching is part of their employment obligations, the context of the learning community can also shape participants' attitudes and experiences with regard to how they approach the learning. The development of collegiality contributes to fostering learning about teaching as intellectual play because it enriches the experience of participation. The notion that experience of participation is important resonates with Gray's (2013) characterizations of play as necessarily motivated by means more than ends, as guided by mental rules, and as fostering imaginative learning. In particular, Gray suggests that undertaking an activity with a playful attitude can result in the consideration of extrinsic outcomes as secondary to the intrinsic experience of the process itself. A shift to focusing on enriching experience facilitates imaginative learning because it lessens the stress and fear of failure that may emerge from a focus on achieving outcomes.

To engage a concept of a Confucian relationality, which envisions people as living in mutuality, draws attention to the phenomena of faculty learning communities that suggest the value of supporting faculty learning. To support the notion of the importance of faculty learning is to situate faculty more complexly than simply as producers but as experts in their fields who are also learning about teaching. In learning communities, the development of collegiality emerges from a willingness of participants and facilitators to take seriously the experience of participation. To focus on the experience, engage in general guidelines to cultivate the space of learning communities, and generate a context in which participants feel comfortable speaking with each other creates the conditions for an attentive state of mind that encourages collaborative learning about teaching that in turn also develops faculty collegiality.

To view universities as learning communities shifts perspective from a product-oriented reflex to attribute contributions driven by a question of responsibility to one that evokes a sharing of responsibility in part through focusing on response. This notion of shared responsibility is reflected in an aspect of Confucian relationality that emphasizes the extensive impacts of personal cultivation. When the world is viewed as process oriented and people live in mutuality, then what people do, including how they learn, influences not only themselves but others too. For universities, this means that faculty who engage in reflective pedagogical research influence not only themselves and those they are in direct contact with but ripple in ways that may be difficult to trace, making attribution difficult. Ellsworth's (1997) responsiveness to her students yields surprising outcomes, including a critique of assumptions about a critical pedagogical approach. Ellsworth, through theorizations about her students' responses to her pedagogical approaches, suggests that notions of teaching as a way to simply convey information from teacher to student is problematic because they assume that direct communication is possible. Instead, Ellsworth argues that faculty should acknowledge the impossibility of such an approach to teaching because they cannot completely control what someone else hears.

Responsiveness, Ellsworth's research suggests, includes viewing disjuncture in communication not as tinged with failure but rather as providing opportunities for those involved to question their assumptions and destabilize what they think they know. Learning, from this perspective, is an integral aspect of teaching. Ellsworth's work reflects a process of personal cultivation by attending to student responses to her pedagogic intents. She adapts her teaching approach as a result of the ongoing process and finds surprisingly that her inquiry leads to a productive critique of the work of some critical pedagogic theorists who assume that teachers can empower students in the classroom. Ellsworth suggests that teachers need to acknowledge they are not all-knowing experts who can address educational inequities by asking students to speak their truths. Teachers, rather, can oppress with their expectations that all students speak to empower themselves.

Responsiveness is a quality that applies to the concept of Confucian relationality itself. Engaging Ellsworth's research from a Confucian relational perspective, for instance, enriches a framework of relationality by providing a contemporary educational context in which to explore it. Ellsworth's discussions about envisioning classroom discussion as conversation instead of dialogue, for instance, provide an opportunity for further inquiry about situating classroom activities from a processual orientation. Ellsworth's exploration of teaching as a performative activity also resonates with a notion of the world as changing when she discusses it as a continual mode of address that may misfire. More broadly, consideration of her work from a Confucian relational perspective provides an opportunity to consider how the juxtaposition of different theoretical frameworks can encourage productive inquiry about the value of her work across disciplines. For instance, while some scholars situate her work as poststructural feminist, juxtaposition of this frame with a Confucian relational one emphasizes how differently each considers a notion of person, furthering inquiry about their implications. A Confucian relational perspective—that people are situated as necessarily constituted by others—suggests that the activity of personal cultivation is unpredictably extensive. Focusing on the relational, it turns out, produces surprising outcomes in ways that focusing on the outcomes at the start might not have returned, and this focus enriches a contemporary notion of a Confucian relationality.

To situate universities as learning communities constituted in large part by faculty activities is to suggest their responsivity, especially when faculty roles are viewed not as separate and competitive but as cohered by an inquiring endeavoring. To view faculty as an intradependent part of the university is to view them as experts and learners, a view that suggests that the university shares responsibility for supporting their endeavoring. For universities, this means that rather than simply linking faculty work to quantifiable outcomes to frame their contributions, they acknowledge the complexity and connectedness of faculty roles. It means being open to inquiring how faculty experiences are shaped more broadly in part by university culture, practices, and expectations.

Embracing the Complexity of Learning: Some Implications

The Confucian relational preoccupation with response situates faculty as continually learning. Engaging this view may compel universities to inquire how institutional expectations influence faculty activities and to consider how a dominant product-oriented framework gets expressed in educational contexts. If relationships constitute people, then the cultivation of relationships and attention to people's experiences must be primary considerations even for educational institutions. But this is a difficult charge, especially as they can be impossible to characterize in the ways a substance-oriented neoliberal framework is wont to demand. If people, following Ellsworth's lead, strive to see the difficulty of measuring or fixing relational space, such as that of conversation, then they may instead see it as a complex space of possibility that fosters learning through the encouragement to ask questions, notice difference, and destabilize notions of what they know.

A Confucian relational orientation insinuates the importance of learning through inquiry because it engages a processual worldview that suggests that people construct who they are by what they do through relationships. People learn through relationships, and they continually challenge what people think they should know. For instance, Ellsworth believed her critical pedagogical approach was effective until she noticed and further inquired about her students' differing responses to her teaching approaches. Confucius strove to become a better person but also realized through his relationships that he could not be the son to his father that he expected his son to be to him. It is through relating that people see difference. If they pay close enough attention and ask about difference—what does it mean and why—it can foster learning.

What does it mean practically to situate universities, then, as learning communities? To consider universities from a Confucian relational perspective suggests that the benefit of making a conceptual shift can show the limits of a neoliberal orientation and emphasize the value of relational aspects of university activities. Put another way, conceptual shifts have practical implications. Hannah Tavares problematizes the notion of a separation between theory and practice. She writes, "our work as scholars entails conceptualizing/re-conceptualizing and I do not simply see that work as a technical matter (i.e., a better or more reliable conceptualization) separate from the so-called 'real' world; rather, our conceptualizations have very real consequences and practical implications because they can (re)orient how we might approach, act, say, and what we might feel and value" (personal communication, April 24, 2017). To engage differing theoretical frameworks will reflect varied interpretations of specific contexts. The two are inextricable—concepts and their practical expressions are necessarily contingently entwined. As a result, it might be of some use to touch upon more specifically how an educational institution like the one I use as a case example might practically express openness toward engaging a Confucian relational framework. These possibilities include making visible processes that already function as part of university activities, using evalutatory processes for inquiry and fact gathering about university responsibilities and culture, and acknowledging process-oriented aspects of university culture and supporting them.

Make Processes Visible

Academic practices emerge from and as processes, but the complexity of these may be overlooked by a neoliberal orientation to link attribution with quantifiable measures. To continually adopt an attitude of reflective inquiry about institutional and academic practices may encourage acknowledgement of the complexity of processes, such as research collaborations and the development of institutional guiding documents. One approach to take to acknowledge the complexity of processes is to consider how to make the processes more visible.

One way to make the processes more visible is to raise awareness of the complexity of academic practices through the use of narratives, even commentaries to accompany the practices. I explore this first by focusing on a common academic practice of attributing sources and authorship. For instance, although normative publication expectations include the request for a sequential byline for authors on papers and books, the complex processes and experiences of faculty collaboration can be difficult to delineate or comprehensively characterize. For example, Roger Ames and David Hall have worked together on six book projects over two decades. Ames writes about his relationship with Hall: "I have been so altered in this relationship that I fully believe that anything I write now even 15 years after his death should be listed as co-authored with him. Collaboration requires that you understand everything and take responsibility for everything" (personal communication, November 28, 2016). Engaging a Confucian relational framework reminds us that even while attempts are made to distribute credit for research, they may be inadequate reflections of the processes of collaboration. Collaboration is intra-action that enriches relationships, which produces a productive space but, like experience, cannot be fully captured. A Confucian relational framework, one that assumes people are constituted by each other, recognizes and accommodates the complexity and nuances of relationships.

Rather than brush by the complexity of collaboration, acknowledging the complexity through narrative can be helpful. From a processual worldview, for example, normative publication practices are not fixed, but persist as they do because people use them. Because they emerge through use, this also means that such practices can change. For instance, bibliographies of academic books are generally located at the end of a book and include an alphabetized list of references. Adopting a position of inquiry encourages experimentation. Thomas Kasulis (2002) notices that bibliography, while it provides a reader with helpful information about other works that influenced the generation of a particular book, also leaves out quite a bit of information. It leaves out mention of the circumstances in which an author encountered a particular work and how the work impacted the development of the author's ideas. While Kasulis writes the majority of the book about two types of cultural orientations, intimacy and integrity, in a straightforward and analytical manner, in the last chapter, he swerves.

Instead of offering readers a list of books in the form of a traditional bibliography that influenced the writing of his book, Kasulis pens what he calls "an intimate bibliography." Kasulis asks, "what might an intimacy-oriented bibliography look like?" and the result becomes an occasion to reflect upon the function of bibliographies in academic contexts and to experiment with the writing of a bibliography as a narrative. Kasulis tells the story of how he encountered the texts that informed the writing of his book, even mentioning moments in college courses he took as an undergraduate. Kasulis's purpose is not only to provide readers with a list of the books and influences that have shaped his work but also to share with readers how he encountered these influences and how they figured into the development of his ideas. Kasulis does not suggest that bibliography formats need to be wholly revised but asks what normative formats leave out, insinuating that all academic endeavors, to some extent, can only be partial. His inquiry serves to remind faculty that it is important to consider how normative formats may be limited.

ACKNOWLEDGE COMPLEXITY

Along the same lines, let's move to consider how foregrounding a process orientation might look if narratives about the construction of public documents accompanied the institutional documents themselves. While narratives may be limited in their ability to comprehensively characterize the process of constructing the content of the documents, they may at least signal to those who read the documents the complexity of their construction. The inclusion of one or even multiple narratives about document content emergence, perhaps provided by the committee members that developed the documents, would provide some indication of the time, effort, and concerns involved in the production of the content. These narratives would remind readers that the documents emerged from specific contextual processes. Similarly, the inclusion of commentaries about the interpretations of the content of the documents might help to legitimize the multiple responses that readers may have about the documents. While it may be impossible to completely make transparent the processes of the construction of the documents, finding varied ways to situate them in specific contexts would acknowledge the complexity of educational endeavors, rather than be a sign of weakness or institutional discord.

Narratives that accompany documents may imply the importance for institutions to continually adopt a position of inquiry by including reflections about what might have been left out of the document construction process and potential future directions. For instance, in the strategic directions document discussed in chapter 4, while the core values were identified early on in the document, they were not mentioned again or in relation to the four institutional goals described. Authors of the document could try to elaborate how the core values might be envisioned to relate to the goals in a narrative document or even in the formal document itself and discuss the potential difficulty of envisioning them as related, acknowledging the tensions that might emerge. Because educational endeavors are complex and difficult to characterize in measurable terms, the document and accompanying narratives could articulate this rather than taking a stance of overt confidence about the ways to achieve the stated goals.

Institutional documents themselves could be revised to show the complexity of the issues they seek to address. Because public documents construct institutional identities and priorities to some extent, revising the documents to include recognition of nuances that may emerge from their interpretation might be useful. Tenure guidelines for instructional faculty could be revised to acknowledge the complexity of the various institutional expectations of faculty roles. In a conversation referenced in chapter 4, the university's assistant vice chancellor of academic personnel stated unequivocally that she felt that tenure evaluation committees should weigh research and teaching equally. If this is indeed the case, that the assistant vice chancellor and other high-level administrators believe this to be true, they could make an effort to share their perspective that teaching and research should be equally considered in a more formal way. For instance, in the tenure and promotion guidelines, while the institutional expectations of instructional faculty with regard to contributions to teaching, research, and service were identified, the document did not mention how the expectations should be weighted in comparison to one another. More directly stating the way faculty roles should be viewed in relation to each other in the tenure guidelines themselves might inform how evaluation committees might consider the categories.

Additionally, the approach of directly articulating the relation among faculty roles might openly address the pressures on faculty to prioritize publishing over teaching. Part of acknowledging the tension could include mention of the difficulties of evaluation, especially the notion of providing evidence for relational aspects like teaching. For instance, it might mention how a request for evidence may overlook the complexity of quality teaching and tend to imply the importance of publications. This might encourage discussion about the primary importance of teaching and of the effort required to develop the craft of teaching, discussions that might spur changes to the tenure guidelines themselves. The mention of tensions might encourage continuing inquiry and critical interpretations of institutional documents with an eye toward the possibility of continuing to revise them.

Enrich Teaching Culture

What engaging a concept of Confucian relationality makes clear as discussed in previous chapters is how the relational aspects of university activities often get overlooked because of a preoccupation with linking contributions to evidence. In particular, relational aspects like the complexity of teaching are often overlooked when institutions place a large responsibility for the development of the craft of teaching on the faculty themselves. Engaging a concept of Confucian relationality suggests that the university should share the responsibility put on faculty to foster global citizens more broadly. To envision the university as a learning community then may include generating inquiry at the departmental and university levels about how to generate the context for discussions and the sharing of resources about teaching that inform a culture of support for the development of the craft of teaching.

Another way to make the complexity of institutional processes more visible is that universities could envision their faculty evaluatory processes as opportunities to assess their own levels of support for faculty endeavors. For instance, while evaluating teaching in a standardized way is difficult, if not impossible, tenure guideline documents could ask that faculty members discuss for nonevaluatory purposes where they may have encountered support for teaching at the institution. In fact, the documents could ask some additional open-ended questions not intended to evaluate faculty members at all but to position the dossiers as resources to some extent that provide the university with a better understanding of faculty experiences. To put it another way, the tenure process could be envisioned not only as a means to evaluate faculty members in individualized ways but also as a chance for institutions to learn about how they could better support faculty members in achieving the various institutional expectations. This reflective approach to evaluation would more clearly situate the university in a position of learning by recognizing the intrarelated aspect of faculty endeavors.

What does it mean to suggest that the university share responsibility for supporting teaching? One way would be to increase departmental discussion of the complexity and the value of teaching with support from the university level. This could happen in varied ways, for instance, in one-on-one conversations with faculty members, as part of faculty meetings, and through encouraging the sharing of reflective pedagogical research or materials. Simply talking more about the value of teaching may assist in influencing how it is perceived as part of faculty roles from departmental and institutional perspectives by drawing attention to it. The attitude about teaching that administrators express may influence how they situate teaching. In addition to talking about teaching, administrators may choose to encourage faculty members to share pedagogical research and experiences. Part of the time allotted for faculty meetings could be used to discuss teaching or share resources, if this does not already occur, to show departmental support for discussions about teaching. Senior faculty members could mentor new faculty if they do not do so already.

Broad recognition of the value of faculty learning communities to enrich universities could contribute to institutional support of such communities. For instance, if faculty learning communities are viewed as creating the conditions for people to engage in dynamic conversation, the groups can be envisioned as forums that promote valuable future cross-disciplinary collaborations. Ellsworth's reflective pedagogical research, which involves rigorous inquiry about her teaching approaches through attention to student actions, generates rich theorizations about what it means to teach-learn that are valuable for faculty in any discipline.

However, more often than not, participation in learning communities may be taken for granted even by the participants themselves. For instance, when I spoke with the chair of the Department of English about learning communities at the case study institution, she mentioned in passing that she was part of an informal writing group. She shared drafts of her articles with a small group of friends and colleagues and received valuable feedback on them. While informal communities may be situated as personal, recognition of their contributions toward supporting faculty endeavors may help encourage institutions to see their value. While institutionalization of learning communities should not necessarily be a goal for universities, acknowledging their potential impact on university communities more broadly could encourage conversation about the complexity of the roles of faculty members and support their work.

While I have suggested some of the broader theoretically practical directions a relational framework might generate, I want to point out that this discussion about possible expressions is not meant to be prescriptive. Academic activities occur at specific moments in time and in ways that construct institutional contexts. From this perspective, a Confucian relational framework could be seen as a resource that inspires imaginative possibilities for all participants of educational systems, with an understanding that how we engage with others not only constitutes who we are but also constructs the institutions we generate through our actions. It also reminds us that those forums that encourage the cultivation of relationships, such as those that support teaching, deserve to be deliberately supported by educational institutions. To view the university as a responsive learning community is to continually inquire how responsibility for faculty expectations may be shared.

How Will You Respond?

A Confucian relationality challenges the assumption that institutions are constituted by individuals who come into relationship. Because people are already configured as part of relationships, to view a university as a responsive learning community can strengthen those relationships through shared learning experiences that emerge through cultivating collegiality. Collegiality develops through conversations that become dynamic when they engage varied perspectives. These intra-actions enrich relationships and the experiences of participation in an institution because they acknowledge the partiality of all perspectives. Because learning communities prioritize the cultivation of relationships, for universities, this implies that relational aspects, for instance, such as support for teaching, should be considered a priority. For if it is relationships that teach, as shown in Ellsworth's research, it is not enough for universities to simply expect that instructional faculty be expert teachers. They need to also share responsibility for these expectations and can do so in part by acknowledging the complexity of teaching, the effort and time required to teach-learn, and their role in supporting it.

For faculty members, engaging a Confucian relationality suggests the value of considering the quality of their professional lives. While newer instructional faculty members may need to respond to very real normative institutional pressures, for instance, to prioritize publishing, they can also make reflective choices while inquiring about the contexts of the pressures, possibly leading to innovative ways to address them, if it's not feasible in the moment then in the future when they may take on leadership and committee positions. A Confucian relationality reminds us that people's actions are always inaugural and that their experiences matter, generating the university through them. While I have focused on the university and its participants as part of the same changing field, I want to point out that engaging a Confucian relationality insinuates that all people are part of the same extensive embodied world field. Our activities create the contexts in which we live not just at work but also in our homes, neighborhoods, and nations. We share responsibility. From this perspective, what we do and how we relate always matters in ways that urgently require us to continually and reflectively foreground the question "How will I, we, respond?

Appendix A

University of Hawai'i Strategic Directions, 2015–2021

As the sole provider of public higher education in Hawai'i, the University of Hawai'i (UH) is committed to improving the social, economic and environmental well-being of current and future generations. These *University of Hawai'i Strategic Directions, 2015–2021* build upon previous work outlined in the *Strategic Outcomes and Performances Measures, 2008–2015 (http://www.hawaii.edu/ovppp/uhplan)* and will guide the university's priorities for the next three biennia to achieve the outcomes directed by the UH Board of Regents (BOR). Productivity and efficiency measures associated with these outcomes provide clear, measurable goals and the ability to effectively monitor progress over time.

Interwoven in the strategic directions are two key imperatives embraced within the BOR-approved UH mission: a commitment to being a foremost indigenous-serving institution and advancing sustainability. To those ends, the directions embrace the work and input of *Hawai'i Papa O Ke Ao* (www.hawaii.edu/offices/op/hpokeao.pdf), a plan for the university to become a model indigenous-serving institution, the Pūko'a Council, and the UH System Sustainability Task Force and their reports. In addition, the President's Task Force on Title IX and Violence Against Women Act (VAWA) has provided recommendations on how to achieve compliance with emerging mandatory federal requirements. The university stands firmly committed to advancing these directions in concert with core values of the institution: academic rigor and excellence, integrity and service, aloha and respect.

The four strategic directions outlined below describe the university's priorities for 2015–2021.

Hawai'i Graduation Initiative (HGI)

Goal: *Increase the educational capital of the state by increasing the participation and completion of students, particularly Native Hawaiians, low-income students and those from underserved regions and populations and preparing them for success in the workforce and their communities.*

An educated labor force and engaged citizenry are essential in today's global, knowledge-based economy. Across the nation, states have set ambitious goals to boost college completion rates. Hawai'i's own *55 by '25 Campaign* goal focuses on increasing the percentage of working age adults with two- or four-year degrees to 55 percent by 2025. According to the most recent data available, 43 percent of Hawai'i's working age adults hold a postsecondary degree. At the state's current rate of degree production, that percentage is expected to reach only 47 percent in 2025, resulting in a shortage of 57,000 degree holders. As the state's sole public higher education system, the University of Hawai'i is committed to doing its part to close the state's projected educational attainment gap.

The university plans to address this gap through expanded access to postsecondary education and training throughout the state and strengthened support for student success. Vigorous support for Native Hawaiians, low-income students and underrepresented and underserved populations and regions remains a top priority for the university.

HGI Action Strategy 1:

Strengthen the pipeline from K–12 to the university to improve college readiness and increase college attendance.

Tactics

- Engage K–12 students and their parents statewide early and often to promote and encourage them to prepare for college
- Emphasize pipeline and college readiness initiatives for Native Hawaiians, rural communities, low-income and under-represented groups, including through UH programs (e.g., *Na Pua No'eau*) and through partnerships with non-UH entities
- Institutionalize early college and "bridge" programs
- Align high school graduation requirements with college entrance requirements and readiness
- Expand outreach services and support to facilitate the completion of college admissions and financial aid applications
- Enhance professional development for K–12 teachers and counselors in support of student preparation for higher education
- Strengthen private school partnerships, including with Kamehameha Schools

HGI Action Strategy 2:

Implement structural improvements that promote persistence to attain a degree and timely completion.

Tactics

- Establish pathways for all degree programs, including transfer pathways from the community colleges
- Strengthen developmental education initiatives that increase preparation, improve placement methods and reduce time spent in developmental education
- Reduce gaps in college completion for Native Hawaiians, low-income and under-represented groups
- Transition from a course-based to a curriculum pathway-based registration system
- Schedule courses to facilitate timely degree completion
- Strengthen and align financial aid resources, policies and practices for increased access and completion
- Improve and stabilize student support services for Native Hawaiians, veterans, returning adults and part-time students.
- Make effective use of summer terms

HGI Action Strategy 3:

Anticipate and align curricula with community and workforce needs.

Tactics

- Obtain accurate information about workforce, employment and salaries from the Department of Labor and Industrial Relations, Economic Modeling Specialist International and other sources
- Follow up with graduates and employers regarding UH students' preparation for the workforce and community
- Engage systematically with community-based groups to inform program offerings and curricula
- Develop new programs that are responsive to community needs, e.g., STEM, data science, sustainability sciences and cybersecurity

HGI Action Strategy 4:

Solidify the foundations for UH West O'ahu, and Hawai'i CC at Palamanui, our "startup" campuses, and establish large-scale student support services for Native Hawaiians, low-income students, and the under-represented populations they serve.

Tactics

- Develop complementary academic and strategic plans that promote UH mission differentiation with applied baccalaureate degrees, offerings of regional interest and need, 2+2 and 3+1 programs with community colleges, programs for returning adults, statewide online and distance learning programs, and development of strong University Centers
- Develop financial and operational plans that support the expected rapid increases in enrollment as the communities embraces their new campuses
- Create capital development plans for facilities that support expected enrollment growth and campus academic and strategic plans
- Develop plans for utilization of non-campus land assets to generate revenue and/or reduce university costs through complementary and compatible activities such as development of a university village and alternate energy generation

Productivity and Efficiency Measures for Hawai'i Graduation Initiative (HGI)

- Number of degrees and certificates
- Graduation rates, graduation and transfer rates (IPEDS 100% and 150%, APLU-SAM)
- Enrollment to degree gap for Native Hawaiian students
- Enrollment to degree gap for Pell students
- Average unmet need of resident students
- Average total debt per undergraduate completer
- Tuition and fees as a percent of median household income

Hawai'i Innovation Initiative (HI2)

Goal: *Create more high-quality jobs and diversify Hawai'i's economy by leading the development of a $1 billion innovation, research, education and training enterprise that addresses the challenges and opportunities faced by Hawai'i and the world.*

The economy of Hawai'i is currently highly dependent on tourism and military spending. The creation of a third economic sector based on research and innovation has been identified as a community priority. As the largest research enterprise in the state, the University of Hawai'i is absolutely essential to achieving this economic diversification. The university, in partnership with the business community, plans to create innovation clusters that link fundamental scientific discovery with applied research and economic development. The university will also provide the training required for technological innovation and economic development to enable Hawai'i's citizens to lead and participate in this sector. With an emphasis on our responsibility to the community, the Hawai'i Innovation Initiative will focus on the following hubs: astronomy, ocean sciences, health sciences and wellness, data intensive sciences and engineering, agriculture and sustainability sciences including energy.

HI2 Action Strategy 1:

Sustain and advance the UH research enterprise.

Tactics
- Empower current UH faculty by identifying and removing administrative and policy barriers that impede research efficiencies and effectiveness
- Achieve financial sustainability for research under declining state investment
- Craft internal incentives and rewards for growth

HI2 Action Strategy 2:

Advance innovation and entrepreneurship within UH and the community.

Tactics
- Integrate entrepreneurship and innovation throughout the UH educational experience for students across the system with strengthened credit and non-credit education, internships, employment opportunities and extra-curricular/co-curricular activities
- Introduce new approaches to UH commercialization and technology acceleration (OTTED 2.0) such as:
  - More flexible licensing
  - Proof-of-Concept/Accelerator to nurture UH technologies
  - Greater community outreach and institutional in-reach
- Strengthen existing partnerships and form new ones to enhance high quality job creation in Hawai'i:
  - Support the Hawai'i Business Roundtable (HBR) and others in the establishment of a Hawai'i version of "CONNECT"

  - Enhance meaningful collaborations with state agencies, incubators and accelerators, national and international agencies and collaborators
- Improve communication within the State and beyond regarding the value of UH research and its critical roles in Hawai'i's economic development, job creation and in addressing the challenges and opportunities facing Hawai'i and the world

HI2 Action Strategy 3:

Invest internal resources and seek external resources for strategic infrastructure requirements and hires that leverage our location and strengths as well as address critical gaps.

- Ocean and climate sciences
- Astronomy
- Health and wellness
- Digital/creative media
- Cybersecurity
- Sustainable agriculture
- Energy
- Data intensive science and engineering initiative to support all research sectors

Productivity and Efficiency Measures for Hawai'i Innovation Initiative (HI2)

- Number of invention disclosures, patents, licenses and start-up companies and jobs
- Total extramural funds
- Number of STEM degrees

21st Century Facilities (21CF)

Goal: Eliminate the university's deferred maintenance backlog and modernize facilities and campus environments to be safe, sustainable and supportive of modern practices in teaching, learning and research.

The University of Hawai'i must eliminate the substantial deferred maintenance backlog and modernize facilities to meet 21st century needs for learning, teaching and research. This systemwide problem exists on all but the newest campus, and is particularly acute at the flagship Mānoa campus. As of June 2014, the university's deferred maintenance backlog for general funded facilities is just over $400 million for its nearly $5 billion dollar capital plant.

UH students, faculty and staff need and deserve well-maintained and up-to-date facilities that support modern teaching, learning, innovation and scholarship. Facilities and campus environments must be safe, sustainable and support 21st century higher education expectations and practices. The university's facilities must be fully digitally enabled; flexible in use; maintainable at low cost; energy, water and waste efficient; and supportive of deep collaborations with partners across the state, nation and the world.

21CF Action Strategy 1:

Adopt model policies and practices for development and management of UH buildings and campuses.

Tactics

- Develop, adopt or adapt new streamlined, accountable, efficient and effective processes and organizational structures for construction, renewal and maintenance of facilities to include all phases from planning and procurement through project management and acceptance
- Develop comprehensive multi-year capital improvement plans for construction, renewal and modernization that minimize disruption to campuses
- Develop a financial plan that responsibly leverages state and university financial capacities to execute capital improvement plans and meet ongoing operating, maintenance and renewal requirements

21CF Action Strategy 2:

Improve the sustainability and resource conservation of the built environment including facilities and grounds by reducing energy consumption, greenhouse gas production, water use and waste production.

Tactics

- Implement full energy metering and monitoring of campus buildings
- Improve energy efficiency of UH campuses and facilities
- Increase the percentage of UH energy generated from renewable sources
- Reduce costs of energy consumed on/by UH campuses
- Improve the sustainability of campus grounds
- Track, report and minimize greenhouse gas emissions
- Re-invest savings and costs avoided from energy conservation and efficiency projects into sustainability projects

21CF Action Strategy 3:

Provide safe, healthy and discrimination free environments for teaching, learning and scholarship for students, employees and visitors.

Tactics

- Collaborate as a system to understand and comply with Title IX and Violence Against Women Act (VAWA) guidance and apply best practices in promoting safety and response to incidents across the state
- Update systemwide and campus policies and guidelines to ensure compliance and promote safety and security
- Ensure availability and accessibility of high-quality confidential resources for victims

- Provide appropriate safety and awareness education for responsible officials and all students and employees
- Ensure that clear and useful information is readily available when needed

Productivity and Efficiency Measures for 21st Century Facilities (21CF)

- Deferred maintenance
- Electricity purchased per gross square foot
- Gallons of water purchased per gross square foot
- Number of criminal offenses on campus

High Performance Mission-Driven System (HPMS)

Goal: Through cost-effective, transparent and accountable practices, ensure financial viability and sustainability to ensure UH's ability to provide a diverse student body throughout Hawai'i with affordable access to a superb higher education experience in support of the institutional mission of the university, which includes commitments to being a foremost indigenous-serving university and advancing sustainability.

UH is committed to accountability, transparency and managing costs including by leveraging our unique status as a unified statewide system of public higher education. Strategies for achieving higher performance will include: providing a diverse student body with multiple entry points and educational pathways across the state; streamlined administrative and support processes; efficient utilization of facilities; exploration and implementation of new instructional approaches; and enhanced use of metrics for productivity and efficiency.

These objectives are achieved with a deep commitment to the institutional mission of UH as a foremost indigenous serving university that advances sustainability at UH and for Hawai'i.

HPMS Action Strategy 1:

Employ best practices in management, administration and operations.

Tactics

- Implement world-class business practices to advance efficiency, transparency and accountability with sound risk management
- Create effective and efficient organizational structures that leverage the advantages of centralization and decentralization to maximize efficiency and responsiveness to internal and external stakeholders
- Maximize efficient use of facilities and classrooms
- Provide professional and leadership development for UH faculty and staff
- Effectively use metrics throughout the system to advance goals and objectives
- Increase transparency in budgeting and expenditures through improved reporting practices

HPMS Action Strategy 2:

Increase opportunity and success for students and overall cost-effectiveness by leveraging academic resources and capabilities across the system.

Tactics

- Expand student-centered distance and online learning to create more educational opportunities through use of technology and by leveraging University Centers on all islands
- Develop degrees and certificates, including with distance delivery, as part of integrated pathways for students enrolled across the UH system
- Promote stronger and more comprehensive transfer and articulation policies that are student-centered, transparent and well communicated in order to support student mobility and success throughout the system.
- Promote mission differentiation through the review of academic offerings to identify unnecessary duplication and opportunities for improved collaboration
- Nurture instructional innovations and institutionalize high impact educational practices
- Standardize, centralize and collaborate on shared services to improve operating efficiencies and effectiveness in student support areas such as transcript evaluation, financial aid processing, admissions, monitoring of student progress, early alerts and intervention strategies
- Reduce cost of textbooks

HPMS Action Strategy 3:

UH aspires to be the world's foremost indigenous serving university and embraces its unique responsibilities to the indigenous people of Hawai'i and to Hawai'i's indigenous language and culture. To fulfill this responsibility, the university ensures active support for the participation of Native Hawaiians and supports vigorous programs of study and support for the Hawaiian language, history and culture. In addition to the Native Hawaiian student success agenda within the Hawai'i Graduation Initiative, the following tactics align with the thematic areas set forth in *Hawai'i Papa O Ke Ao*, UH's plan for a model indigenous serving university.

Tactics

- Prepare more Native Hawaiians to assume leadership roles within UH and the community
- Develop community and public-private partnerships locally and globally that advance UH's indigenous serving goals and share practices globally
- Advance the utilization and understanding of the Hawaiian language and culture throughout the UH System, including through articulated programs of study as well as through informal learning
- Impart a Hawaiian sense of place on campuses through landscaping, signage and the creation of Pu'u Honua

HPMS Action Strategy 4:

UH will be a global leader in the integration of sustainability in its teaching, research, operations and service. The university must embrace both indigenous practitioners and global experts to advance Hawai'i's stewardship and use of energy, food, water, land and sea for the well-being of the state and the world.

Tactics

- Integrate sustainability across the curriculum using common criteria such as an 'S' designation
- Develop academic programs in sustainability sciences collaboratively throughout the system
- Support research and service around issues of sustainability
- Incorporate sustainability practices, including those derived from indigenous wisdom, throughout the university
- Encourage alternate modes of transportation
- Support Hawai'i's local food economy

HPMS Action Strategy 5:

Diversify resource base beyond state appropriations and tuition to support public higher education in Hawai'i.

Tactics

- Execute a successful fundraising campaign across all campuses to provide additional support for students, faculty, facilities, priorities and programs
- Actively manage UH land assets to generate revenue, reduce costs and support UH's mission activities statewide
- Execute a coherent strategy for international and non-resident recruitment and enrollment, including through partnerships, that advances revenue goals as well as the educational benefits to Hawai'i students of a globally diverse student body
- Improve revenue generation associated with UH innovations and intellectual property through the Hawai'i Innovation Initiative

Productivity and Efficiency Measures for High Performance Mission-Driven System (HPMS)

- Education and related expenditures per completion
- SSH/instructional faculty FTE
- FTE Students/FTE staff (non-instructional, non-EM) ratios
- FTE Students/FTE Executive/Managerial ratios
- Number of programs with low number of graduates per year
- Classroom utilization
- Number of Native Hawaiian employees and graduate assistants (faculty/staff/administrators)

- Student enrollment in Native Hawaiian courses in language and culture (unduplicated count)
- Number of international undergraduate students enrolled in credit courses
- Number of degrees in Health, Education, and Agriculture

Appendix B

CRITERIA AND GUIDELINES FOR

FACULTY TENURE/PROMOTION APPLICATION

UNIVERSITY OF HAWAIʻI AT MĀNOA

September 2015

SUBMISSION DEADLINE TO DEPARTMENT:

FRIDAY, October 2, 2015

PLEASE SUBMIT AN ORIGINAL PLUS SEVEN (7) COPIES

NOTE:

ALL REFERENCES ARE TO THE *2015-2017 UHPA/UH AGREEMENT*

TABLE OF CONTENTS

I. Instructions for Tenure Applicants ... 3

II. Instructions for Promotion Applicants ... 4-5

III. Joint Appointments and Split Appointments ... 5

IV. Criteria for Tenure: General Comments ... 5-6

A. For Instructional Faculty ... 6-7

B. For Research Faculty ... 7-8

C. For Specialist and Librarian Faculty ... 8-9

D. For Extension Agent Faculty ... 9

V. Criteria for Promotion: General Comments ... 9-10

A. For Instructional Faculty ... 10-11
(including Law and Clinical Medicine)

B. For Research Faculty ... 11-12

C. For Specialist Faculty ... 12-13

D. For Librarian Faculty ... 13-14

E. For Extension Agent Faculty ... 14-15

VI. The Tenure/Promotion Review Process ... 15-16

VII. Guidelines for Preparing the Application ... 16-22

Appendix A: Executive Policy - Classification of Faculty (E5.221)

Appendix B: Supplemental Guidelines

Appendix C: Tenure/Promotion Application Form

I. Instructions for Tenure Applicants

The 2015-2017 *Agreement between the University of Hawai'i Professional Assembly and the Board of Regents of the University of Hawai'i* (*Agreement*) requires that all eligible faculty must apply for tenure by their final year of probationary service according to a timetable established and published by the University. Probationary service is defined in Article XII, Section C of the *Agreement*. Failure to apply results automatically in the issuance of a terminal year contract. If you have doubts about which is your final year of probation, check your most recent PNF (Payroll Notification Form). Assistance in obtaining this information will be provided by your Department Chair or comparable unit head.

The information submitted by you in your tenure application, and that appended to your application by its reviewers, are the principal bases on which your case for tenure will be assessed. It is your responsibility to see that all pertinent information has been included in your application. Guidelines for preparing the application are provided in Section VII below.

The Available Options. Article XII of the *Agreement* defines when you should normally apply for tenure. There are several options available to you:

A. If you are in your final year of probationary service, or in your terminal year of service but have a written agreement that the University will accept your application during the 2015-2016 academic year, you must elect whether or not to apply.

1. After familiarizing yourself with the criteria contained in Section IV below, and any additional college and/or departmental criteria appropriate to your application, you may proceed by signing the statements in Part II on p. 2.2 of the application form. **If your Department Personnel Committee Procedures for Tenure, Promotion and Contract Renewal have been revised, you may elect to have your tenure application reviewed under the procedures in effect for 2012-2013.** Be sure to complete the application by **October 2, 2015** and submit it to your Department Chair or comparable unit head. To assist you, the Department Chair is required to be available for consultation but is neither required nor permitted to prepare the application for you. Procedures for review of your application are outlined in Section VI below. You should also be familiar with Article XII, "Tenure and Service" of the *2015 – 2017 UHPA/UH Agreement*.

2. You may elect not to apply, in which case you should sign the form for this purpose by **October 2, 2015.** The form is available in your Dean's/Director's office. **IMPORTANT**: If you make this choice, your contract for 2015-2016 will be your last probationary year and you will receive a terminal year contract commencing August 1, 2016 and your appointment with the University will terminate on **July 31, 2017** unless you resign before that date.

B. You may apply for tenure before your final year of probationary service. If you wish to do so, however, you must submit a signed letter requesting that the University reduce your normal probationary period. This letter must contain a statement that you understand that, in the event the request is approved, the **2015-2016** academic year will become your final year of probationary service and that a negative decision on your application for tenure will result in a terminal year's contract for **2016-2017**. Your request should be submitted to your Department Chair and will be forwarded for appropriate review and action by your Dean/Director. You may attach a copy of the request to your application form and submit the application according to the procedures outlined in Section VI below. However, the University will take no action on your application for tenure until a decision is made on your request for a reduction in your probationary period.

For Instructional (including Law and Medicine) and Research Faculty (Rank 3):
If your initial appointment was at Rank 3 on or after July 1, 1977, you will be promoted to Associate rank if you are awarded tenure. This means you will be evaluated for promotion to Rank 4 as well as for tenure at Rank 4.

For All Specialist, Librarian, and Agent Faculty and Instructional and Research Faculty (Rank 4):
All Specialist, Librarian, Agent faculty members and Instructional and Research faculty members at Rank 4 may use a single application to apply for: 1) tenure only at the current rank, and 2) tenure and promotion **(please note, the second action requires a separate vote for tenure and a separate vote for promotion by each level of review)**. If the recommendation for promotion is negative, but the recommendation for tenure is positive, your tenure-only application will be forwarded to the Board of Regents for positive action.

II. Instructions for Promotion Applicants

The *Agreement* between the University of Hawai'i Professional Assembly and the University of Hawai'i provides that any faculty member may apply for promotion in any year in accordance with the guidelines set forth below.

The information submitted by you in your promotion application, and that appended to your application by its reviewers, are the principal bases on which your case for promotion will be assessed. **If your Department Personnel Committee Procedures for Tenure, Promotion and Contract Renewal have been revised, you may elect to have your promotion application reviewed under the procedures in effect for 2012 - 2013.** It is your responsibility to see that relevant supportive information has been included in the application. Guidelines for preparing the application are given in Section VII below.

A. You may apply for promotion in any year you meet the minimum qualifications for the rank to which you seek promotion. If you do not meet the minimum qualifications, you may still apply, but in this case, you must request a waiver of one or more of the specified minimum qualifications. For the 2015-2016 review cycle, the deadline for all requests for waivers of minimum qualifications is **August 26, 2015.** The authority to approve waivers of minimal education requirements has been retained by the Chancellor; the authority to approve waivers of time in rank has been delegated to the Deans/Directors. By this date all requests recommended by the Department Chair and Dean/Director must be sent to the Mānoa Chancellor's Office, Hawai'i Hall 209.

B. You may apply for promotion in the same year that you apply for tenure, provided that you meet the requirements outlined above.

III. Joint Appointments and Split Appointments

If you are affiliated with and receive payment for your services from more than one unit, such as two departments or a department and a research institute, you have at least two responsibilities and must, in general, be assessed on your performance in these responsibilities. Page 1.1 of the application defines joint appointments and split appointments (only in the College of Tropical Agriculture and Human Resources). If you have either a joint or split appointment, make sure that page 1.1 is completed so that the reviewing bodies have an appreciation of your multiple responsibilities and give proper consideration to them.

If you have a joint appointment, then you must prepare duplicate applications and assure that each of the units or departments has a copy for review. You should give one copy of the application to the Department Chair, or equivalent, of your primary unit. If you have a joint appointment between two departments in the same College or School, then you should consult with the Dean/Director of the College or School involved and get a signed statement designating the primary unit without ambiguity. Correspondingly, if your appointment is between departments or organizations not in the same College, you should consult the Mānoa Chancellor's Office (Dr. Beverly A. McCreary, 956-9429 or bmccrear@hawaii.edu).

A second copy of your application should go to the secondary unit head at the same time. Each department or unit will then forward copies of your application through its chain of review and the results will be consolidated by the Dean/Director of the primary unit prior to submission to the Tenure and Promotion Review Committee.

If you have an appointment in which one component is administration, then your application will be based only on your non-administrative activities. Due consideration will be given by reviewing bodies to the reduced time you have or have had for your professional activities, but your administrative duties and skills are not a substitute for these professional activities in your application for tenure/promotion.

IV. Criteria for Tenure: General Comments

Article XII.G.1 of the *Agreement* provides that a faculty member applying for tenure in the final year of the normal probationary period shall have the option of being considered under the criteria contained in the *Criteria and Guidelines* distributed in the year of application or those contained in the *Criteria and Guidelines* distributed two years earlier. The campus criteria contained in these 2015-2016 *Criteria and Guidelines* are similar to those distributed for 2012-2013. There are changes to the dossier based on several faculty senate resolutions designed to simplify the tenure and promotion application. Please see Section VII.C for specific changes. Additionally, there are four other changes to the Criteria and Guidelines that took effect 2012-2013, one reflects a change in the *2015-2017 Agreement* (see page 15) and the other three provide clarification. The first provides language clarifying criteria for promotion to associate professor and researcher (pages 10-12); the second recommends articulation of authorship convention within the faculty member's field (pages 7-8 & 10); the third further delineates the conflict of interest requirements for the external evaluators (page 19-21). You should determine with your Department Chair if departmental and/or college criteria have changed. If such criteria have changed, you would have the option of using the criteria distributed two years ago.

The general reasons for granting tenure are that the University has concluded that you are and will continue to be a productive and valuable member of your department, school/college, and campus, that your pattern of continuing professional growth is positive, and that the University anticipates a long-term need for your professional specialty and services. This is a matter of judgment, and there may be honest differences of opinion based on fair and thorough consideration of the evidence.

Because the granting of tenure involves a long-term commitment of the University's resources, the review process is essentially conservative. Unless there is a clear case for tenure, the practice is not to recommend tenure. The Board of Regents must approve all tenure recommendations.

In assessing the evidence for tenure, reviewers will assign the greatest weight to accomplishments and performance during the period since your initial hire at the University of Hawai'i and your pattern and rate of professional growth. In order to be awarded tenure in a given rank, a faculty member must meet the minimum qualifications, including the requirements for education and experience, in addition to any criteria which may be established by the University for that rank. If you do not meet the minimum qualifications, as specified in Executive Policy – Classification of Faculty, E5.221 (see Appendix A), you may still apply, but in this case, you must request a waiver of one or more of the specified minimum qualifications. For the 2015-2016 review cycle, the deadline for all requests for waivers of minimum qualifications is **August 26, 2015**. By this date all requests recommended by the Department Chair and Dean/Director must be sent to the Mānoa Chancellor's Office (attention: Dr. Beverly A. McCreary, Hawai'i Hall 209).

A. Tenure Criteria for Instructional Faculty (including Law and Clinical Medicine)

1. The University must have a present and long-term need for a faculty member with the particular combination of qualifications, expertise, and abilities possessed by the applicant for tenure.

2. The faculty member must have demonstrated a high level of competence as a teacher during the probationary period. In the rank of Assistant Professor, there should be evidence of increasing professional accomplishment as a teacher. For the Associate and full Professor ranks, there should be evidence of a mature level of performance and the versatility to contribute to all levels of the department's instructional program. In all cases, the evidence should include summaries of student evaluations, how your classes contribute to programmatic and institutional learning outcomes, or other objective assessments of a significant sample of the courses taught during the probationary period.

3. The faculty member must have demonstrated a level of scholarly achievement appropriate to the rank at which tenure is sought in comparison with peers active in the same discipline. The comparison peer group consists not only of departmental colleagues but also of the whole of the appropriate community of scholars active at major research universities. For the Assistant Professor seeking tenure as an Associate Professor, the applicant should be well on the way to becoming an established scholar in his or her discipline. The Associate Professor seeking tenure should be an established scholar whose scholarly contributions and recognition during the probationary period reflect this stature. The full Professor must be among the leaders in the scholarly discipline. In general, publication in a form that involves review by independent referees is of first importance in establishing scholarly achievement. Other means by which scholarly and creative contributions to the discipline are reviewed, utilized and evaluated by peers outside the University are also important. A more detailed listing of the criteria that will be used at each rank may be found in the promotion criteria (Part V) and the Executive Policy – Classification of Faculty, E5.221 (Appendix A).

   Collaborative research and joint and shared publications may be the norm in some fields or disciplines. In such cases, departments should include a discussion of authorship conventions - including the significance of authorship order - in their policies and procedures used for tenure and promotion. If not, applicants in such fields or disciplines should provide Department Personnel Committees and Department Chairs with documentation that such is the norm to aid the review process. The significance of such work within the discipline or field should be described to assist the review. Both 1) the proportion of time among given tasks and functions in research and/or writing, and 2) the total proportion of time and effort in the research or publication should be described to aid the review process. Co-author or researcher concurrence or an independent report on such contributions is needed to aid in review.

4. The faculty member should have participated in the academic affairs of the University, such as through service on appropriate faculty committees, and have shown a willingness to use professional competence in the service of the profession and the general community.

B. Tenure Criteria for Research Faculty

1. The University must have a present and long-term need for a faculty member with the particular combination of qualifications, expertise, and abilities possessed by the applicant for tenure.

2. The faculty member must have demonstrated a level of research achievement and productivity appropriate to the rank at which tenure is sought in comparison with peers active in the same field. The comparison peer group consists not only of local colleagues but also of the whole of the appropriate research community active at major research centers. For the Assistant Researcher seeking tenure as an Associate Researcher, the faculty member should be well on the way to becoming an established

researcher in his or her field. The Associate Researcher seeking tenure should be an established researcher whose productivity during the probationary period reflects this stature. The full Researcher must be among the leaders in the research field. In general, publication of research results in a form that involves review by independent referees is of first importance in establishing research competence and productivity. A more detailed listing of the criteria that will be used at each rank may be found in the promotion criteria (Part V) and the Executive Policy – Classification of Faculty, E5.221 (Appendix A).

Collaborative research and joint and shared publications may be the norm in some fields or disciplines. In such cases, departments should include a discussion of authorship conventions - including the significance of authorship order - in their policies and procedures used for tenure and promotion. If not, applicants in such fields or disciplines should provide Department Personnel Committees and Department Chairs with documentation that such is the norm to aid the review process. The significance of such work within the discipline or field should be described to assist the review. Both 1) the proportion of time among given tasks and functions in research and/or writing, and 2) the total proportion of time and effort in the research or publication should be described to aid the review process. Co-author or researcher concurrence or an independent report on such contributions is needed to aid in review.

3. The faculty member should have participated in the academic affairs of the University, such as through service on appropriate faculty committees, and have shown a willingness to use professional competence in the service of the profession and the general community.

C. Tenure Criteria for Specialist and Librarian Faculty

1. The University must have a present and long-term need for a faculty member with the particular combination of qualifications, expertise, and abilities possessed by the applicant for tenure.

2. The faculty member must have demonstrated a level of professional achievement and productivity in the field of specialization appropriate to the rank at which tenure is sought in comparison with peers active in the same field. The comparison peer group consists not only of local colleagues but also of the whole of the appropriate professional community active at major institutions of higher education. At the ranks of Junior and Assistant Specialist and Librarian II and III, the applicant should demonstrate clear evidence of professional growth in the specialty. The Associate Specialist and Librarian IV seeking tenure should be an established contributor to the standards, techniques, and methodology of the profession. The full Specialist and Librarian V must show evidence of interaction with the broader professional community beyond the University of Hawaiʻi and have made significant contributions to the standards, techniques, and methodology of the profession. For the senior ranks, there should be evidence of a high level of professional maturity and the capacity to assume responsibilities calling for the extensive exercise of independent judgment. A

more detailed listing of the criteria that will be used at each rank may be found in the promotion criteria (Part V) and the statement of minimum qualifications (Appendix A).

3. The faculty member should have participated in the academic affairs of the University, such as through service on appropriate faculty committees, have shown a willingness to use professional competence in the service of the profession and the general community, and have demonstrated the ability to work effectively with faculty, staff, and administrators as necessary.

D. Tenure Criteria for Extension Agent Faculty

1. The University must have a present and long-term need for a faculty member with the particular combination of qualifications, expertise, and abilities possessed by the applicant for tenure.

2. The faculty member must have demonstrated a level of professional achievement and productivity in extension service appropriate to the rank at which tenure is sought in comparison with peers active in extension. The comparison peer group consists not only of local colleagues but also of the whole of the community of extension professionals active in major extension service programs nationwide. At the ranks of Junior and Assistant Extension Agent, the applicant should demonstrate clear evidence of professional growth. The Associate Extension Agent seeking tenure should provide evidence of interaction with the nationwide extension profession and of contributions to extension as a profession. The full Extension Agent should provide evidence of significant interaction with the nationwide extension profession and of substantial contributions to extension as a profession. A more detailed listing of the criteria that will be used at each rank may be found in the promotion criteria (Part V) and the Executive Policy – Classification of Faculty, E5.221 (Appendix A).

3. The faculty member should have participated in the academic affairs of the University, such as through service on appropriate faculty committees, and have shown a willingness to use professional competence in the service of the profession and the general community. The faculty member should have rendered other services to the community as appropriate and have shown an ability to work effectively in an integrated extension program.

V. Criteria for Promotion: General Comments

In order to be considered for promotion, an applicant must meet the minimum qualifications established by the Board of Regents for the rank to which promotion is sought. The applicant must also meet additional criteria which may be established by the department/unit, school/college and campus. The mere satisfaction of minimum qualifications does not guarantee promotion, nor is promotion granted to recognize "satisfactory" service on the part of a faculty member. Instead, promotion represents important transitions in the faculty member's professional growth, development, and status. In general, competent or even superior performance in one area of activity or responsibility is not sufficient to justify promotion. It is expected that an applicant will demonstrate the level of academic achievement and reputation that is commensurate with the rank sought as found at major research universities in the United States. The exact stage of a faculty member's career at which promotion is merited is a matter of judgment, and there may be honest differences of opinion based on fair and thorough consideration of the evidence.

Collaborative research and joint and shared publications may be the norm in some fields or disciplines. In such cases, departments should include a discussion of authorship conventions - including the significance of authorship order - in their policies and procedures used for tenure and promotion. If not, applicants in such fields or disciplines should provide Department Personnel Committees and Department Chairs with documentation that such is the norm to aid the review process. The significance of such work within the discipline or field should be described to assist the review. Both 1) the proportion of time among given tasks and functions in research and/or writing, and 2) the total proportion of time and effort in the research or publication should be described to aid the review process. Co-author or researcher concurrence or an independent report on such contributions is needed to aid in review.

The granting of promotion has implications for the University's standards and its standing in the academic community. Therefore, the review process is essentially conservative. Unless there is a clear case for promotion, the practice is not to recommend promotion to the Board of Regents. In the case of promotion to Rank 3, the final decision has been delegated to the President by the Board of Regents.

In assessing the evidence for promotion, reviewers will assign the greatest weight to accomplishments and performance during the period since the last promotion, or since initial hire at the University of Hawai'i if you have not been previously promoted during your service here.

A. Promotion Criteria for Instructional Faculty (including Law and Clinical Medicine)

1. Promotion to Assistant Professor. An earned doctorate in the relevant field or other appropriate terminal degree is required. The faculty member must provide evidence of competence and increasing professional maturity as a teacher. This evidence should include summaries of student evaluations, how your classes contribute to programmatic and institutional learning outcomes, or other objective assessments of a significant sample of the courses taught while in the rank of Instructor. There must be evidence of scholarly research and contribution to scholarship or other related creative activity which shows scholarly ability, accomplishment and promise.

2. Promotion to Associate Professor. The faculty member must provide evidence of a mature level of performance as a teacher and the versatility to contribute to all levels of the department's instructional program. This evidence should include summaries of student evaluations, how your classes contribute to programmatic and institutional learning outcomes, or other objective assessments of a significant sample of the courses taught while in the rank of Assistant Professor. The Assistant Professor seeking promotion to Associate Professor should be well on the way to becoming an established

scholar in his or her discipline. The comparison peer group consists not only of departmental colleagues, but the whole of the community of scholars active at major research universities. In general, publications and other creative activities of a type that permit review by independent referees are of first importance in establishing scholarly achievement. Other means by which scholarly and creative contribution to the discipline are reviewed, utilized and evaluated by peers outside the University are also important. The faculty member should have participated in the academic affairs of the University, such as through service on appropriate faculty committees and should have shown a willingness to use professional competence in the service of the profession and the general community.

3. Promotion to Professor. The faculty member must provide evidence of a mature level of performance and achievement as a teacher and the versatility to contribute to all levels of the department's instructional program. This evidence should include summaries of student evaluations, how your classes contribute to programmatic and institutional learning outcomes, or other objective assessments of a significant sample of the courses taught while in the rank of Associate Professor. The significance and distinction of the scholarly achievement should clearly place the faculty member at the forefront of the discipline or field. In general, publication in the major journals and presses in the field is of first importance in establishing this level of scholarly achievement. Funded research grants and other means by which scholarly and creative contribution to the discipline are reviewed, utilized and evaluated by peers outside the University are also important. The faculty member should be a leader in the academic affairs of the University, should have shown a willingness to use professional competence in the service of the profession and the general community, and should have shown significant accomplishment in the profession and the appropriate discipline.

B. Promotion Criteria for Research Faculty

1. Promotion to Assistant Researcher. An earned doctorate in the relevant field or other appropriate terminal degree is required. The faculty member must provide evidence of competence and increasing professional maturity in the performance of professional and scientific work in the field of research indicated by the title of the class. There must be evidence of ability and promise in independent professional and scientific research documented by independent research activities, publications and contributions to scholarship.

2. Promotion to Associate Researcher. The faculty member seeking promotion to Associate Researcher should be well on the way to becoming an established scholar in his or her discipline in comparison with peers active in the same area of research. The comparison peer group consists not only of departmental colleagues, but the whole of the community of scholars active at major research centers. Publication in a form that involves review by independent referees is of first importance in establishing research achievement. Other means by which scholarly and creative research contributions to the discipline are reviewed, utilized and evaluated by peers outside the University are also important. The faculty member must provide evidence of independent ability to

plan and organize funded research activities, including effective interactions with students and assistants as appropriate. The faculty member should have participated in the academic affairs of the University, such as through service on appropriate faculty committees, and have shown a willingness to use professional competence in the service of the profession and the general community.

3. Promotion to Researcher. The faculty member must demonstrate a level of research achievement and productivity which establishes stature among the leaders in the relevant research field or sub-field. This leadership position is not only with respect to departmental colleagues, but the international community of scholars active at major research centers. Publications and funded research grants that involve review by independent referees are of first importance in establishing research achievement. Other means by which research contributions to the discipline are reviewed, utilized and evaluated by peers outside the University are also important. The faculty member should have participated in the academic affairs of the University, such as through service on appropriate faculty committees, and have shown a willingness to use professional competence in the service of the profession and the general community.

C. Promotion Criteria for Specialist Faculty

1. Promotion to Assistant Specialist. The faculty member must provide evidence of competence, productivity and increasing professional achievement and maturity in the performance of assigned duties. Training represented by a Master's degree and 30 credits of graduate study beyond the Master's from a college or university of recognized standing with major work in a field closely related to the position involved is required. There should be evidence of ability to perform duties calling for independent professional judgment in the field of specialization, evidence of productivity and an indication of the capacity to supervise clerical help and at least three years previous experience at the next lower rank or equivalent.

2. Promotion to Associate Specialist. The faculty member must provide evidence of increasing professional maturity in the professional specialization and in the performance of duties in the rank of Assistant Specialist, including evidence of the ability to exercise independent professional judgment competently in the field of specialization. Training represented by a doctorate from a college or university of recognized standing with major course work and dissertation in a relevant field is required. At least four years of experience in the appropriate specialty in the next lower rank or equivalent are required. The faculty member must demonstrate the ability to plan and organize assigned activities and to supervise the work of assistants, if appropriate. The faculty member must demonstrate a level of professional achievement which reflects his or her stature as a contributor to the standards, techniques and methodology of the profession in comparison with peers active in the same field. The comparison peer group consists not only of local colleagues but the whole of the professional community active at major institutions of higher education. In general, contributions of such a nature as to permit critical review and facilitate use by other professionals are of first importance in establishing professional achievement. There

must be evidence of interaction with the broader professional community beyond the University of Hawai'i.

3. Promotion to Specialist. The faculty member must provide evidence of increasing productivity and professional maturity in the performance of duties in the rank of Associate Specialist, including evidence of the competent exercise of independent professional judgment in the field of specialization. Training represented by a doctorate from a college or university of recognized standing with major course work and dissertation in a relevant field is required. At least four years of experience in the appropriate specialty in the next lower rank or equivalent are required. The faculty member must provide evidence of successful planning and organization of assigned activities, including the supervision of assistants, if appropriate. The faculty member must demonstrate a level of professional achievement which establishes his or her stature as a substantial contributor to the standards, techniques and methodology of the profession. This stature is not only with respect to local colleagues, but the whole of the professional community active at major institutions of higher education. In general, contributions of such a nature as to permit critical review and facilitate use by other professionals are of first importance in establishing professional achievement. There must also be evidence of significant interaction and leadership with the broader professional community beyond the University.

D. Promotion Criteria for Librarian Faculty

1. Promotion to Librarian III. The Librarian must provide evidence of competence, productivity and increasing professional achievement and maturity in the performance of assigned duties. Training represented by a Master's degree in Library or Information Science and in addition to the Master's degree, 24 post-baccalaureate credits of academic study, and at least three years of appropriate experience is required. There should be evidence of ability to perform duties calling for independent judgment as well as evidence of initiative, analytical and problem-solving ability and familiarity with departmental functions, library-wide goals and University programs. The Librarian should demonstrate awareness of current professional literature and development.

2. Promotion to Librarian IV. The Librarian must provide evidence of increasing professional maturity in the professional specialization and in the performance of duties in the rank of Librarian III, including evidence of the ability to exercise independent professional judgment. Training represented by two Master's degrees is required: one in Library or Information Science, and one in a specialized subject area. Seven years of appropriate experience or four years in the rank of Librarian III are also required. The Librarian should show ability to anticipate and recommend changes in accordance with the changing needs of the Library and University as a whole and should also exhibit independence and creativity in the provision of service and/or program development or evaluation. The Librarian should demonstrate participation in academic or professional activities within the University and beyond. If managerial or supervisory responsibilities are an aspect of the Librarian's assigned position or function, there should be demonstration of maturing competence in this area.

3. Promotion to Librarian V. The Librarian must provide evidence of increasing productivity and professional maturity in the performance of duties in the rank of Librarian IV including evidence of the competent exercise of independent professional judgment. Training represented by two Master's degrees is required: one in Library or Information Science and one in a specialized subject area. The Librarian also must have 12 years of appropriate experience or four years in the rank of Librarian IV. The Librarian must demonstrate academic and professional leadership, functioning in responsible positions in academic and professional affairs. The comparison group consists not only of local colleagues, but the whole of the professional community active at major institutions of higher education. Leadership can be at the state or national level and may be demonstrated by contributions to the field through activities such as publication, committee work, presentation of papers, etc. In general, contributions should be of such a nature as to permit critical assessment and to facilitate use by the population the Library serves. If supervisory or managerial responsibilities are an aspect of the Librarian's assigned position or function, there should be demonstration of mature competence and effectiveness in this area.

E. Promotion Criteria for Extension Agent Faculty

1. Promotion to Assistant Extension Agent. A Master's degree from a college or university of recognized standing, with major work in agriculture, home economics, marine science, resource management or a related field, as appropriate, or, in addition to the Bachelor's degree, 30 credits of post-baccalaureate academic work in a field appropriate to the individual's job is normally required. Three years of successful experience in Cooperative Extension work, Sea Grant Extension work, or equivalent in closely related fields are required. The faculty member must provide evidence of competence, productivity and increasing professional maturity in the performance of assigned extension activities. In addition, there should be evidence of ability to perform duties calling for independent professional judgment, and of the capacity to assume responsibility for the development of an extension program. The faculty member must have shown an ability to work effectively with other agents in an integrated extension system.

2. Promotion to Associate Extension Agent. A Master's degree from a college or university of recognized standing in agriculture, home economics, marine science, resource management or a related field, whichever is appropriate; in addition to the Master's, 15 credit hours of post-baccalaureate academic work in an appropriate field; at least four years experience as an Extension faculty member or its equivalent in related fields in the next lower rank is required. The faculty member must provide evidence of increasing productivity and professional maturity in the performance of extension activities in the rank of Assistant Extension Agent. There must be evidence of a high level of leadership ability, including the capacity to develop leadership in others. The faculty member must demonstrate the successful administration of a well-organized extension program and the capacity to work effectively with agents in other jurisdictions and with related public agencies. There must be evidence of interaction

with the profession and of contributions to the appropriate subject matter discipline or to extension as a profession.

3. Promotion to Extension Agent. A Master's degree from a college or university of recognized standing with major work in agriculture, home economics, marine science, resource management or a related field, whichever is appropriate; in addition to the Master's degree, 30 credit hours of post-baccalaureate academic work beyond the Master's degree in an appropriate field; and at least four years of experience as an Extension faculty member or similar and equivalent work in the next lower rank are required. The faculty member must provide evidence of continued professional growth as an Associate Extension Agent. There must be evidence of exceptional leadership ability and success in a position with significant program or administrative responsibilities covering major subject areas or large geographic areas. The faculty member must provide evidence of ability to perceive and implement broad educational programs relevant to community needs, and the capacity to work harmoniously with agents in other jurisdictions and with other governmental agencies in an integrated extension program. There must be evidence of significant interaction and leadership with the nationwide extension profession, and of substantial contributions to the appropriate subject matter discipline or to extension as a profession.

VI. The Tenure/Promotion Review Process

The procedures for review of your application for tenure/promotion are given in detail in Article XII, and Article XIV of the *2015-2017 UHPA/UH Agreement*. In summary, you should complete your application in accordance with the guidelines in Section VII as described below and submit it by **October 2, 2015.**

A. The application for tenure/promotion must be submitted to the Department Chair. He/she and the Department Personnel Committee will make written assessments of your strengths and weaknesses, append recommendations if they so desire, and transmit the dossier to the Dean/Director.

B. The Dean/Director will make his or her independent assessment and recommendation and transmit the dossier to a Tenure and Promotion Review Committee (TPRC) which has been appointed to review your case.

C. The TPRC "shall review the dossier and make a recommendation, then return it to the Dean/Director for consideration and transmission to the Chancellor." [1]

D. Faculty Members will be notified of the TPRC's recommendation after it has been received by the Mānoa Chancellor's Office.

[1] From *2015-2017 Agreement between the University of Hawai'i Professional Assembly and the Board of Regents of the University of Hawai'i*, Article XII.G.2.F.

E. If, after the TPRC review, the dossier contains only positive recommendations, the dossier will be transmitted to the Mānoa Chancellor for review. If the Chancellor's assessment is positive, a recommendation for tenure/promotion will be made to the President and to the Board of Regents.

F. If, after the TPRC review, the dossier contains a negative recommendation, you will be permitted to examine the dossier and to submit written comments and additional materials. If the negative recommendation occurred at the TPRC, the dossier will be returned to the same TPRC for a second review. The dossier will then be forwarded to the Mānoa Chancellor who will make an independent assessment of the application, reviewing all materials, including any additional materials that may have been submitted in accordance with the procedure described. If the negative review did not occur at the TPRC, then the additional materials will be forwarded directly to the Mānoa Chancellor. The Mānoa Chancellor will then decide to either recommend tenure/promotion or deny tenure/promotion. If the latter, you will be so notified and permitted to examine the dossier and meet with the Mānoa Chancellor, if you desire.

G. If you are denied tenure, the options available to you are explained in Article XII.H of the *2015-2017 UHPA/UH Agreement*.

H. If you are denied promotion, under certain circumstances, as specified in Article XIV.D of the *2015-2017 UHPA/UH Agreement*, you may request a further review.

VII. Guidelines for Preparing the Application

The tenure/promotion application is the means by which you convince those involved in the review process of your achievements and ability. Therefore, you should document your accomplishments with as much objective evidence as possible. The sections below indicate some of the kinds of evidence that are of particular value to the reviewers. If you include letters of support from colleagues, students, or others as part of your application, it is wise to select those that evaluate specific contributions or achievements rather than those which simply express support for your case. The reviewers of your application are charged with making an independent assessment of your record, and specific information and evaluation by peers is more useful for this purpose than general statements or opinions. Inclusion of testimonials that do not provide specific substantive support may detract from the effectiveness of your presentation.

You are required to complete Parts I, II, III and IV of the application form. If you have questions about Parts I, II or III, your Department Chair will be able to assist you. Some guidelines for completing Part IV are as follows:

A. Pagination. Be sure that every page of material you submit has a page number, starting with 4.2 and proceeding sequentially. **Please type or use labels to put your legal on the upper right hand corner of each page you submit (Last, First M.I.)**. To guard against the loss of any material, enter the number of the last page submitted in the appropriate space on page 4.1 of the application.

B. Language. The Constitution of the State of Hawai'i identifies two official languages in the State, English and Hawaiian (Ōlelo Hawai'i). Please indicate the language in which you are submitting your dossier on page 2.1.

C. Statement of endeavors. (Recommended length: 1-9 pages, 12 point) You are required to give a well-documented and clear report of your teaching, research and service activities and achievements since the last promotion or since initial hire, whichever is appropriate. This report should be more than a list of activities. Where appropriate, an analysis of the quality and value of your research, a statement of your instructional philosophy and a statement about the impact of your professional service will be expected. You can provide a statement about the unique aspects and special significance of your accomplishments and future plans in teaching, research and/or service. Discussions of departmental/University service and community service are in Sections D.4 and D.6 below. Please read these in order to fully understand the weight given to these activities in comparison with research and teaching.

D. Supporting materials. Appropriate supporting materials depend on your faculty classification. Faculty in the Instructional classification must submit documented evidence of teaching accomplishments, as suggested in Section D.1, "Teaching," outlined below.

For both Instructional and Research faculty, a bibliography or other objective record of scholarly work is essential. Section D.2, "Bibliography," below gives the format you should use in compiling your bibliography. Faculty in fields such as the fine arts may substitute a list of shows, performances, etc., in lieu of a bibliography. Professional reviews of your work by peers not associated with University of Hawai'i at Mānoa (UH Mānoa) are important and should be included if available.

1. Teaching. If you are in the Instructional classification, you must have documented evidence of your teaching ability and of your contributions to the curriculum.

   a) Teaching ability is usually documented by means of teaching evaluations. These should reflect a representative sample of all of the courses you have taught in recent years. You should include coverage of all the recent courses you have taught which used the standard evaluation procedures adopted by your department, college or school. Special recognition by awards or citations for excellence in teaching should be recorded. Evidence of progress over the years in the scope, depth and effectiveness of your teaching may be helpful to reviewers in evaluating your maturity as an instructor.

   b) Contributions to the curriculum may be documented by materials from courses you have helped to create or modify; materials from classes you have taught as writing intensive, as part of the honors program, or to serve special needs; and evidence of innovations in teaching or teacher training, including the development of textbooks and innovation in the publication of educational materials (e.g., electronic publication, CD ROMs, etc).

2. Bibliography. Your bibliography provides an invaluable objective record of your scholarly activity. The format which should be used is as follows:

   a) Separate your published works, conference presentations and manuscripts into appropriate groupings. The following categories may be adapted to your discipline. Additional categories may be created as necessary.

      - Books of original scholarship–author/co-author
      - Chapters in books
      - Edited volumes
      - Textbooks
      - Articles in international or national refereed journals
      - Articles in other periodicals
      - Unpublished work, accepted for publication (with documentation: submitted, conditionally accepted, in press, etc.)
      - Internal reports and other unpublished work
      - Invited conference presentations
      - Refereed conference contributions
      - Departmental seminars
      - Published abstracts
      - Other scholarly products (such as major software, video or film)
      - Grants (indicate funded, approved but not funded, submitted but not approved, etc.)

   b) Within each category, list your works in order of publication or completion, with the most recent works first. Make a clear division between work published or completed since your last promotion (or initial hire if you have not previously been promoted at the University of Hawai'i) and earlier work.

   c) For each item, give complete citation. An entry for a published article, for example, should include all the authors as listed in order by the journal, complete title, volume, year and pagination.

   d) Make a clear distinction between works for which you were an author and those for which you were an editor.

   e) For all jointly authored and edited works, you must indicate your estimate of the extent of your contributions.

   f) Faculty in disciplines such as the fine arts, music, drama, etc., should provide a complete listing of exhibitions, performances or other appropriate presentations of their creative work. A clear division should be made between presentations since your last promotion (or initial hire if you have not previously been promoted here) and earlier ones. Complete information as to the nature of each presentation, place, dates, etc., should be provided.

3. Peer evaluations of contributions. You should include all relevant external reviews of your published work or creative productions. These include published reviews, grant reviewers' comments, letters to the editor, readers' comments of manuscripts submitted for publication and unsolicited letters from peers in response to publication of your work.

4. University service. Your statement concerning service on departmental committees or special projects should be included in the narrative. Academic service activities may include (but are not limited to): participation in faculty governance by membership in standing and ad hoc organizations, committees and task forces at the college/school and/or university levels, activities contributing to the improvement of teacher education, etc.

5. Professional service. You should include activities related to service to your discipline and professional organizations. Professional service activities may include (but are not limited to): serving as an officer in a professional organization, editing a professional publication, organizing conferences/workshops, creating discipline-related instructional models and resource materials for use in K-12 education, etc.

6. Community service. Public service that is related to your profession is considered a positive factor in reviewing faculty for promotion. Still, for Instructional and Research faculty, the lack of professional public service accomplishments (unlike University service) is not detrimental to advancement–a recognition that the opportunity for such work in some fields is quite limited. Public service is not a substitute for research and teaching achievements. It is complementary to these other types of activities for Instructional and Research faculty. Public service (as other faculty achievements) should be documented, including an assessment of quality and impact. In sum, public service is a generally marginal but sometimes significant factor in the advancement of UH Mānoa faculty. While not weighted equally with research and teaching, meritorious public service activities–if linked closely to the other two areas–can have a favorable impact on tenure and promotion decisions.

E. Solicitation of external evaluations by Department Chair, Chair of Department Personnel Committee, or Dean/Director. Departments should seek external evaluations of each applicant's work. An evaluator should be at, or above the rank aspired to by the applicant. External evaluators should be professionally capable to assess the applicant's work objectively and comment on its significance in the discipline.

Normally, the applicant is asked to provide in writing three to five names and addresses of respected scholars in related fields who are not at the University of Hawai'i, Mānoa. Applicants should not contact possible external evaluators. It is the obligation of the Department to secure external evaluations. It is recommended that the Department Chair, in consultation with the Chair of the Department Personnel Committee, should secure letters from 2-3 of these people and a comparable number of letters from known scholars proposed by the Department who can evaluate the applicant's work.

Approximately the same cover letter soliciting the evaluation should be sent to each evaluator. The Department Chair should keep a copy of each letter. A curriculum vita will be included with the letter and if possible copies of reprints of the applicant's major publications, if practical. The purpose of the request is to obtain an opinion about the scholarly contributions which the applicant has made and not to determine whether or not the applicant would receive tenure/promotion at another institution.

The confidentiality of such evaluations is of great concern. The following paragraphs should be included in the letter to external evaluators:

> Your review of Professor_____ is for the sole purpose of helping the faculty and administration of the University of Hawaiʻi at Mānoa to evaluate this faculty member for promotion and/or tenure (use appropriate phase). Your identity as a confidential referee will not be shared with this applicant and we will do our best to maintain the confidentiality of your evaluation.
>
> The faculty and administration of the University of Hawaiʻi greatly appreciate your willingness and efforts in evaluating and commenting on the work of this faculty member.

When the external evaluations arrive in the departmental office, necessary steps should be taken to ensure that the evaluation is kept confidential. The procedure for handling the evaluation should include the following:

1. Mark the letter "Confidential" as soon as it arrives. Do not show the letter to the applicant at any time.

2. Make seven (7) copies of the letter and assemble eight (8) sets of confidential letters (original + 7 copies). One set of confidential letters should be included with each copy of the dossier.

3. Place the confidential letters in eight (8) manila envelopes marked "CONFIDENTIAL" and with the applicant's name. Include inside each envelope a listing of the reviewers, their institutional and disciplinary affiliations and whether they came from the candidate's or the department's list. Also include a copy of the letter sent to external reviewers.

4. On page 5.2, Department Assessment (Section E, Confidential Letters of Evaluation), indicate the number of confidential letters solicited by the department and the number of confidential letters received by the department. Do not list the authors of the confidential letters in this section.

5. In **Summer 2016**, when the final decisions are announced, a brief letter should be sent to each of the external reviewers informing them of the disposition of the case and

thanking them once again for their efforts on behalf of the department, the college, and the UH Mānoa. In the case of a negative decision, departments must confirm with the Mānoa Chancellor's Office that any appeal has been resolved prior to contacting the reviewers.

F. Compiling dossiers.

- Each appended page should be numbered at the bottom center and have the applicant's full name (Last, First M.I.) at the top right corner; labels may be utilized for names and page numbers.
- The margins for each appended page should be wide enough to ensure that no part of the text is obscured when the dossier is bound.
- Dossiers should be bound in a manila file folder or three-ring binder.
- Fasten at the left side of the page with a prong paper fastener. Set the two-hole punch at 11" for the pages and 12" for the manila folder. **If using manila folders, please make sure that the fastener opens at the back of the folder**.
- Label the original dossier as "Original" and number it "Copy 1". Number the subsequent copies "2" through "8".
- Place a file label with the applicant's full name, college/unit, department, and copy number on the manila file folder tab, or the front of the three-ring binder.
- When using a three-ring binder the dossiers may be printed double-sided.
- Confidential letters in their own manila envelope should be included in the folder (but not attached) by the Department Chair.

. Special instructions for Specialists, Librarian, and Extension Agent faculty and Instructional and Research faculty at Rank 4 who may apply in two categories simultaneously. Faculty who are Specialists (S), Librarians (B) or Extension Agents (A) may receive tenure at ranks 2 and 3 without being promoted. Specialist, Librarian, and Agent faculty members who wish to be considered for tenure with promotion to the next rank may use a single application for these two options. **Please note – these actions require a separate vote for tenure and a separate vote for promotion by each level of review**. For example, faculty with S, B, or A classifications may complete the top of page 1.1 of the application form as follows:

_X_ Tenure only at ________ (indicate current rank)
(Rank)

_X_ Tenure and Promotion to _______

(Rank)

Thus, if the faculty member is recommended for tenure but is not recommended for promotion, the faculty member will still be awarded tenure at his/her current rank.

In the event that an applicant receives tenure but is denied promotion, he/she is eligible for the remedies for denial of promotion (see Article XIV.D-J). In the event that tenure is also denied, the applicant may elect the remedies in Article XII.H.

Bibliography

Alcoff, L. (1988). *New versions of the coherence theory: Gadamer, Davidson, Foucault, and Putnam* (Unpublished doctoral dissertation). Brown University, Providence, RI.

Ames, R. T. (2011). *Confucian role ethics: A vocabulary*. Honolulu, HI: University of Hawai'i Press.

Ames, R. T. (2016). On teaching and learning (*Xue Ji* 學記): Setting the root in Confucian education. In D. Xu, H. McEwan, & L. X. Yang (Eds.), *Chinese philosophy on teaching and learning: Xue Ji (學記) in the 21st century*. Albany, NY: State University of New York Press.

Ames, R. T., & Hall, D. L. (2001). *Focusing the familiar: A translation and philosophical interpretation of the Zhongyong*. Honolulu, HI: University of Hawai'i Press.

Barad, K. (2007). *Meeting the universe halfway: Quantum physics and the entanglement of matter and meaning*. Durham, NC: Duke University Press.

Becher, T. (1989). *Academic tribes and territories: Intellectual enquiry and the cultures of disciplines*. Milton Keynes, U.K. and Bristol, PA: The Society for Research into Higher Education & Open University Press.

Bennett, J. (2010). *Vibrant matter: A political ecology of things*. Durham, NC: Duke University Press.

Bevir, M. (1999). Foucault and critique: Deploying agency against autonomy. *Political Theory, 27*(1), 65–84.

Biesta, G. (2010). *Good education in an age of measurement: Ethics, politics, democracy*. Boulder, CO: Paradigm Publishers.

Boyer, E. L. (1990). *Scholarship reconsidered: Priorities of the professoriate*. Princeton, NJ: Carnegie Foundation for the Advancement of Teaching.

Brown, W. (2015). *Undoing the demos: Neoliberalism's stealth revolution*. New York, NY: Zone Books.

Chang, M. K. (2017). Reevaluating collegiality: Relationality, learning communities and possibilities. *Policy Futures in Education, 16*(7), 851–865.

Cox, M. D. (2004). Introduction to faculty learning communities. In M. D. Cox & L. Richlin (Eds.), *Building faculty learning communities* (pp. 5–23). San Francisco, CA: Jossey-Bass.

Dewey, J. (1916). *Democracy and education: An introduction to the philosophy of education.* New York, NY: Macmillan.

Dewey, J. (1933). *How we think.* Lexington, MA: Heath.

Dewey, J. (1957). *Human nature and conduct: An introduction to social psychology.* New York, NY: The Modern Library.

Dill, B. (1983/2013). Race, class, and gender: Prospects for an all-inclusive sisterhood. In B. J. Thayer-Bacon, L. Stone, & K. M. Sprecher (eds.), *Education feminism: Classic and contemporary readings* (pp. 59–74). Albany, NY: State University of New York Press.

Elman, B. A. (2000). *A cultural history of civil examinations in late imperial China.* Berkeley, CA: University of California Press.

Ellsworth, E. A. (1997). *Teaching positions: Difference, pedagogy, and the power of address.* New York, NY: Teachers College Press.

Ellsworth, E. A. (1989/2013). Why doesn't this feel empowering? Working through the repressive myths of critical pedagogy. In B. J. Thayer-Bacon, L. Stone, & K. M. Sprecher (eds.), *Education feminism: Classic and contemporary readings* (pp. 187–214). Albany, NY: State University of New York Press.

Ellsworth, E. A. (2005). *Places of learning: Media, architecture, pedagogy.* New York, NY: Routledge.

Eno, R. (2015). *The Analects of Confucius.* Retrieved from http://www.indiana.edu/~p374/Analects_of_Confucius_(Eno-2015).pdf

Epstein, E. (2018, January 16). How China infiltrated U.S. classrooms. *Politico Magazine.* Retrieved from https://www.politico.com/magazine/story/2018/01/16/how-china-infiltrated-us-classrooms-216327

Fendler, L. (2006). Others and the problem of community. *Curriculum Inquiry,* 36(3), 303–326.

Fitzsimons, P. (2002). Neoliberalism and education: the autonomous chooser. *Radical Pedagogy.* Retrieved from http://www.radicalpedagogy.org/radicalpedagogy/Neoliberalism_and_education__the_autonomous_chooser.html

Foucault, M. (1995). *Discipline and punish: The birth of the prison.* New York, NY: Vintage Books.

Friedman, D. B., Crews, T. B., Caicedo, J. M., Besley, J. C., Weinberg, J., & Freeman, M. L. (2010). An exploration into inquiry-based learning by a multidisciplinary group of higher education faculty. *Higher Education: The International Journal of Higher Education and Educational Planning,* 59(6), 765–783.

Furco, A., & Moely, B. E. (2012). Using learning communities to build faculty support for pedagogical innovation: A multi-campus study. *Journal of Higher Education,* 83(1), 128–153.

Gardner, D. K. (1998). Confucian commentary and Chinese intellectual history. *The Journal of Asian Studies*, *57*(2), 397–422.

Gardner, D. K. (2003). *Zhu Xi's reading of the Analects: Canon, commentary, and the classical tradition*. New York, NY: Columbia University Press.

Gardner, D. K. (2007). *The four books: The basic teachings of the later Confucian tradition*. Indianapolis, IN: Hackett.

Gardner, S., & Veliz, D. (2014). Evincing the ratchet: A thematic analysis of the promotion and tenure guidelines at a striving university. *The Review of Higher Education*, 38(1), 105–132.

Germain, M., & Scandura, T. A. (2005). Grade inflation and student individual differences as systematic bias in faculty evaluations. *Journal of Instructional Psychology*, *32*(1), 58–67.

Giroux, H., & McLaren, P. (1986). Teacher education and the politics of engagement: the case for democratic schooling. *Harvard Educational Review*, 56, 213–238.

Glowacki-Dudka, M., & Brown, M. P. (2008). Professional development through faculty learning communities. *New Horizons in Adult Education and Human Resource Development*, *21*, 29–39.

Glyer, D., & Weeks, D. L. (1998). *The liberal arts in higher education: Challenging assumptions, exploring possibilities*. Lanham, MD: University Press of America.

Gray, P. (2015). *Free to learn: Why unleashing the instinct to play will make our children happier, more self-reliant, and better students for life*. New York, NY: Basic Books.

Green, T. F., Ericson, D. P., & Seidman, R. H. (1997). *Predicting the behavior of the educational system*. Troy, NY: Educator's International Press.

Harvard University (2017). *Harvard's president & leadership*. Retrieved from http://www.harvard.edu/about-harvard/harvards-president-leadership

Hourdequin, M., & Wong, D. (2005). A relational approach to environmental ethics. *Journal of Chinese Philosophy*, *32*(1), 19–33.

Ingold, T. (2018). *Anthropology and/as education*. New York, NY: Routledge.

Kasulis, T. (2002). *Intimacy or integrity: Philosophy and cultural difference*. Honolulu, HI: University of Hawai'i Press.

Komisar, E. (2017). *Being there: Why prioritizing motherhood in the first three years matters*. New York, NY: TarcherPerigee.

Lather, P., & St. Pierre, E. A. (2013). Post qualitative research. *International Journal of Qualitative Studies in Education*, *26*(6), 629–633.

Latour, B. (2004). Why has critique run out of steam? From matters of fact to matters of concern. *Critical Inquiry*, *20*(2), 225–248.

Lave, J. (1988). *Cognition in practice: Mind, mathematics, and culture in everyday life*. Cambridge: Cambridge University Press.

Lave, J., & Wenger, E. (1991). *Situated learning: Legitimate peripheral participation*. Cambridge: Cambridge University Press.

Lillard, P. P., & Jessen, L. L. (2003). *Montessori from the start: The child at home from birth to age three*. New York, NY: Schocken Books.

Limbrick, L., & Knight, N. (2005). Close reading of students' writing: What teachers learn about writing. *English Teaching: Practice and Critique*, *4*, 5–22.

Liston, D. D., Hansman, C. A., Kenney, S. L., & Breton, C. C. (1998). Teaching portfolio use in the absence of institutional support. *Journal on Excellence in College Teaching*, *9*(1), 121–134.

Liston, D., & Zeichner, K. (1987). Critical pedagogy and teacher education. *Journal of Education*, *169*, 117–137.

Liu, Y., Xu, S., & Zhang, B. (2019). Thriving at work: How a paradox mindset influences innovative work behavior. *The Journal of Applied Behavioral Science*, *56*(3), 347–366.

Marsden, G. M. (1994). *The soul of the American university: From Protestant establishment to established nonbelief*. New York, NY: Oxford University Press.

Mead, G. H., & Morris, C. W. (1934). *Mind, self & society from the standpoint of a social behaviorist*. Chicago, IL: University of Chicago Press.

Meiklejohn, A. (1932). *The experimental college*. New York, NY: HarperCollins.

Mengel, F., Sauermann, J., & Zölitz, U. (2019). Gender bias in teaching evaluations. *Journal of the European Economic Association*, *17*(2), 535–566.

Miyazaki, I (1981). *China's examination hell: The civil service examinations of imperial China*. New Haven, CT: Yale University Press.

Neufeld, G., & Maté, G. (2004). *Hold on to your kids: Why parents need to matter more than peers*. Toronto: A.A. Knopf Canada.

Nylan, M. (2001). *The five "Confucian" classics*. New Haven, CT: Yale University Press.

Nylan, M. (2005). Toward an archaeology of writing: Text, ritual, and the culture of public display in the classical period (475 B.C.E.–220 C.E.). In M. Kern (Ed.), *Text and ritual in early China* (pp. 3–49). Seattle, WA: University of Washington Press.

O'Boyle, L. (1983). Learning for its own sake: The German university as nineteenth-century model. *Comparative Studies in Society and History*, *25*(1), 3–25.

Ozcan, K. (2013). Student evaluation of lecture and teaching effectiveness in higher education. *Educational Research and Reviews*, *8*(8), 378–389.

Pinnegar, S. (1995). (Re-)Experiencing beginning. *Teacher Education Quarterly*, *22*(3), 65–83.

Ritter, J. K. (2011). On the affective challenges of developing a pedagogy of teacher education. *Studying Teacher Education*, *7*(3), 219–233.

Rosemont, H. (1991). Rights-bearing individuals and role-bearing persons. In M. I. Bockover (Ed.), *Rules, rituals, and responsibilities: Essays dedicated to Herbert Fingarette* (pp. 71–102). LaSalle, IL: Open Court Press.

Rosenlee, L.-H. L. (2006). *Confucianism and women: A philosophical interpretation*. Albany, NY: State University of New York Press.

Reinharz, S., & Davidman, L. (1992). *Feminist methods in social research.* New York, NY: Oxford University Press.

Schön, D. A. (1983). *Reflective practitioner: How professionals think in action.* New York, NY: Basic Books, Inc.

Shor, I., & Freire, P. (1987). What is the dialogical method of teaching? *Journal of Education, 169*, 11–31.

Siegel, D. J., & Bryson, T. P. (2016). *No-drama discipline: The whole-brain way to calm the chaos and nurture your child's developing mind.* New York, NY: Bantam Books.

Siegel, D. J., & Hartzell, M. (2014). *Parenting from the inside out: How a deeper self-understanding can help you raise children who thrive.* New York, NY: Jeremy P. Tarcher/Penguin.

St. Pierre, E. A. (2014). A brief and personal history of post qualitative research: Toward "post" inquiry. *Journal of Curriculum Theorizing, 30*(2), 2–19.

Stanford University. (2018, May 18). *President outlines new vision for Stanford's future.* Retrieved from https://parents.stanford.edu/2018/05/18/president-outlines-new-vision-for-stanfords-future/

Stanford University. (2019, September 1). *Chapter 3: Promotion to tenure (tenure line).* Retrieved from https://facultyaffairs-humsci.stanford.edu/handbook/chapter-3-promotion-tenure-tenure-line

St. Pierre, E. A. (2000). Poststructural feminism in education: An overview. *International Journal of Qualitative Studies in Education, 13*(5), 477–515.

Stone, L. (1988/2013). Toward a transformational theory of teaching. In B. J. Thayer-Bacon, L. Stone, & K. M. Sprecher (eds.), *Education feminism: Classic and contemporary readings* (pp. 127–135). Albany, NY: State University of New York Press.

Stone, L. (2013). Epilogue. In B. J. Thayer-Bacon, L. Stone, & K. M. Sprecher (eds.), *Education feminism: Classic and contemporary readings* (pp. 469–471). Albany, NY: State University of New York Press.

Subtirelu, N. C. (2015). "She does have an accent but . . .": Race and language ideology in students' evaluations of mathematics instructors on RateMyProfessors.com. *Language in Society, 44*(1), 35–62.

Thayer-Bacon, B. (2010). A pragmatist and feminist relational (e)pistemology. *European Journal of Pragmatism and American Philosophy*, 2(1), 1–20.

Teo, C. W. (2015, November 20). Stepping back in time at China's schools for traditional culture and Confucianism [Blog post]. *Straits Times.* Retrieved from https://www.straitstimes.com/asia/east-asia/stepping-back-in-time-at-chinas-schools-for-traditional-culture-and-confucianism

Tan, S. (2003). *Confucian democracy: A Deweyan reconstruction.* Albany, NY: State University of New York Press.

Tuhiwai-Smith, L. (2012). *Decolonizing methodologies: Research and indigenous peoples.* London: Zed.

University of California, Berkeley (2002). *UC Berkeley strategic academic plan*. Retrieved from http://vpsafp.berkeley.edu/media/Strategic-Academic-Plan-02.pdf

University of Hawai'i. (2015). *University of Hawai'i strategic directions, 2015–2021*. Retrieved from http://blog.hawaii.edu/strategicdirections/files/2015/01/StrategicDirectionsFINAL-013015.pdf

University of Michigan. (n.d.). *Mission statement*. Retrieved March 3, 2021, from https://president.umich.edu/about/mission/

University of Michigan (1954, April). *Promotion guidelines*. Retrieved from https://www.provost.umich.edu/faculty/promotion_guidelines/AttachmentA.html

University of Michigan, Ann Arbor (2016). *The academic innovation initiative*. Retrieved from http://ai.umich.edu/events/ai-initiative/

Vassar College. (n.d.). *Mission statement*. Retrieved March 3, 2021, from http://info.vassar.edu/about/vassar/mission.html

Vassar College. (2019, July). *Faculty handbook Vassar College 2020–21*. Retrieved from https://deanofthefaculty.vassar.edu/docs/VassarFacultyHandbook.pdf

Vescio, V., Ross, D., & Adams, A. (2008). A review of research on the impact of professional learning communities on teaching practice and student learning. *Teaching and Teacher Education*, *24*(1), 80–91.

Wang, H. (2001). *The call from the stranger on a journey home: Curriculum as creative transformation of selfhood* (Doctoral dissertation). Louisiana State University, Baton Rouge, Louisiana.

Ward, H., & Selvester, P. (2012). Faculty learning communities: Improving teaching in higher education. *Educational Studies*, *38*, 111–121.

Wenger, E. (1998). *Communities of practice: Learning, meaning, and identity*. Cambridge: Cambridge University Press.

Yayli, D. (2012). Professional language use by pre-service English as a foreign language teachers in a teaching certificate program. *Teachers and Teaching: Theory and Practice*, *18*, 59–73.

Index

academic freedom, 125, 144
accumulation of light, 79
Adams, A., 127
affinity groups, 158
agential
  reading, 37, 59–60
  realism, Barad, 17
Alcoff, L., 154
Ames, Roger, 6, 22, 38, 42, 55, 62, 65–70, 72–74, 78–79, 81, 84–85, 117, 156, 160–161, 183
Analects, 40, 41, 47, 56
analytic dialogue, 150, 152, 165
attachment, 85, 88
  theory, importance of, 70–73, 76–77
attention, agency and value of, 99
attitude, value of attending to, 84–85, 131, 179, 183
attribution, complexity of determining, 175, 180, 183
axe handle, 85

Barad, Karen, 17–18, 21
Becher, Tony, 121, 141
Bennett, Jane, 81
Besley, John, 125
Bevir, Mark, 14, 15
bibliography
  as narrative, 184
  section of dossier, 107–108, 110–111
Biesta, Gert, 9–11, 95
Book of Songs, 67, 85
Bowlby, John, 71
Boyer, Ernest, 21
brainwriting, 134
Breton, C. C., 110
Brown, M. P., 23, 122, 127
Brown, Wendy, 3, 9, 11
Bryson, Tina, 81
Buddhism, 48

Caicedo, Juan, 125
centripetal participation, 128
Ch'eng-Chu learning, 50
challenges, globally scaled, 4
Chang, M., 55
Cheng Hao, 50
Cheng Yi, 50, 57
citizens, global, wise, cultivation of, 4–5, 93, 95–111, 175, 186
civil service examination
  context: disciplinary mechanism of, 51; extreme nature of, 59; institutionalization of, 49, 54–55; spectacle of, 51; visibility of, 49
  historical: contextualization of, 44–45, 49; periods, 45, 50, 52, 54
  link to social status, 52, 58
  odds of passing, 53

civil service examination *(continued)*
preparation, 54, 63
uses: political purpose, 45; restriction of military power, 46; social stability, 46
classical Chinese texts
conflation with exams, 58
historical contextualization of, 62–63
interdisciplinary implications: democracy, 62; environmental ethics, 62; feminism, 62
interpretive approach, 61–62: genuine engagement of, 57
normative views of, 60: abstraction of, 55; appropriation of, 57, 60
pedagogical implications, 61–62
translator challenges, 63
classical scholars, objects and subjects of power, 51–52, 59
collegiality
development of, 33, 121, 133, 137–139, 142, 179, 188
in faculty learning communities, 23, 121, 139
networks of, 140
relationships, value of, 5, 29, 122–123
commentarial tradition, Confucian, 39–41, 44, 66, 68, 176
pedagogical implications of, 61
communication, dynamic, 134, 136
communicative dialogue, 150–152
communities of practice
concept of, 123, 127–130
outcomes orientation focus, 129
comparative inquiry, 61
comparative philosophers, influences of, 6, 66, 176
Confucian relational framework
as collaborative resource, 119, 183, 186, 188
concept of person, 32, 166–169
process orientation, 8, 156
reading from, 26, 146, 157
Confucian relationality, 98, 176–181
aspects of: complexity of, 16; foregrounding experience, 8, 16; link to personal cultivation, 83; process-oriented nature of, 15, 20, 73, 112; promoting longer term view, 8
background, 6, 65–66
people: as embodied, 189; in relation, 15–16, 19–22, 30–33; living in mutuality, 80, 90; reframing faculty activities, 7
use of, 4–5, 23–25, 94, 99, 104–106, 118–122, 124, 130, 133, 142–144, 154, 169–171, 173, 186–189
views of: as radical framework, 32–33; attention to core values, 117; communication, 151; faculty, 5; worldview, 19
Confucian tradition and Confucianism
background of, 37–42: ancestor role, 78; classical texts, 41; translator interpretations, 42
commentarial aspect of, 37
nature of: dynamic 20, 43, 62–63; multivocal, 40, 42, 62, 176
views: Eurocentric, 38, 43; interpretive, 39, 41, 43
Confucius, 78, 84, 88–89, 156, 182
life of, 37, 41
relation to tradition, 38–39
Confucius Institutes, 60
conversation instead of dialogue in classrooms, 148, 151–153, 180
core values, institutional, 100, 110, 116, 120, 177–178, 185
challenges to, 117–118

correlative cosmology, 81
Cox, M. D., 23
Crews, Tena, 125
critical friends, 121, 137
  developing inner circles of, 141
critical pedagogy. *See* pedagogy
culture of measurement, 3, 11–13, 25, 110–111

Davidman, L. 163
Dewey, John, 21–23, 82–83
Dill, Bonnie, 163
disciplinary methods, educational, 13–14
disjunctures, responses to, 31–32, 112, 148
display culture, 49–50. *See also* spectacle culture
Doctrine of the Mean. See *Zhongyong*
Duke of Zhou, 78

education (*jiao*)
  as leading life, 22, 99
  as process of personal cultivation, 84
  "improving upon this way," 69–70
  responsibility of, 73
educational theories
  Platonic and Rousseauian, 16, 166
efficiency as method, 101
Ellsworth, Elizabeth, 12, 24, 30, 145–166, 170, 180, 182
  teaching as contextually responsive, 147, 173
Elman, Benjamin, 45, 46, 49, 50, 53
embodied, people as, 19, 80–81
emotional maturity, development of, 66, 74, 86
empathy, value of capacity, 90
Eno, Robert, 41
Epstein, E., 60
Ericson, D. P., 9
exemplary character, attitude of, 68, 74, 85. See also *junzi*
experiences, value of, 29–30, 82, 84
  enrichment of, 140
  participation, 131–132
  participation in learning communities, 133–134
experiment, imaginative thinking, 118, 141, 178

faculty
  as experts and adaptive learners, 4, 6, 8, 144, 176, 181
  as producers, 2, 6, 11, 93, 98, 102, 111, 115
  enrichment of experiences, 124
faculty activities
  as intraconnected, 176
  as open-ended, 138
  as way-making, 117
  big three, 2
  complexity of, 2
  institutional silence about various roles, 2
  market view of, 96
  normative value of, 26
  paradox of, 93, 95, 97–98, 112
  pressure to find evidence of contributions, 96
faculty learning communities. *See* learning communities
faculty learning, supporting, 179
faculty roles
  aspectual nature of, 94
  professionalization of, 144
familial and kin relationships, importance of, 67, 69
feminism, 163
  framework of, 165
  poststructural, 162, 164–165
Fendler, Lynn, 129

Fitzsimons, Patrick, 9, 10, 11, 25
foci, people as, 78–79
focus and field, concept of, 161
Foucault, Michel, 13–15, 47, 51, 58, 164
Four Books, 47–48, 56–66
Fredrickson, Barbara, 132
Freeman, Miriam, 125
Friedman, Daniela 125–126, 134, 136–137, 139
Furco, Andrew, 24, 125, 134, 136–137

Gardner, Daniel K., 40, 48, 56, 61
Gardner, S., 98
gendered, different perspectives of, 166–167
Germain, M., 109
Glowacki-Dudka, M., 23, 122, 127
Glyer, D., 144
governance, responsibility of, 37, 47, 56, 75
Gray, Peter, 123, 130–132, 135, 141, 179
Great Learning (Daxue), 40, 47
Green, T. F., 9
guoxue, (also known as Chinese cultural schools) 54, 63

habits as "active means," 82–83
Hall, 6, 38, 42, 62, 65–70, 72–73, 78–79, 84–85, 117, 156, 161, 183
Hansman, C. A., 110
Hartzell, Mary, 81, 86, 88
He Yan, 40
hierarchy, challenges to, 77–78
higher education, contextual field of, 8
historical recontextualization, 61
Hourdequin, M., 62
how will I respond? 145, 150, 153, 189

identities, performance of, 83
imperial power, relation to examination process, 51
individualization, Foucault, 13–14
individuals, normative notion of, 4, 13–16, 55, 80–81, 129, 165–168, 175
Ingold, Tim, 22, 99, 153–154
inquiry-based learning, 125–126, 134–135, 137
inquiry as method. *See* juxtaposition
inquiry as project, 124
institutions (institutional)
  dominant paradigms, 94: goals, 97
  messages of documents, 94
  of disciplinary power, 111
  visibility of complex processes, 183, 186
intellectual play, collaboratives of, 130
  space for, 142
intentionality, 18
intra-action, 17, 19, 21, 75, 94, 124, 130, 150, 177, 188: collaboration as, 183
intraconnected, people as, 32, 176

Jessen, L. L., 73
jiao, 70, 73, 84. *See also* education
junzi, 67–69
juxtaposition, 31, 146
  frameworks, of, 146, 161, 162, 169, 181: Confucian and feminist, 163, 165, 168, 170
  implications of, 61, 97
  inquiry as method, 30–32

Kasulis, Thomas, 6, 183–184
Kenney, S. L., 110
King Wu, 68, 78
Knight, N., 122

knowledge
 dualistic approaches, 166
 partiality of, 165
 power/knowledge, 14–15
 transactional, 17
Komisar, Erica, 71
Kong Ji, 65–66

language, performativity of, 164
Lather, P., 31
Latour, Bruno, 18
Lave, Jean, 127–128
learning
 as continual endeavoring, 118
 as embodied, 155
 as training, 111
 complexity of, 181
 imaginative, 132, 142: as interference of distress, 133
 inquiry-based, 135, 137, 182
learning communities
 development of collegiality, 131, 133–136
 faculty, 122–123, 130, 133, 135, 138: collegiality within, 24; concept of, 23; example of, 26; value of, 187
 framing, 130
 meeting norms, 135
 participation. *See under* experiences
 research about, 125–126, 135, 139
 space of, 138
 university affiliated, 123
 university as responsive. *See under* universities
Liji, 66
Lillard, P. P., 73
Limbrick, L., 122
Liston, D. D., 110, 160
Liu, Y., 137
Lyotard, Jean-François, 25

market orientation, 3. *See also* product orientation
 language, use of, 100, 106, 115, 174
 outcomes focus, 7
Marsden, G. M., 144
Maté, Gabor, 70, 72, 76, 85
Mead, George Herbert, 82–83
measurable outcomes, looking beyond, 139–140
Meiklejohn, Alexander, 23
Mencius, 40, 47, 57
Mengel, F., 12, 109
mission statements, 3, 96. *See also under* institutions
Miyazaki, I., 46, 54
modes of address, complexity of, 148, 150–153, 164
Moely, Barbara, 24, 125, 134, 136–137

Neo-Confucian perspectives, 48, 50, 55–57
neoliberal pressure on institutions, 174
neoliberalism, 8–9, 33. *See also* product-oriented paradigm
 ethic of, 11
 framework, 16
 rationality, 14
 view of people, 13–14
Neufeld, Gordon, 70, 72, 76, 85
norms, 4–5, 32–33, 44, 55, 59, 129, 149
 meetings, 135–136
 power of, 14–16
Nylan, Michael, 38–39, 49–50, 52–53

Ozcan, K., 109

parents and children's relationships, 76–77, 85

patriarchy, function in world, 163, 168
pedagogical spaces, 155
pedagogy, 150
  Confucian relational view, 150, 154, 160
  critical: critique of, 159; oppressive aspects, 157–158; language of, 158; theorists of, 160
  Ellsworth, 24, 143, 156, 170
  performative, 148–149, 162, 164, 166
  responsive, 143, 147–148, 150, 159
people
  as events (framing of), 80, 82
  as intradependent, 176
  as narrative, acknowledging complexity of, 184–185
personal cultivation, 7, 24, 176, 181
  attuning to others, 5, 74, 84
  Ellsworth, 145, 180
  extensivity of, 25, 32–33, 65–68, 80, 83, 168, 177, 179, 181
  harmonizing relationships, 67, 79
  kin relationships, 69
  parent and child, 72–73, 76
  parental role, 86
  reflective inquiry, 61, 89
  relational perspective of, 90, 169–170
  teaching as occasion for, 156–157, 159–160
Pinnegar, S., 23
play, work of, 132, 137–138, 141, 179
positionality, 17, 154, 165
poststructuralist interests, 16. *See also* feminism
process orientation. *See also* relationality
  aspects of, 5–6, 30, 73, 79
  parenting perspective, 76–78
  university context, aspects of, 120
  worldview, 6, 65, 80
product orientation
  implications of (focusing on what is more easily measurable), 99, 111
  limits of, 2–5, 13
product-oriented paradigm
  complications of, 105, 107
  influence on higher education, 32–33
  power/knowledge regime, 14
  producing labor force, 25
  rationality of, 14
  teaching: business of, 25; deemphasis of, 107, 112
reading ability in the classical age, 52–53
reflective inquiry, 85, 89
regard, respect for others, 76–77, 80
Reinharz, S., 163
relation-ing, 6–7, 65–66, 73, 75–77, 81, 85–86, 88, 90, 141
relationality
  Confucian. *See* Confucian relationality
  epistemology, 17, 19
  Eurocentric perspectives, 16
  matters of fact and concerns, 18
  pragmatist social feminist view of, 17
relationships, harmonizing of, 85, 124
research endeavors, partiality of, 30
research production (role in faculty evaluation), 107
response as inquiry, 173, 179
reverse discourse, concept of, 168
Ritter, J. K., 23
Rosemont, H., 62
Rosenlee, Lisa Li-Hsiang, 54, 56, 77, 166–167
Ross, D., 127

ruxue, 38–39, 41, 43, 54. *See also* Confucianism

Sauermann, J., 12, 109
Scandura, T. A., 109
Schön, Donald, 22
Seidman, R. H., 9
Selvester, Paula, 122–123, 126, 135–137, 139–140
service-learning initiatives, 125
Siegel, Daniel, 81, 86, 88
situated learning, theory of, 127
social positions, shifting of, 77
space of possibility, 182
spectacle culture, 50
St. Pierre, E. A., 17, 31, 162, 164–165, 167–168
Stanford University, 95–96
Stone, Lynda, 16, 163, 166–167, 169
strategic directions, 3
  documents, 1, 8, 174
  language of, 10
  University of Hawai'i, 9–10, 93, 97, 100–101, 103–105, 110, 114–118, 120, 177, 185
students as laborers, 101
study the way, 89
substance ontology, 38
Subtirelu, N. C., 12, 109

Tan, Sor-hoon, 6, 56–57, 78
Tavares, Hannah, 182
teachers and students
  relationship, 149
  roles, 154–156
teaching
  as conversation, 24
  as experimental improvisation, 153–154
  as synergistic learning, 22
  Confucian relational view, 5
  culture, enrichment of, 186
  evaluations, 108, 110: biases, 12, 109; difficulty of the process, 113; inadequacy of, 110
  importance and effort, 146, 186
  impossibility of, 12, 152
  portfolios, 110
  process orientation of, 146–147: complexity of, 145; responsive, 148, 171, 180; sharing responsibility for, 187, 189
  value of craft, 4
tenure and promotion guidelines, 94–96
  University of Hawai'i, 93, 100, 103–104, 107–109, 113–114, 118, 124, 174, 185
tenure evaluation process
  ambiguity of, 3, 119
  engaging a process view, 115
  subjectivity of, 113
  uncertainty of, 115
Thayer-Bacon, Barbara, 17
tian, productivity of, 38, 42, 68–71, 84
time and space, link between, 5, 26, 28–30, 33, 98
triggered or triggers, parental feelings, 87–88
Tuhiwai-Smith, Linda, 28

universal design for learning, 126, 137
university or universities
  as businesses, 96
  as responsive learning community, 25, 175–180, 182, 188
  German model of, 143–144
  history of, 144
University of California, Berkeley, strategic academic plan, 10
University of Hawai'i. *See under* strategic directions *and* tenure and promotion guidelines

University of Michigan, 95–96
  academic innovation, 10

Vassar College, 95–96
Veliz, D., 98
Vescio, V., 127

Wang, Hongyu, 55, 57
Wang Yangming, 160
Ward, Hsuying, 122–123, 126, 135–137, 139–140
ways forward, five, 67–68, 90, 112, 117
  natural contexts of, 81
Weeks, D. L., 144
Weinberg, Justin, 125
Wenger, Etienne, 127–128
Western Association of Schools and Colleges (WASC), 100
Wong, D., 62

Xu, S., 137

Yayli, D., 122

Zhang, B., 137
Zhongyong, 6, 20, 39, 42, 47, 54, 65–69, 72–75, 78–79, 81, 83–85, 88–90, 117, 156, 169, 176
Zhu Xi, 40, 47–48, 50, 56–57, 66
Zölitz, U., 12, 109